Survival

GLOBAL POLITICS AND STRATEGY

Volume 66 Number 4 | August–September 2024

'If Beijing and Moscow's "no-limits friendship"
did extend to some form of loose nuclear alliance
– and this remains a very big if – any US response
predicated on matching its two nuclear peers
warhead for warhead, delivery system for delivery
system, would be costly folly.'

Douglas Barrie and Timothy Wright, Not More, But More Assured: Optimising US
Nuclear Posture, p. 9.

'Should Trump be elected, Ukraine's membership
in NATO is almost unimaginable. Once closed, the
window is unlikely to be reopened.'

Liana Fix, NATO and Ukraine: The Peril of Indecision, p. 75.

'The deeper flaw in equating the French and Italian
far right is that Italy's citizens, however bruised,
are, as they have always been, overwhelmingly
pro-European and feel that their very survival is
tied to the EU.'

Catherine Fieschi, France's Political Crisis, p. 122.

Survival

GLOBAL POLITICS AND STRATEGY

Volume 66 Number 4 | August–September 2024

Contents

On the cover
A US Air Force AGM-86 air-launched cruise missile takes flight in 1979.

On the web
Visit www.iiss.org/publications/survival for brief notices on new books on Russia and Eurasia, Asia-Pacific, and Cyber Security and Emerging Technologies.

***Survival* editors' blog**
For ideas and commentary from *Survival* editors and contributors, visit https://www.iiss.org/online-analysis/survival-online.

Survival

GLOBAL POLITICS AND STRATEGY

The International Institute for Strategic Studies

2121 K Street, NW | Suite 600 | Washington DC 20037 | USA
Tel +1 202 659 1490   Fax +1 202 659 1499   E-mail survival@iiss.org   Web www.iiss.org

Arundel House | 6 Temple Place | London | WC2R 2PG | UK
Tel +44 (0)20 7379 7676   Fax +44 (0)20 7836 3108   E-mail iiss@iiss.org

14th Floor, GFH Tower | Bahrain Financial Harbour | Manama | Kingdom of Bahrain
Tel +973 1718 1155   Fax +973 1710 0155   E-mail iiss-middleeast@iiss.org

9 Raffles Place | #49-01 Republic Plaza | Singapore 048619
Tel +65 6499 0055   Fax +65 6499 0059   E-mail iiss-asia@iiss.org

Pariser Platz 6A | 10117 Berlin | Germany
Tel +49 30 311 99 300   E-mail iiss-europe@iiss.org

Survival Online www.tandfonline.com/survival and www.iiss.org/publications/survival

Aims and Scope *Survival* is one of the world's leading forums for analysis and debate of international and strategic affairs. Shaped by its editors to be both timely and forward thinking, the journal encourages writers to challenge conventional wisdom and bring fresh, often controversial, perspectives to bear on the strategic issues of the moment. With a diverse range of authors, *Survival* aims to be scholarly in depth while vivid, well written and policy-relevant in approach. Through commentary, analytical articles, case studies, forums, review essays, reviews and letters to the editor, the journal promotes lively, critical debate on issues of international politics and strategy.

Editor **Dana Allin**
Managing Editor **Jonathan Stevenson**
Associate Editor **Carolyn West**
Editorial Assistant **Conor Hodges**
Production and Cartography **Alessandra Beluffi, Ravi Gopar, Jade Panganiban, James Parker, Kelly Verity**

Contributing Editors

William Alberque	Franz-Stefan Gady	Nigel Inkster	Benjamin Rhode	Robert Ward
Aaron Connelly	Bastian Giegerich	Jeffrey Mazo	Ben Schreer	Marcus Willett
James Crabtree	Nigel Gould-Davies	Fenella McGerty	Maria Shagina	Lanxin Xiang
Chester A. Crocker	Melissa K. Griffith	Irene Mia	Karen Smith	
Bill Emmott	Emile Hokayem	Meia Nouwens	Angela Stent	

Published for the IISS by
Routledge Journals, an imprint of Taylor & Francis, an Informa business.

ISBN 978-1-032-80662-4 paperback / 978-1-003-49800-1 ebook

About the IISS The IISS, a registered charity with offices in Washington, London, Manama, Singapore and Berlin, is the world's leading authority on political–military conflict. It is the primary independent source of accurate, objective information on international strategic issues. Publications include *The Military Balance*, an annual reference work on each nation's defence capabilities; *Survival*, a bimonthly journal on international affairs; *Strategic Comments*, an online analysis of topical issues in international affairs; and the *Adelphi* series of books on issues of international security.

SUBMISSIONS

To submit an article, authors are advised to follow these guidelines:

- *Survival* articles are around 4,000–10,000 words long including endnotes. A word count should be included with a draft.
- All text, including endnotes, should be double-spaced with wide margins.
- Any tables or artwork should be supplied in separate files, ideally not embedded in the document or linked to text around it.
- All *Survival* articles are expected to include endnote references. These should be complete and include first and last names of authors, titles of articles (even from newspapers), place of publication, publisher, exact publication dates, volume and issue number (if from a journal) and page numbers. Web sources should include complete URLs and DOIs if available.
- A summary of up to 150 words should be included with the article. The summary should state the main argument clearly and concisely, not simply say what the article is about.

- A short author's biography of one or two lines should also be included. This information will appear at the foot of the first page of the article.

Please note that *Survival* has a strict policy of listing multiple authors in alphabetical order.

Submissions should be made by email, in Microsoft Word format, to survival@iiss.org. Alternatively, hard copies may be sent to *Survival*, IISS–US, 2121 K Street NW, Suite 801, Washington, DC 20037, USA.

The editorial review process can take up to three months. *Survival*'s acceptance rate for unsolicited manuscripts is less than 20%. *Survival* does not normally provide referees' comments in the event of rejection. Authors are permitted to submit simultaneously elsewhere so long as this is consistent with the policy of the other publication and the Editors of *Survival* are informed of the dual submission.

Readers are encouraged to comment on articles from the previous issue. Letters should be concise, no longer than 750 words and relate directly to the argument or points made in the original article.

Survival: Global Politics and Strategy (Print ISSN 0039-6338, Online ISSN 1468-2699) is published bimonthly for a total of 6 issues per year by Taylor & Francis Group, 4 Park Square, Milton Park, Abingdon, Oxon, OX14 4RN, UK. Periodicals postage paid (Permit no. 13095) at Brooklyn, NY 11256.

Airfreight and mailing in the USA by agent named World Container Inc., c/o BBT 150-15, 183rd Street, Jamaica, NY 11413, USA.

US Postmaster: Send address changes to Survival, World Container Inc., c/o BBT 150-15, 183rd Street, Jamaica, NY 11413, USA.

Subscription records are maintained at Taylor & Francis Group, 4 Park Square, Milton Park, Abingdon, OX14 4RN, UK.

Subscription information: For more information and subscription rates, please see tandfonline.com/pricing/journal/TSUR. Taylor & Francis journals are available in a range of different packages, designed to suit every library's needs and budget. This journal is available for institutional subscriptions with online-only or print & online options. This journal may also be available as part of our libraries, subject collections or archives. For more information on our sales packages, please visit librarianresources.taylorandfrancis.com.

For support with any institutional subscription, please visit help.tandfonline.com or email our dedicated team at subscriptions@tandf.co.uk.

Subscriptions purchased at the personal rate are strictly for personal, non-commercial use only. The reselling of personal subscriptions is prohibited. Personal subscriptions must be purchased with a personal cheque, credit card or BAC/wire transfer. Proof of personal status may be requested.

Back issues: Please visit https://taylorandfrancis.com/journals/customer-services/ for more information on how to purchase back issues.

Ordering information: To subscribe to the journal, please contact T&F Customer Services, Informa UK Ltd, Sheepen Place, Colchester, Essex, CO3 3LP, UK. Tel: +44 (0) 20 8052 2030; email subscriptions@tandf.co.uk.

Taylor & Francis journals are priced in USD, GBP and EUR (as well as AUD and CAD for a limited number of journals). All subscriptions are charged depending on where the end customer is based. If you are unsure which rate applies to you, please contact Customer Services. All subscriptions are payable in advance and all rates include postage. We are required to charge applicable VAT/GST on all print and online combination subscriptions, in addition to our online-only journals. Subscriptions are entered on an annual basis, i.e., January to December. Payment may be made by sterling cheque, dollar cheque, euro cheque, international money order, National Giro or credit cards (Amex, Visa and Mastercard).

Disclaimer: The International Institute for Strategic Studies (IISS) and our publisher Informa UK Limited, trading as Taylor & Francis Group ('T&F'), make every effort to ensure the accuracy of all the information (the 'Content') contained in our publications. However, IISS and our publisher T&F, our agents and our licensors make no representations or warranties whatsoever as to the accuracy, completeness or suitability for any purpose of the Content. Any opinions and views expressed in this publication are the opinions and views of the authors, and are not the views of or endorsed by IISS or our publisher T&F. The accuracy of the Content should not be relied upon and should be independently verified with primary sources of information, and any reliance on the Content is at your own risk. IISS and our publisher T&F make no representations, warranties or guarantees, whether express or implied, that the Content is accurate, complete or up to date. IISS and our publisher T&F shall not be liable for any losses, actions, claims, proceedings, demands, costs, expenses, damages and other liabilities whatsoever or howsoever caused arising directly or indirectly in connection with, in relation to or arising out of the use of the Content. Full Terms & Conditions of access and use can be found at http://www.tandfonline.com/page/terms-and-conditions.

Informa UK Limited, trading as Taylor & Francis Group, grants authorisation for individuals to photocopy copyright material for private research use, on the sole basis that requests for such use are referred directly to the requestor's local Reproduction Rights Organization (RRO). The copyright fee is exclusive of any charge or fee levied. In order to contact your local RRO, please contact International Federation of Reproduction Rights Organizations (IFRRO), rue du Prince Royal, 87, B-1050 Brussels, Belgium; email ifrro@skynet.be; Copyright Clearance Center Inc., 222 Rosewood Drive, Danvers, MA 01923, USA; email info@copyright.com; or Copyright Licensing Agency, 90 Tottenham Court Road, London, W1P 0LP, UK; email cla@cla.co.uk. This authorisation does not extend to any other kind of copying, by any means, in any form, for any purpose other than private research use.

Submission information: See https://www.tandfonline.com/journals/tsur20

Advertising: See https://taylorandfrancis.com/contact/advertising/

Permissions: See help.tandfonline.com/Librarian/s/article/Permissions

All Taylor & Francis Group journals are printed on paper from renewable sources by accredited partners.

August–September 2024

Not More, But More Assured: Optimising US Nuclear Posture

Douglas Barrie and Timothy Wright

The United States is facing two nuclear rivals in an already deteriorating security environment. China is a rising power aiming to triple its warhead holdings and substantially increase its delivery systems. It is moving away – with a concerning lack of transparency – from a minimum-deterrence posture. Russia is a weakened state but one with a strategic arsenal broadly the size of the United States'. It continues to modernise its strategic triad while simultaneously attempting to develop so-called novel delivery systems. Moscow issued nuclear-tinged warnings to those supporting Ukraine following its full-scale invasion in February 2022 and may revise its nuclear posture in the near future.[1] Meanwhile, China and Russia are growing strategically closer. The United States is compelled to respond to these developments practically without the guardrails of strategic arms control.

One of the most notable responses so far to this darkening backdrop has been the work of the Congressional Commission on the Strategic Posture of the United States.[2] Authorised by Congress in 2022, the commission's intent was to review the US strategic posture as the country potentially faces two nuclear-peer rivals and to make recommendations to President Joe Biden and Congress concerning the long-term stance of the United States. Twelve months in the making, the commission's October 2023 report indicated

Douglas Barrie is IISS Senior Fellow for Military Aerospace. **Timothy Wright** is a research associate in the IISS Defence and Military Analysis Programme.

Survival | vol. 66 no. 4 | August–September 2024 | pp. 7–28   https://doi.org/10.1080/00396338.2024.2380194

how the United States' nuclear posture could evolve. There is considerable value in the report, not least in its recognition that the post-Cold War benign neglect of the United States' nuclear-weapons manufacturing and support infrastructure needs to be redressed, and the present nuclear-systems-modernisation programme sustained and expedited; as well as its acknowledgement that conventional capabilities are an important element of deterrence. But the report's most urgent recommendation is that the confluence of burgeoning threats and a worsening security environment require Washington to adopt new measures if it is to maintain a credible nuclear deterrent.[3]

A central recommendation of the report is that the US should be able to simultaneously deter China and Russia and, if deterrence fails, to fight at the conventional level and, implicitly, the nuclear level. The compulsion to deliver a 'consensus report' precluded the commission as a whole from endorsing an increase in the size of the US stockpile.[4] Some of its members, however, considered this 'inevitable' and stated that the 'number of delivery systems should increase'.[5]

The US already has a modernisation programme under way, known as the 'Program(s) of Record', or POR. The commission said that while it remains essential, it has been rendered inadequate by the deterioration in US relations with Russia and China, and emerging challenges posed by changes to their nuclear postures.[6] The commission also cited Beijing's and Moscow's ongoing efforts to improve their integrated air and missile defences (IAMD) as reasons for the US to modify its strategic- and theatre-nuclear-force postures.[7] Indeed, it would take near wilful ignorance to argue that the world today is as stable and peer rivalry no more abrasive or fraught than they were in the first decade of this century. As the report stated: 'The size and composition of the nuclear force must account for the possibility of combined aggression from Russia and China. U.S. strategy should no longer treat China's nuclear forces as a "lesser included" threat. The United States needs a nuclear posture capable of simultaneously deterring both countries.'[8]

A more insecure world, however, does not necessarily mean that Beijing and Moscow will be marching in nuclear lockstep to undermine US strategic deterrence. Russian President Vladimir Putin's repeated invocations in 2023 of Russia's nuclear capabilities in attempting to cow those backing Ukraine did not gain unbridled support from China.[9] Furthermore, during the last decade, Russia has continued war-gaming against China, and simulations have included the employment of nuclear weapons.[10] If Beijing and Moscow's 'no-limits friendship' did extend to some form of loose nuclear alliance – and this remains a very big if – any US response predicated on matching its two nuclear peers warhead for warhead, delivery system for delivery system, would be costly folly. Beijing, Moscow or both might simply respond in kind by building more, and the Cold War arms race would be sadly reprised.

It is unlikely that Beijing's projected extra 1,000 warheads by the mid-2030s, even when combined with Russia's deployed forces and warhead-upload capacity, would fundamentally undermine the US deterrent, even excluding the United States' upload capacity and the 500 or so warheads that France and the United Kingdom will probably retain. It is also unlikely that Beijing and Moscow will actually calculate that daring the US to unleash upwards of 2,500 warheads is a good wager. Nevertheless, for the United States to ensure that its deterrent options remain durably credible, it should make qualitative rather than quantitative changes to its force posture that will better meet potential military requirements.

Adversarial backdrop

China has historically relied on a small nuclear force as part of its strategic posture, establishing deterrence by way of a credible second-strike nuclear capability. This approach, described in Chinese defence White Papers as 'lean and effective', obviated the need for Beijing to match the size of much larger Soviet/Russian and US arsenals, as Chinese policymakers believed that the threat of using even a small number of nuclear weapons to retaliate against an adversary was sufficient to prevent a first strike.[11] The size and capability of China's nuclear forces, however, have changed considerably in the past decade as Chinese President Xi Jinping has increasingly directed the People's Liberation Army (PLA) to improve its capabilities and 'establish a strong system of strategic deterrence'.[12] Accordingly, Beijing has made qualitative and quantitative changes to its nuclear forces.

Although Chinese leaders have vowed that it 'will not participate in any form of arms race', its nuclear forces' expansion casts doubt on this claim.[13] The United States assesses that China's nuclear arsenal will probably grow from its present 500 nuclear warheads to over 1,000 by 2030.[14] In 2021, three large fields were identified in central and western China that together included 330 intercontinental ballistic missile (ICBM) silos, some of which the US assesses have since been loaded with ICBMs.[15] China has also improved the accuracy, mobility, readiness and survivability of its nuclear forces, especially the PLA Rocket Force, which is responsible for most of its nuclear capabilities. The US contends that China is probably also developing new types of strategic weaponry, including a strategic-range hypersonic glide vehicle (HGV) and a fractional orbital bombardment (FOB) system.[16]

Beijing now has a nascent triad, the most important element of which remains its land-based systems. Statements by China's leadership and Chinese national-policy documents direct the PLA to improve its nuclear capabilities across all domains.[17] The PLA Air Force is developing a nuclear-delivery capability, though it will at least initially be confined to theatre range. China's deployment of the JL-3 submarine-launched ballistic missile (SLBM), which has a greater range and larger payload than its predecessor, and its ongoing development of a new nuclear-powered ballistic-missile submarine (SSBN) support a stronger sea-based deterrent more easily capable of threatening the continental United States.[18]

While the qualitative and quantitative growth of China's nuclear forces is evident, the purpose driving its strategy is less so, and is characterised by US officials as opaque.[19] Beijing has routinely rejected accusations that it is expanding its nuclear arsenal. Some Chinese officials have said, however, that the perceived threat from the US requires that China adapt its security posture.[20] Some Chinese analysts have argued that China's historical approach to nuclear deterrence is no longer sustainable due to improved US conventional precision-strike capabilities in combination with rising strategic competition.[21] It is also possible that China's leadership views a larger nuclear arsenal as the hallmark of a great power, advancing Xi's objective of the 'great rejuvenation of the Chinese nation' and symbolising a 'strong country with a strong military'.[22]

Russia is less opaque regarding changes to its nuclear forces. Details about ongoing developments and the rationale behind them, however, remain thin. Faced with serious economic travails in the 1990s and early 2000s, Moscow directed much of its limited defence budget towards maintaining nuclear parity with the United States. That consideration remains the key factor guiding Moscow's decision-making with respect to its nuclear forces.[23] Through its 20-year modernisation programme, Russia has developed and deployed new platforms and delivery vehicles, replaced older launchers with more modern systems, upgraded warhead storage and basing sites, and improved nuclear command and control. The Russian government said in 2023 that the percentage of 'modern' – possibly meaning post-Soviet – weapons and equipment had reached 95% across Russia's strategic forces.[24] Furthermore, Russia could deploy an additional 1,000 warheads within a short time frame on deployed strategic systems if New START collapsed or expired without a replacement treaty.[25]

In addition to modernising its 'traditional' triad, Russia is working on several types of 'novel' strategic systems that currently have no known analogue in China or the US. These include an intercontinental-range nuclear-armed HGV known as *Avangard* (RS-SS-19 *Stiletto* Mod 4), a nuclear-powered and nuclear-armed cruise missile called *Burevestnik* (RS-SSC-X-09 *Skyfall*), and *Poseidon* (*Kanyon*), a nuclear-powered and -armed uninhabited underwater vehicle. Russia's leadership has argued that the development of these strategic systems is a response to what it claims is the United States' pursuit of a 'global missile defence system'. Russia's leadership believes US missile defences have degraded the credibility of its deterrent and forced Moscow to develop systems that can circumvent them.[26] Thus, Russia is modernising its large arsenal of an estimated minimum of 2,000 non-strategic nuclear weapons with new systems and possibly expanding this stockpile by operationalising older nuclear ordnance long thought retired.[27]

Getting defensive

Adversaries' strategic missile defences are now a greater concern for Washington. The commission noted that advances in Russian and Chinese IAMD require addressing by both US strategic and theatre nuclear forces, and that the US should 'accelerate efforts to develop advanced counter-measures to adversary IAMD'.[28] Although it did not directly address how Chinese and Russian missile defence threatened potential US response options, it noted the importance of the US being able to potentially 'absorb a first strike and respond effectively with enough forces to cause unaccept-able damage to the aggressor while still posing a credible threat to the other nuclear power'.[29]

China has one of the world's largest IAMD architectures for defending against aircraft and cruise missiles. Furthermore, the PLA is undertaking a coordinated effort to develop multi-tiered missile defence against strategic- and theatre-range ballistic missiles. Beyond its existing inventory, China is developing several new types of land- and sea-based missile-interceptor systems that would represent a capability leap if successfully developed and deployed. This includes an exo-atmospheric mid-course interceptor known as the DN-3, which appears somewhat similar to the United States' deployed Ground-based Midcourse Defense (GMD) interceptor.[30] Like the GMD, the DN-3 uses a kinetic kill vehicle that could defeat incoming nuclear warheads during the mid-course phase of flight. China has conducted mul-tiple mid-course tests of the DN-3 since at least 2010. It most recently tested the system in April 2023, when, according to Chinese defence officials, it intercepted a simulated warhead.[31]

China has also strengthened its IAMD-supporting infrastructure with ground- and spaced-based radars – part of an integrated early-warning system that can be used to detect, track and intercept strategic-range bal-listic missiles.[32] Beijing and Moscow have also cooperated in 2016, 2017 and possibly 2019 on joint ballistic-missile-defence exercises to improve their respective IAMD capabilities.[33] Whether these exercises include sharing detection and tracking data is unclear.

China has criticised the US for its development of certain types of missile defences by claiming that this has 'undermined global strategic stability'.[34] Thus far, however, it has not provided an explanation for its pursuit of what appears to be an analogous system other than the boilerplate mantra that it is 'defensive in nature and not targeted against any country'.[35] Likewise, Russia regularly criticises US missile-defence developments as threatening strategic stability even though it too has devoted significant resources to developing ballistic-missile defences.[36]

Russia has also researched nuclear-armed and conventional hit-to-kill technologies as part of long-standing efforts to protect Moscow and Russia's nuclear command and control from attack. Efforts along these lines began in the 1950s, and by 1974 the A-35 (RS-AB-1 *Galosh*) system had entered experimental service. This was followed by the A-135 (RS-AB-3), which came onstream in the mid-1990s. A new interceptor system, the A-235, is now in development. A large, mobile surface-to-air missile system, the S-500, is also nearing service entry. Former Russian defence minister Sergei Shoigu said in April 2024 that the first S-500 systems would be provided to the Aerospace Forces this year. He added that their purpose was to provide, among other things, 'high-quality cover for the most important objects of the command and control system, strategic nuclear forces, and groups of forces'.[37]

US modernisation plans

The US is more than a decade into upgrading delivery systems and warheads across all three legs of its nuclear triad. It committed to modernising its deterrent in 2010, before most of the changes in China's and Russia's nuclear postures became apparent. Yet Washington has appeared slow to react to those changes and needs to do more than simply stay the course on modernisation. The near-term American steps that would be of greatest value in countering Chinese and Russian missile-defence developments appear confined mainly to replacing existing components and ensuring their operability as opposed to developing new types of advanced countermeasures to defeat adversary capabilities.[38] To the extent that plans for enhancing US penetration capabilities are in place, they have not been accelerated despite the challenge of advanced IAMD. While the existing arrangements and tempo of US modernisation were sufficient in a less threatening era, it is not clear that they are now.

The US Air Force (USAF) plans to replace its existing 400 LGM-30G *Minuteman* III ICBMs with an equivalent number of a new missile known as the LGM-35 *Sentinel*. This missile will carry an upgraded warhead and re-entry vehicle known respectively as the W78-1 and Mk21A. US officials have said that the *Sentinel* will offer advantages over the *Minuteman* III, but whether these are attributable to a more advanced missile design (for instance, a shorter boost phase or protective coatings to shield the missile against radiation) or to wider improvement across the whole architecture of the land-based leg of the triad (including command, control and communications upgrades, and refurbished and modernised launch facilities) is uncertain. Information from the US Department of Defense and the National Nuclear Security Administration (NNSA) does make clear that risk and costs minimisation are the main drivers behind the W78-1/Mk21A programme, which the NNSA says 'does not provide new military capabilities'.[39] *Sentinel* will eventually be equipped with a re-entry vehicle currently known as the Next Generation Re-entry Vehicle (NGRV), aimed at improving the survivability, lethality and accuracy of the re-entry vehicle, but Defense Department documents do not specify when the NGRV will enter service, and Washington has not accelerated the new re-entry vehicle's development.[40]

In the maritime realm, Washington will keep its continuous at-sea deterrent through the replacement of its 14 *Ohio*-class SSBNs with 12 *Columbia*-class submarines. The commission criticised the *Columbia*-class programme for delivery delays and raised concerns about the smaller number of submarines that the US Navy will procure, as well as the smaller number of launch tubes the design will have compared to the *Ohio* class.[41] But the commission did not appear to consider that fewer *Columbia*-class SSBNs will be necessary to maintain the navy requirement of having ten boats at sea at any given time because the new submarines will be fitted with a life-of-the-ship reactor. This should eliminate the need to conduct a lengthy mid-life refuel, during which an *Ohio*-class boat would be in drydock for an extended period and unavailable for patrols.[42]

Although the navy will have a new submarine, it will continue to use the UGM-133 *Trident* II SLBM possibly until the 2080s, meaning the missile may be in service for roughly 90 years before it is retired. *Trident* will benefit from a second life-extension programme by which the navy will replace solid rocket motors and ignitors and update the missile's guidance packages, eyeing upgraded operational capacity in the late 2030s.[43] The missile will be equipped with a replacement warhead and aeroshell collectively known as the W93/MK 7 beginning sometime in the mid-2030s. The new warhead and aeroshell will 'incorporate modern technologies' that allow it to 'keep pace with future adversary threats' and provide the navy 'with a more survivable weapon', suggesting that it may feature new penetration aids or potentially more advanced passive and active defences.[44]

The US bomber fleet's nuclear capability will be stronger by virtue of the introduction of the very-low-observable B-21 *Raider* bomber, particularly if the USAF's goal of acquiring more than 100 aircraft is met. The USAF currently fields 20 low-observable B-2 *Spirit* bombers alongside a larger number of less-survivable B-52H *Stratofortresse*s. The nuclear-capable B-52 will remain in service until around 2050 and will receive new engines, radar and avionics in an upgrade programme. The B-21 fleet will succeed the USAF's 20 nuclear-capable B-2 and 44 conventional Rockwell B-1B *Lancer* bombers. The USAF plans to procure at least 100 B-21 aircraft, with some suggestions from senior US personnel that it may well require more aircraft to meet future needs.[45]

The B-21 is intended to challenge Chinese or Russian air defences

The commission also advocates purchasing additional B-21s.[46] The B-21 will not only fulfil the nuclear role but also provide conventional long-range-strike capacity across the globe, not least in the Asia-Pacific and Euro-Atlantic theatres. The B-21 is intended to operate within highly contested airspace and, when combined with the AGM-181 Long-range Stand-off (LRSO) nuclear-armed cruise missile, to pose a challenge to Chinese or Russian air defences due to what USAF officials have described as the missile's 'improved survivability and standoff range'.[47] The AGM-181 will replace the Boeing AGM-86B, of which the International Institute for Strategic Studies estimates there are around 536 in the United States' active inventory. The original acquisition number of the AGM-181 was for 1,020 missiles, though more recently the USAF has declined to discuss the total number it plans to purchase. There is little detail in the public domain about the LRSO's capabilities, but testimony provided by US defence officials regarding US hypersonics programmes have made it clear that the weapon will not be capable of hypersonic (Mach 5+) speeds.[48]

Inflated concerns?

Threat inflation was a hazard throughout the Cold War, even with the very real risk of war with the Soviet Union, and the tenor of parts of the commission's report suggests that it remains a residual risk. Bomber gaps, missile gaps and windows of vulnerability were all at one point common parlance in Washington. By the 1980s, the US intelligence community was projecting that by the late 1990s, 'all elements of Soviet strategic offensive forces [would] be extensively modernized'.[49] In the event, by then the Soviet Union had ceased to exist, and its modernisation programme was in tatters.

Of course, the early bomber and missile gaps turned out to favour the United States, while the chief vulnerability proved to be that of the Soviet economy. None of the concerns were born initially out of an intention to mislead. Rather, they seemed to stem from a mixture of lacking or inaccurate information, confirmation bias and an understandable tendency towards worst-case planning.

Bombers featured in the commission's report, which painted a comparative picture unfavourable to the US. The commission flagged concern over what it viewed as a 'general lack of urgency' in meeting the schedule for the nuclear-modernisation POR and the fact that the B-21 was 'already experiencing delays'.[50] The B-21 is in fact behind schedule and was flown for the first time around a year later than envisaged, but this is far from unusual in combat-aircraft development, similar delays having arisen with the B-2.[51] Still, the report noted that 'as of 2020, the People's Liberation Army Air Force had operationally fielded the nuclear-capable H-6N bomber, providing a platform for the air component of the [People's Republic of China's] nascent nuclear triad'.[52] Absent from the report, however, was any acknowledgement that the B-21 is an advanced, very-low-observable platform, while the Xian H-6N is merely a variant, albeit much upgraded, of the Tupolev Tu-16 *Badger*, the prototype for which was first flown in 1952. The H-6 is a medium-range rather than a long-range aircraft and cannot threaten the continental United States. China is developing a low-observable, long-range bomber, the H-20, but a prototype has yet to be flown and the aircraft is probably at least a decade away from being available in operationally significant numbers.[53]

A similar lightness of touch, or lack of detail, is apparent in the commission's discussion of the air-launched element of Moscow's modernisation programme. Describing the overall programme as nearly complete, it does not acknowledge that Moscow has repeatedly been unable to meet its ambition to field a new bomber. A Soviet-era requirement for a low-observable strategic bomber was never realised, while the more recent bomber-modernisation road map has had to be repeatedly redrawn. In the mid-2010s, the prototype for the Russian air force's next-generation bomber was to be delivered in 2023.[54] As of 2024, the status of the project was unclear, but no prototype has been flown or even rolled out. A first airframe may be under construction, but even this remains open to doubt. Russia has resorted to restarting production of the Tu-160 *Blackjack* long-range bomber, the design of which began in the early 1970s, and has probably further delayed any plan to introduce a low-observable strategic bomber.[55]

Prior to the publication of the commission report in October 2023, the Biden administration had argued there was no need to increase the size of the US arsenal to guarantee deterrence, and implied that to do so would be foolhardy.[56] By mid-2024, however, the US government was cautioning that 'we may reach a point in the coming years where an increase from current deployed numbers is required'.[57] A key element in the assessment of a nuclear arsenal's size has been the persistent presence of an arms-control architecture that dictated the size of US nuclear forces. This architecture's ongoing erosion risks undermining strategic stability. Russia and the US have not exchanged New START biannual data since September 2022, and the information Moscow and Washington possess on each other's nuclear-force structure is growing outdated. This has already begun to affect each country's level of confidence in its ability to assess compliance with the central limitations of New START while it remains in force.[58] It will also almost certainly reduce each one's understanding of the size of the other's arsenal if the agreement is not replaced.

The lack of verification and transparency mechanisms, and mutual suspicion concerning potential increases in warhead or launcher numbers, risk worst-case assessments that could inadvertently generate quantitative increases, whether the assessments are accurate or not. Just such a worst-case analysis seemed apparent in the Defense Department's annual report on Chinese military capabilities in 2023. The report raised its estimate of Chinese ICBM launchers to 500, compared to the 100 listed in the 2021 report. This was because it chose to count all potential launchers, including more than 300 silos discovered in 2021, rather than just operational systems.[59] The information prompted some Republicans with leadership positions in the House Armed Services subcommittees to advocate 'higher numbers and new capabilities'.[60]

Quantity or quality?

In an increasingly fraught security environment with fast-eroding arms control in which two nuclear rivals are preoccupied with deterring each other, US policymakers may be tempted to consider withdrawing from its few remaining arms-control commitments and increasing the size of its nuclear forces. This approach has support within the Republican Party.[61] If Donald Trump wins the November 2024 presidential election, it could become US policy, assuming the 2016–20 Trump administration's hostility towards arms control, evident from the United States' withdrawal from the 1987 US–Russia Intermediate-Range Nuclear Forces Treaty and the 2015 Joint Comprehensive Plan of Action on Iran's nuclear programme, and from Trump's enthusiasm for strengthening US nuclear capabilities, are indicative of his current views.[62] As noted, even Biden's re-election would not guarantee that US stockpile holdings would be held at their current level.

Increasing the number of deployed warheads and delivery systems is clearly an option, even if the commission was constrained from openly recommending this. Such a move would also likely be ineffective and counterproductive. The response in Beijing and Moscow might simply be to match US increases, while a US increase in holdings would not adequately address either Chinese and Russian capability developments or changes in doctrine.

A qualitative rather than quantitative response may well be more effective, while also allowing the US to hold the ethical high ground as a responsible actor. Such an approach would align with what one senior US official in June 2024 called a 'better' as opposed to a 'more' approach, calling for 'discrete capabilities that fill an important niche'.[63]

Assured delivery

Given the forward lean of the report with respect to improving theatre and strategic nuclear capabilities, there are some potentially significant lacunae in the air domain. The commission noted that the pending introduction of the Lockheed Martin F-35A *Lighting* II/B61-12 nuclear-bomb combination is bolstering NATO's dual-capable-aircraft capability. But this observation sits curiously alongside its recommendation that US theatre nuclear forces be capable of penetrating advanced IAMD with high confidence. Irrespective of the capability of the F-35A – and it is a highly capable platform – relying only on a free-fall bomb requiring near over-flight of the target raises the question of survivability.

Notwithstanding lengthy recommendations on improving US strategic capabilities, the commission did not suggest that Washington reconsider its present position on hypersonic cruise-missile and boost-glide systems. The US has so far maintained that these classes of Mach 5+ weapons will be conventional only, but US officials have highlighted the value of their capacity to 'credibly threaten and, if necessary, defeat heavily defended targets' and to credibly deter adversaries.[64] Given the challenges of detection and interception, very-high-speed, in-atmosphere weapons could provide Washington with a formidable means of addressing concerns over Chinese and Russian IAMD capabilities without necessarily increasing the size of the United States' nuclear stockpile. Moscow has already fielded a nuclear-armed boost-glide system and is working on dual-capable very-high-speed cruise-missile designs. In all likelihood, the same goes for Beijing. Some US allies are also developing this technology. France has advocated very-high-speed technology as a way of overcoming IAMD and is working on a nuclear-armed hypersonic or very-high-supersonic cruise missile known as the ASN4G.[65]

Developing and deploying hypersonic glide vehicles and cruise missiles as nuclear-delivery vehicles while accelerating the time frame for developing new re-entry vehicles such as the NGRV and W93/MK 7 argu-ably would enhance the US deterrent. The *Sentinel* ICBM and *Trident* SLBM could both theoretically be adapted as delivery vehicles for a nuclear-armed HGV, Russia having adapted its UR-100 (RS-SS-19 *Stiletto*) ICBM to deliver the *Avangard* HGV. The US is already developing an HGV design known as the Common Hypersonic Glide Body (C-HGB), which could potentially be equipped with a nuclear warhead and integrated into either launch vehicle. However, because the glider is not equipped with a high-explosive warhead and will use kinetic energy to destroy targets, the C-HGB might be too small to accommodate a nuclear payload.[66] A new HGV design might require the NNSA to either develop a new warhead or modify an existing one to be incorporated into a glider design. Given the demands of its other warhead programmes, this would be time-consuming and expensive, but might still reward the effort.

*   *   *

Although hypersonic glide vehicles and hypersonic cruise missiles have been criticised as destabilising because of warhead and target ambiguity, it is worth noting that warhead ambiguity is a characteristic of many existing Chinese and Russian systems, and, in the past, has featured in US systems. Multiple independently targetable re-entry vehicles – long constituents of strategic nuclear arsenals and capable of manoeuvring in flight – already arguably create target ambiguity, as their warheads are individually tar-getable and can be dispersed over wide areas.

Despite the challenges of developing and deploying hypersonic glide vehicles and cruise missiles as nuclear-delivery vehicles, they would improve Washington's ability to shape an opponent's decision calculus and reduce its capacity to pursue deterrence by denial. Possessing these systems – especially more manoeuvrable ones – would also enhance the United States' ability to hold at risk multiple high-value, well-defended targets and reinforce plan-ners' confidence in retaliatory strikes on such targets if deterrence fails.

A qualitative approach to modernisation could actually benefit arms control. By focusing on qualitative rather than quantitative improvements,

Washington can enhance the capability of its nuclear forces without significantly increasing warhead or launcher numbers, and thereby maintain its international non-proliferation commitments and avoid fuelling a quantitative arms race. There is precedent for accommodating such systems within already agreed treaty definitions. For example, Russia's nuclear-armed HGV *Avangard* is accountable under New START. If strategic relations among the United States, China and Russia eventually become more conducive to arms-control negotiations, the United States will be in a stronger position to argue for central limitations at levels that are similar or lower than those existing today.

Notes

1   See 'Ryabkov dopustil izmeneniye yadernoy doktriny RF iz-za deystviy SSHA' Рябков допустил изменение ядерной доктрины РФ из-за действий США [Ryabkov allowed a change in the Russian nuclear doctrine due to US actions], TASS, 11 June 2024, https://tass.ru/politika/21067077; and 'MID RF schitayet neobkhodimym utochnit' nekotoryye parametry yadernoy doktriny' МИД РФ считает необходимым уточнить некоторые параметры ядерной доктрины [The Russian Foreign Ministry considers it necessary to clarify some parameters of the nuclear doctrine], TASS, 18 June 2024, https://tass.ru/politika/21132395.

2   Congressional Commission on the Strategic Posture of the United States, 'America's Strategic Posture: The Final Report of the Congressional Commission on the Strategic Posture of the United States', October 2023, available at https://www.ida.org/-/media/feature/publications/a/am/americas-strategic-posture/strategic-posture-commission-report.ashx.

3   *Ibid.*, p. v.
4   *Ibid.*, p. vi.
5   *Ibid.*, p. vi.
6   *Ibid.*, p. vi.
7   *Ibid.*, p. vi.
8   *Ibid.*, p. viii.
9   See Max Seddon et al., 'Xi Jinping Warned Vladimir Putin Against Nuclear Attack in Ukraine', *Financial Times*, 5 July 2023, https://www.ft.com/content/c5ce76df-9b1b-4dfc-a619-07da1d40cbd3.
10 See Max Seddon and Chris Cook, 'Leaked Russian Military Files Reveal Criteria for Nuclear Strike', *Financial Times*, 28 February 2024, https://www.ft.com/content/f18e6e1f-5c3d-4554-aee5-50a730b306b7.
11 China's defence White Papers consistently used 'lean and effective' to describe its nuclear capabilities from 2005. It stopped using this language to describe its nuclear forces in 2019. See State Council Information Office of the People's Republic of China, 'China's Military Strategy', May 2015, https://www.andrewerickson.

com/wp-content/uploads/2019/07/ China-Defense-White-Paper_2015_ English-Chinese_Annotated.pdf; and Jeffrey Lewis, *Paper Tigers: China's Nuclear Posture*, Adelphi 446 (Abingdon: Routledge for the International Institute for Strategic Studies, 2014), p. 35.

12 See State Council of the People's Republic of China, 'Full Text of the Report to the 20th National Congress of the Communist Party of China', 25 October 2022, https://english.www.gov.cn/ news/topnews/202210/25/content_ WS6357df20c6d0a757729e1bfc.html.

13 See Ministry of Foreign Affairs of the People's Republic of China, 'Remarks by Director-General Mr. Sun Xiaobo at the High-level Segment of the Conference on Disarmament', 26 February 2024, https://www.fmprc.gov.cn/ mfa_eng/wjb_663304/zzjg_663340/ jks_665232/kjfywj_665252/202402/ t20240229_11252086.html.

14 See State Council of the People's Republic of China, 'Full Text of the Report to the 20th National Congress of the Communist Party of China'; and US Department of Defense, 'Military and Security Developments Involving the People's Republic of China: 2023', 19 October 2023, p. 66, https://media.defense.gov/2023/ Oct/19/2003323409/-1/-1/1/2023-MILITARY-AND-SECURITY-DEVELOPMENTS-INVOLVING-THE-PEOPLES-REPUBLIC-OF-CHINA.PDF.

15 US Department of Defense, 'Military and Security Developments Involving the People's Republic of China: 2023'.

16 *Ibid.*, p. 67.

17 See State Council of the People's Republic of China, 'China's National Defense in the New Era', July 2019, https://english.www.gov.cn/atts/stream/ files/5d3943eec6d0a15c923d2036.

18 See Anthony Capaccio, 'China Has Put Longer-range ICBMs on Its Nuclear Subs, US Says', Bloomberg, 18 November 2022, https://www.bloomberg. com/news/articles/2022-11-18/ us-says-china-s-subs-armed-with-longer-range-ballistic-missiles; and Timothy Wright, 'China Beyond Minimum Deterrence: Reading Beijing's Nuclear Developments', Military Balance Blog, 13 January 2023, https://www.iiss.org/en/online-analysis/ military-balance/2023/01/china-beyond-minimum-deterrence-reading-beijings-nuclear-developments/.

19 See US Department of State, 'Testimony Before the Senate Foreign Relations Committee: The Future of Arms Control and Deterrence', 15 May 2024, https://www.state.gov/ testimony-before-the-senate-foreign-relations-committee-the-future-of-arms-control-and-deterrence/.

20 See Timothy Wright (@Wright_T_J), post to X, 8 December 2021, https://twitter.com/Wright_T_J/ status/1468544694950977544.

21 See Bin Li and Riqiang Wu, 'U.S. Strategy of Damage Limitation Vis-à-vis China: Long-term Programs and Effects', *China International Strategy Review*, 25 April 2024, https://link. springer.com/article/10.1007/s42533-024-00153-w; and Yao Yunzhu, 'China Will Not Change Its Nuclear Policy', *China US Focus*, 22 April 2013, https://www.

chinausfocus.com/peace-security/china-will-not-change-its-no-first-use-policy.

22 See, respectively, Tong Zhao, 'The Real Motives for China's Nuclear Expansion', *Foreign Affairs*, 3 May 2024, https://www.foreignaffairs.com/china/real-motives-chinas-nuclear-expansion; National Ethnic Affairs Commission, 'Achieving Rejuvenation Is the Dream of the Chinese People', 29 November 2012, https://www.neac.gov.cn/seac/c103372/202201/1156514.shtml; and Xi Jinping, 'Secure a Decisive Victory in Building a Moderately Prosperous Society in All Respects and Strive for the Great Success of Socialism with Chinese Characteristics for a New Era', Xinhuanet, 18 October 2017, p. 47, http://www.xinhuanet.com/english/download/Xi_Jinping's_report_at_19th_CPC_National_Congress.pdf.

23 See 'Russia Suspends New START to Make Sure Nuclear Parity Is Observed – Kremlin Spokesman', TASS, 21 February 2023, https://tass.com/politics/1579973.

24 See President of Russia, 'Expanded Meeting of Defence Ministry Board', 19 December 2023, http://en.kremlin.ru/events/president/news/73035.

25 See Matt Korda, 'If Arms Control Collapses, US and Russian Strategic Nuclear Arsenals Could Double in Size', Federation of American Scientists, 7 February 2023, https://fas.org/publication/if-arms-control-collapses-us-and-russian-strategic-nuclear-arsenals-could-double-in-size/.

26 President of Russia, 'Presidential Address to the Federal Assembly', 1 March 2018, http://en.kremlin.ru/events/president/news/56957.

27 See US State Department, 'Report to the Senate on the Status of Tactical (Nonstrategic) Nuclear Weapons Negotiations Pursuant to Subparagraph (a)(12)(B) of the Senate Resolution of Advice and Consent to Ratification of the New START Treaty', 16 April 2024, https://www.state.gov/report-on-the-status-of-tactical-nonstrategic-nuclear-weapons-negotiations/.

28 Congressional Commission on the Strategic Posture of the United States, 'America's Strategic Posture', pp. viii, 48.

29 *Ibid.*, p. 97.

30 See Ankit Panda, 'Revealed: The Details of China's Latest Hit-to-kill Interceptor Test', *Diplomat*, 21 February 2018, https://thediplomat.com/2018/02/revealed-the-details-of-chinas-latest-hit-to-kill-interceptor-test/.

31 See Ministry of National Defense of the People's Republic of China, 'China Successfully Conducts Land-based Mid-course Missile Interception Test', 14 April 2023, http://eng.mod.gov.cn/xb/News_213114/NewsRelease/16217684.html.

32 See 'Zhōngguó P bōduàn xiàng kòng zhèn yùjǐng léidá néng fāxiàn shù qiān gōnglǐ wài dàndào dǎodàn' 中国P波段相控阵预警雷达 能发现数千公里外弹道导弹 [China's P-band phased-array early-warning radar can detect ballistic missiles thousands of kilometres away], Sina Military, 8 February 2021, https://mil.sina.cn/zm/2021-02-08/detail-ikftssap4752743.d.html.

33 See Ministry of Defence of the Russian Federation, 'Aerospace Security 2017 Russian–Chinese ABM Defence Computer CPX Kicks Off in Beijing', 11 December 2017, https://

eng.mil.ru/en/news_page/country/
more.htm?id=12154544@egNews;
and 'Komandno-shtabnyye ucheniya
Kitaya i Rossii po PRO proydut v
2019 godu v RF' Командно-штабные
учения Китая и России по ПРО
пройдут в 2019 году в РФ [Command-
post exercises between China and
Russia on missile defence will be held
in 2019 in the Russian Federation],
TASS, 25 April 2019, https://tass.ru/
mezhdunarodnaya-panorama/6375197.

34 Ministry of Foreign Affairs of the
People's Republic of China, 'Foreign
Ministry Spokesperson Zhao Lijian's
Regular Press Conference on April
14, 2021', 14 April 2021, https://www.
fmprc.gov.cn/mfa_eng/xwfw_665399/
s2510_665401/2511_665403/202104/
t20210414_9170725.html.

35 See Ministry of National Defense
of the People's Republic of China,
'China Successfully Conducts Land-
based Mid-course Missile Interception
Test'. The United States has proffered
similar justifications for global missile
defence but developed it expressly to
defend against so-called rogue states,
such as North Korea.

36 See Keir Giles, 'Russian Ballistic
Missile Defense: Rhetoric and Reality',
US Army War College Press, 1 June
2015, https://press.armywarcollege.
edu/cgi/viewcontent.cgi?article=1451&
context=monographs.

37 See Ministry of Defence of the Russian
Federation, 'Defence Ministry Board
Session Takes Place in Moscow',
23 April 2024, https://eng.mil.
ru/en/news_page/country/more.
htm?id=12510122@egNews.

38 See Anthony Cappacio, 'US Nuclear-
missile Sub Delayed up to 16 Months

Over Bow, Generators', Bloomberg, 17
April 2024, https://www.bloomberg.
com/news/articles/2024-04-17/
nuclear-missile-sub-delayed-up-to-
16-months-over-bow-generators; and
Brad Dress, 'Sentinel Missile Test
Flight Delayed by 2 Years Until 2026',
Hill, 28 March 2024, https://thehill.
com/policy/defense/4562509-sentinel-
missile-test-flight-delayed-by-two-
years-until-2026.

39 US Department of Defense, 'Contracts
For Oct. 30, 2023', 30 October 2023,
https://www.defense.gov/News/
Contracts/Contract/Article/3573405/;
and National Nuclear Security
Administration, 'W87-1 Modification
Program', November 2023, https://
www.energy.gov/sites/default/
files/2023-11/W87-1_1123.pdf.

40 See US Department of Defense,
'Department of Defense Fiscal Year
(FY) 2024 Budget Estimates', March
2023, p. 589, https://www.saffm.
hq.af.mil/Portals/84/documents/
FY24/Research%20and%20
Development%20Test%20and%20
Evaluation/FY24%20Air%20Force%20
Research%20and%20Development%20
Test%20and%20Evaluation%20
Vol%20IIIa.pdf?ver=XlpR81Vas-
iawp8KzshPww%3d%3d; and 'Next
Generation Reentry Vehicle', SAM.gov,
5 April 2023, https://sam.gov/opp/756fc
6956c104f34b78e41c449d22d1c/view.

41 See Congressional Commission on the
Strategic Posture of the United States,
'America's Strategic Posture', p. 43.

42 See Government Accountability
Office, 'Columbia Class Submarine:
Immature Technologies Present
Risks to Achieving Cost, Schedule,
and Performance Goals', December

2017, p. 10, https://www.gao.gov/assets/690/689426.pdf.

43 See US House Armed Services Committee, Strategic Forces Subcommittee, 'Statement of Vice Admiral Johnny Wolfe, USN Director, Strategic Systems Programs Before the Subcommittee on Strategic Forces of the House Armed Services Committee on FY 2025 Budget Request for Nuclear Forces and Atomic Energy Defense Activities', 30 April 2024, pp. 4–5, https://armedservices.house.gov/sites/republicans.armedservices.house.gov/files/04.30.24%20Wolfe%20Statement.pdf; and US Department of Defense, 'Trident II (D-5) Sea-launched Ballistic Missile UGM 133A (Trident II Missile) as of FY 2021 President's Budget', December 2019, p. 8, https://www.esd.whs.mil/Portals/54/Documents/FOID/Reading%20Room/Selected_Acquisition_Reports/FY_2019_SARS/20-F-0568_DOC_78_Trident_II_Missile_SAR_Dec_2019_Full.pdf.

44 National Nuclear Security Administration, 'W93/Mk7 Acquisition Program', November 2023, https://www.energy.gov/sites/default/files/2023-11/W93_1123.pdf; and National Nuclear Security Administration, 'Fiscal Year 2024 Stockpile Stewardship and Management Plan', November 2023, p. viii, https://www.energy.gov/sites/default/files/2023-11/FY24SSMP_FINAL_NOVEMBER_2023_0.pdf.

45 See US House Armed Services Committee on Strategic Forces, 'Statement of Anthony J. Cotton, Commander United States Strategic Command, Before the House Armed Services Committee on Strategic Forces, 21 March 2024', 21 March 2024, https://armedservices.house.gov/sites/evo-subsites/republicans-armedservices.house.gov/files/03.21.24%20Cotton%20Statement.pdf.

46 See Congressional Commission on the Strategic Posture of the United States, 'America's Strategic Posture', p. 48.

47 US House Armed Services Committee on Strategic Forces, 'Statement of Lieutenant General Andrew J. Gebara, USAF Deputy Chief of Staff for Strategic Deterrence and Nuclear Integration Before the Subcommittee on Strategic Forces of the House Armed Services Committee on Nuclear Forces', 30 April 2024, p. 2, https://armedservices.house.gov/sites/evo-subsites/armedservices.house.gov/files/evo-media-document/04.30.24%20Gebara%20Statement.pdf.

48 See US House Armed Services Committee on Strategic Forces, 'Statement of Dr. Michael Horowitz, Deputy Assistant Secretary of Defense, Force Development and Emerging Capabilities OUSD Policy/Strategy, Plans, and Capabilities Before the House Arms Services Committee Subcommittee on Strategic Forces', 12 March 2024, https://armedservices.house.gov/sites/evo-subsites/republicans-armedservices.house.gov/files/03.12.24%20Horowitz%20Statement.pdf.

49 CIA, 'Soviet Forces and Capabilities for Strategic Nuclear Conflict Through the Late 1990s', July 1987, p. 3, https://www.cia.gov/readingroom/docs/CIA-RDP09T00367R000200280001-6.pdf.

50   Congressional Commission on the
     Strategic Posture of the United States,
     'America's Strategic Posture', p. 44.
51   See 'Maiden Flight of Stealth Bomber
     Aborted by Low Pressure Reading',
     New York Times, 16 July 1989, https://
     www.nytimes.com/1989/07/16/us/
     maiden-flight-of-stealth-bomber-
     aborted-by-low-pressure-reading.html.
52   Congressional Commission on the
     Strategic Posture of the United States,
     'America's Strategic Posture', p. 13.
53   See Audrey Decker, 'China's New
     Stealth Bomber "Nowhere Near as
     Good" as US's, Intel Official Says',
     Defense One, 22 April 2024, https://
     www.defenseone.com/threats/2024/04/
     china-bomber/395972/.
54   See 'Russia's New Generation
     Strategic Bomber to Make First Flight
     in 2019 – Air Force', TASS, 13 February
     2015, https://tass.com/russia/777542.
55   See 'Rostec Breathes New Life
     into Production of Tupolev-160
     Strategic Bombers – CEO', TASS,
     21 February 2024, https://tass.com/
     defense/1749797.
56   See White House, 'Remarks by
     National Security Advisor Jake
     Sullivan for the Arms Control
     Association (ACA) Annual
     Forum', 2 June 2023, https://www.
     whitehouse.gov/briefing-room/
     speeches-remarks/2023/06/02/
     remarks-by-national-security-advisor-
     jake-sullivan-for-the-arms-control-
     association-aca-annual-forum/.
57   Arms Control Association, 'Adapting
     the U.S. Approach to Arms Control
     and Nonproliferation to a New
     Era: Remarks from Pranay Vaddi,
     Special Assistant to the President and
     Senior Director for Arms Control,
     Disarmament, and Nonproliferation
     at the National Security Council',
     7 June 2024, https://www.
     armscontrol.org/2024AnnualMeeting/
     Pranay-Vaddi-remarks.
58   See US Department of State, '2023
     Report to Congress on Implementation
     of the New START Treaty', 31 January
     2024, https://www.state.gov/2023-
     report-to-congress-on-implementation-
     of-the-new-start-treaty/.
59   See US Department of Defense,
     'Military and Security Developments
     Involving the People's Republic of
     China: 2021', 3 November 2021, p.
     162, https://media.defense.gov/2021/
     Nov/03/2002885874/-1/-1/0/2021-CMPR-
     FINAL.PDF; and US Department
     of Defense, 'Military and Security
     Developments Involving the People's
     Republic of China: 2023', 19 October
     2023, p. 186, https://media.defense.
     gov/2023/Oct/19/2003323409/-1/-
     1/1/2023-MILITARY-AND-SECURITY-
     DEVELOPMENTS-INVOLVING-THE-
     PEOPLES-REPUBLIC-OF-CHINA.PDF.
60   US House Armed Services
     Committee, 'Republican Armed
     Services Leaders Comment on
     China's Rapidly Expanding Nuclear
     Deterrent', 7 February 2023, https://
     armedservices.house.gov/news/
     press-releases/republican-armed-
     services-leaders-comment-china-s-
     rapidly-expanding-nuclear.
61   See Tom Cotton, 'Cotton,
     Colleagues: U.S. Should Withdraw
     from New START Treaty', 18
     May 2023, https://www.cotton.
     senate.gov/news/press-releases/
     cotton-colleagues-us-should-
     withdraw-from-new-start-treaty;
     US House Armed Services

Committee, 'Republican Armed Services Leaders Comment on Russian New Start Violations', 31 January 2023, https://armedservices.house.gov/news/press-releases/republican-armed-services-leaders-comment-russian-new-start-violations; and US House Armed Services Committee, 'Rogers Statement on Russia Suspending Participation in New Start', 21 February 2023, https://armedservices.house.gov/news/press-releases/rogers-statement-russia-suspending-participation-new-start.

62 See Daryl G. Kimball, 'Nuclear Dangers and the 2024 Election', *Arms Control Today*, January/February 2024, https://www.armscontrol.org/act/2024-02/focus/nuclear-dangers-and-2024-election; 'Donald Trump: US Must Greatly Expand Nuclear Capabilities', BBC News, 22 December 2016, https://www.bbc.com/news/world-us-canada-38410027; and US Department of State, 'Secretary Michael R. Pompeo at a Press Availability', 21 October 2020, https://2017-2021-translations.state.gov/2020/10/21/secretary-michael-r-pompeo-at-a-press-availability-14/.

63 Arms Control Association, 'Adapting the U.S. Approach to Arms Control and Nonproliferation to a New Era'.

64 US House Armed Services Committee on Strategic Forces, 'Statement of Dr. Michael Horowitz, Deputy Assistant Secretary of Defense, Force Development and Emerging Capabilities OUSD Policy/Strategy, Plans, and Capabilities Before the House Arms Services Committee Subcommittee on Strategic Forces'; and US House Armed Services Committee on Strategic Forces, 'Statement of Dr. James Weber, Principal Director for Hypersonics, Office of the Assistant Secretary of Defense for Critical Technologies and Mr. George Rumford, Director, Test Resource Management Center Before the House Armed Services Committee Subcommittee on Strategic Forces on U.S. and Adversary Hypersonics Programs', 12 March 2024, p. 3, https://armedservices.house.gov/sites/evo-subsites/republicans-armedservices.house.gov/files/03.12.24%20Weber%20-%20Rumford%20Statement.pdf.

65 See Assemblée Nationale, 'Rapport d'information n°1112' [Information report no. 1112], 24 April 2023, https://www.assemblee-nationale.fr/dyn/16/rapports/cion_def/l16b1112_rapport-information#_Toc256000011.

66 See US House Armed Services Committee on Strategic Forces, 'Statement of Dr. James Weber, Principal Director for Hypersonics, Office of the Assistant Secretary of Defense for Critical Technologies and Mr. George Rumford, Director, Test Resource Management Center Before the House Armed Services Committee Subcommittee on Strategic Forces on U.S. and Adversary Hypersonics Programs'.

Legion of Doom? China, Russia, Iran and North Korea

Daniel Byman and Seth G. Jones

On 17 May 2024, Russian President Vladimir Putin concluded a two-day visit to China by highlighting the deepening relationship between the two countries and emphasising his growing affinity for Chinese President Xi Jinping. It was the 43rd meeting between the leaders, and state media showed Putin and Xi strolling through manicured gardens past shimmering lakes and giant willow trees, and sipping tea at a pavilion on the expansive grounds of the Zhongnanhai, the walled compound in Beijing that serves as a residence for Chinese Communist Party leaders. As they said goodbye later that evening, Xi hugged Putin and then gently patted his back.[1]

Shortly before Russia invaded Ukraine in February 2022, Putin and Xi publicly declared that they had a friendship 'with no limits'.[2] At the time, this could be dismissed as mere words, but two and a half years later it is clear that a deep relationship has developed. Iran and North Korea, two other autocratic regimes the West has opposed, have also deepened their cooperation with Moscow and Beijing.

Sceptics contend that there is little trust and minimal real cooperation between the countries.[3] One Council on Foreign Relations analysis concluded that 'many Chinese and Russian officials, business leaders, and citizens distrust each other – a dynamic often motivated by historical

Daniel Byman is a Senior Fellow at the Center for Strategic and International Studies and a professor at Georgetown University's School of Foreign Service. **Seth G. Jones** is a Senior Vice President and Director of the International Security Program at the Center for Strategic and International Studies, as well as the author, most recently, of *Three Dangerous Men: Russia, China, Iran, and the Rise of Irregular Warfare* (W. W. Norton & Co., 2021).

Survival | vol. 66 no. 4 | August–September 2024 | pp. 29–50   https://doi.org/10.1080/00396338.2024.2380195

grievances or overt racism'.[4] Others insist that their relationship is 'mostly transactional' and does not pose a serious threat to the West.[5] Yet another assessment concludes that 'this axis is, currently, more rhetorical than real'.[6]

These arguments are wrong. A growing body of evidence indicates that security cooperation between China, Iran, Russia and North Korea has increased substantially over the past several years, particularly since Russia's Ukraine invasion. Support from these countries has allowed Russia to wage a protracted war in Ukraine. In early 2022, virtually no experts – including us – guessed that China, Iran and North Korea would all ship arms and dual-use components to Russia to support its invasion of Ukraine. Yet Chinese dual-use components, Iranian drones and artillery shells, and North Korean missiles, rockets and artillery shells have been critical to Russia's military effort.

There are, of course, constraints on their relations. But the growing cooperation among China, Russia, Iran and North Korea remains a profound development in the global balance of power and has major implications for the West. In future crises, it will likely be difficult for Western countries to deal with these countries in isolation. What happens in East Asia will not stay there.[7]

What is driving cooperation?

Greater cooperation between China, Iran, North Korea and Russia is not surprising. The surprise is that it took so long to develop in earnest. In different ways, each country sees the United States as its main enemy or rival. All four countries see aspects of the Western-led liberal order as a set of rules designed to benefit the United States and its allies while hindering potential rivals. Russia, for example, sees former Soviet republics such as Belarus, Georgia, Ukraine and the Central Asian countries as part of its sphere of influence, while the West sees them as independent, sovereign countries that can pick their own institutions and allies. The four countries also believe US and European efforts to promote democracy and encourage the free flow of ideas directly undermine their regime stability.[8]

All four powers are revisionist. As Philip Zelikow argues, 'their leaders regard themselves as men of destiny, with values and historical perspectives quite different from the consumerist or social metrics that suffuse much of the world'.[9] For Putin, Russian military expansion was – and is – about returning what rightly belongs to Russia. 'Peter the Great', he has claimed,

> waged the Great Northern War for 21 years. He was not taking away anything, he was returning ... From time immemorial, the Slavs lived there along with the Finno-Ugric peoples, and this territory was under Russia's control. The same is true of the western direction, Narva and his first campaigns. Why would he go there? He was returning and reinforcing, that is what he was doing. Clearly, it fell to our lot to return and reinforce as well.[10]

Xi, Putin, North Korean leader Kim Jong-un and Iranian Supreme Leader Sayyid Ali Khamenei all see the United States and other Western countries as major obstacles to the changes they want to see in the world. Indeed, Russia already sees itself as in an undeclared war with the United States and Europe due to their support for Ukraine.

Furthermore, each country has its own particular goals that call for greater cooperation. Russia's disastrous military performance following the invasion of Ukraine and the broad sanctions the United States and its European allies have imposed on Moscow made outside help vital for keeping Russia's economy afloat, energising its industrial base and ensuring its ability to continue waging war in Ukraine. Iran and North Korea both seek to circumvent international sanctions, are desperate for outside investment, and seek diplomatic protection at the United Nations and military aid in the event of a conflict with the United States or their US-aligned neighbours, such as Israel and South Korea respectively. Russia and China can also help smaller partners improve their air and space capabilities, and otherwise bolster their militaries. China, for its part, likely wants to keep the West busy in Ukraine while enjoying discounted Russian oil and gas.[11] Meanwhile, US policy compounds their hostility. The more the United States builds alliances in Asia against China, works with Israel against Iran, pushes sanctions against North Korea, and backs Ukraine against Russia, the greater the incentives for these countries to work together.

Growing cooperation

Cooperation has been most consequential in the military and dual-use areas, particularly around the Russia–Ukraine war.

Russia–China

Since the Russian invasion of Ukraine, China has ramped up dual-use aid to the Russian military and intelligence services, which Russia uses in missiles, drones, main battle tanks, artillery and other weapons systems. Beijing has hidden much of this aid using shell companies and cut-outs, and clandestine tactics, techniques and procedures.[12] The US intelligence community's 2024 Annual Threat Assessment concluded that 'trade between China and Russia has been increasing since the start of the war in Ukraine, and [People's Republic of China] exports of goods with potential military use rose *more than threefold* since 2022'.[13]

Chinese officials have claimed that Beijing has not provided weapons to Russia for use in Ukraine.[14] Following a statement by British defence minister Grant Shapps that lethal assistance is 'flowing from China to Russia and into Ukraine', the Chinese embassy in London responded that the accusations were 'totally groundless' and accused the United Kingdom of spreading 'baseless accusations'.[15] Although China has refrained from providing entire weapons systems to Russia, it has provided a wide range of components of different systems without which they could not function. China has probably provided navigation equipment for M-17 military-transport helicopters, machine tools for ballistic missiles and other weapons systems, parts for fighter jets, antennas for military vehicles used for communication jamming, drones, engines for drones and cruise missiles, optical components for Russian tanks and armoured vehicles, parts for mobile radar units used on S-400 anti-aircraft missile systems, military helmets and body armour, and front-end shovel loaders and excavators for digging trenches on the battlefield.[16] In addition, China has probably supplied global-navigation-satellite system boards for Russian attack drones, electronic integrated circuits for Russian drones, infrared detectors, communications equipment, pressure sensors and microcontrollers used in Russian missile systems and drones, and a wide range of microelectronics and semiconductors for use in Russian weapons systems.[17]

China appears to have provided satellite-imagery analysis and aid to improve Russian satellite and other space-based capabilities for use in Ukraine.[18] According to the US government, Chinese companies have even provided cotton cellulose, nitrocellulose and critical ingredients for nitrocellulose (such as cotton pulp), which are explosive precursors that the Russian military uses to produce rocket propellants, gunpowder and other explosives.[19] In 2023, roughly 70% of Russia's imported machine tools and 90% of its imported microelectronics came from China, according to US government estimates.[20] And that does not include many systems and components that are shipped clandestinely and whose status is not reported.[21]

Russian exports to China have been more limited. Russian arms sales to China flourished in the 1990s and early 2000s, but they have dropped off in recent years as the quality of China's own arms industry has grown. Still, China depends on Russian-made engines for some People's Liberation Army aircraft. Some of China's Chengdu J-20 stealth fighters are equipped with Russian Saturn AL-31 engines, and versions of China's developmental Shenyang J-35/FC-31 jet fighter have used Russian RD-93 engines.[22] Russia has also exported some helicopter systems to China and cooperated in such areas as space and counter-space.[23] And of course, Russia has exported oil, gas, liquefied petroleum and other non-defence goods to China.

Russia–Iran

Iran – including the Islamic Revolutionary Guard Corps – has ramped up war-related assistance to Russia since the 2022 invasion, including hundreds of *Shahed*-136 (*Geran*-2), *Shahed*-131 (*Geran*-1) and *Mohajer*-6 drones; artillery shells; more than one million rounds of ammunition; and several hundred *Fateh*-110 short-range ballistic missiles.[24] Iran is also building a sprawling drone factory in the Russian town of Yelabuga; it could produce thousands of drones and loitering munitions for battlefield use by 2025.[25] In addition, there is some evidence that Iran may deliver additional drones such as the *Shahed*-101 and its modified version, the *Shahed*-107, which is outfitted with technology that can seek out high-value battlefield targets, such as UK and

US multiple-launch rocket systems.[26] These weapons systems have helped Moscow sustain pressure on Ukraine despite its having depleted its own stores of precision-guided munitions.

In response, Russia has supplied – or is expected to supply – Iran with Yak-130 pilot-training aircraft, Su-35 multi-role fighter jets, Mi-28 attack helicopters and potentially S-400 air-defence systems, as well as aid to Iran's space and missile programmes.[27] Russian technology and weapons systems could turn Iran into a significantly more formidable military power with fourth-generation aircraft, substantial air-defence capabilities and more advanced missiles.

Russia–North Korea

Russia has imported from North Korea over 3m artillery rounds; rockets; solid-propellant, short-range ballistic missiles; and other munitions and components for them. North Korea has multiple ways to ship weapons to Russia, including by cargo ships, rail and trucks.[28] Overall, North Korea has provided Russia with 11,000 shipping containers full of arms.[29] Although some munitions have been faulty, the sheer volume of military aid to Russia has been helpful on the battlefield.[30] Moscow has also expressed interest in warm-water ports on the Korean Peninsula for its Pacific Fleet, and in energy and transport-infrastructure projects that connect Northeast Asia to Siberia and the Eurasian land mass through the Korean Peninsula.[31]

Russia has supplied North Korea with advanced technology for satellites, nuclear-powered submarines and ballistic missiles.[32] Russia's use of North Korean weapons in Ukraine has allowed Pyongyang to assess the performance of its weapons on the battlefield, including against advanced missile-defence systems.[33] In November 2023, North Korea launched its new *Chollima-1* rocket from its satellite-launching station in Tongchang-ri, thanks in part to technical help from Russia.[34] In addition, North Korea has apparently sought from Russia fighter aircraft, surface-to-air missiles, armoured vehicles, ballistic-missile production equipment and other advanced systems and technologies, though for now Russia may be unwilling to export assets it could use in Ukraine.[35]

Table 1: **Examples of military and dual-use cooperation among Russia, China, Iran and North Korea**

Country	Provided to Russia	Received from Russia
China	• Navigation equipment for M-17 military-transport helicopters • Machine tools for ballistic missiles and other weapons systems • Parts for fighter jets • Antennas for military vehicles used for communication jamming • Drones, drone parts, and engines for drones and cruise missiles • Optical components for Russian tanks and armoured vehicles • Parts for mobile radar units used on S-400 anti-aircraft missile systems • Military helmets and body armour • Front-end shovel loaders and excavators for digging trenches and other purposes • Global-navigation-satellite system boards for Russian attack drones • Electronic integrated circuits for Russian drones, infrared detectors, communications equipment, and pressure sensors and microcontrollers used in Russian missile systems and drones • Satellite-imagery analysis and aid to improve Russian satellite and other space-based capabilities for use in Ukraine • Cotton cellulose, nitrocellulose and critical ingredients for nitrocellulose (such as cotton pulp), which are used to produce gunpowder, rocket propellants and other explosives	• Aircraft engines • Helicopter systems • Space and counter-space cooperation
Iran	• *Shahed*-136 (*Geran*-2), *Shahed*-131 (*Geran*-1), *Mohajer*-6, and possibly *Shahed*-101 and *Shahed*-107 drones • Drone-production facilities • Artillery shells • Ammunition • *Fateh*-110 short-range ballistic missiles	• Yak-130 pilot-training aircraft • Possibly Su-35 multi-role fighter jets • Mi-28 attack helicopters • Possibly S-400 air-defence systems • Space cooperation
North Korea	• Artillery rounds (including 152 mm and 122 mm) • Rockets • KN-23, KN-24 and KN-25 short-range ballistic missiles • Other munitions and components for munitions	• Technology for satellites • Technology for nuclear-powered submarines • Technology for ballistic missiles

In June 2024, Putin and Kim agreed to additional military cooperation.[36] Putin cast this revived military relationship as a response to greater US support for Ukraine and threatened to arm North Korea and other foes in response: 'Those who supply these weapons believe that they are not at war with us … We reserve the right to supply weapons to other regions of the world.'[37]

Other types of cooperation

Military and dual-use cooperation is also occurring between other pairs, such as China and North Korea, which renewed a mutual-defence treaty in 2021.[38] China and Iran have participated in joint military drills and cooperated in maritime operations, counter-piracy and search-and-rescue operations. China has also exported to Iran dual-use components such as drone parts.[39]

China, Russia, Iran and North Korea have also coordinated in other ways. Shortly before the invasion of Ukraine, China and Russia issued a joint statement declaring their intention to cooperate on the Arctic, trade and climate while expressing concerns about the AUKUS security agreement and condemning US efforts to impose its version of democracy on other countries, among other issues.[40] China refrained from condemning Russia's actions in Ukraine and has criticised Western sanctions on Russia. North Korea is benefiting from its ties, with China and Russia vetoing UN Security Council resolutions on the North Korean nuclear programme. Iran has signed a 25-year cooperation agreement with Beijing that stands to yield economic and technical cooperation worth hundreds of billions of dollars. After Israel and Iran exchanged attacks in April 2024, China issued a statement assuring Iran that cooperation would continue.[41] Iran, for its part, has been silent about China's brutal treatment of Uyghurs and other Muslim minorities in Xinjiang.[42] It has also helped Russia evade sanctions imposed after its invasion of Ukraine.[43]

Furthermore, trade between China and Russia reached a record high of $240bn in 2023, an increase of more than 64% since 2021. Russia surpassed Saudi Arabia to become China's top crude-oil supplier in 2023, the 107m tonnes of crude it imported from Russia that year representing a 24% increase from the previous year. And China imported 8m tonnes of liquefied petroleum gas from Russia in 2023, a 77% increase from 2021.[44]

Growing cooperation among the four countries has been enormously beneficial to Russia's war effort in Ukraine, particularly after Russia failed to seize Kyiv and faced a protracted war of attrition. Russia's battlefield successes in 2024 depended on plentiful ammunition stocks, and its terror-bombing of Ukrainian cities usually has involved less advanced systems that are regularly shot down and require replacements supplied in part by Russia's partners. Russia has fired up to 70,000 rounds per day in Ukraine and is spending roughly 40% of its overall budget on defence.[45] Moscow cannot sustain this level of effort without outside support from its three partners. Defence and dual-use cooperation mutually benefits their militaries and strengthens their defence-industrial bases, allowing each country to enhance the scale and scope of weapons systems they can produce.

The limits of cooperation

The expansion of cooperation among the four countries is not open-ended. Firstly, it is largely bilateral. Beijing, Moscow, Tehran and Pyongyang have not created a formal alliance that commits the signatories to mutual defence. They have not even established a multilateral security institution to facilitate cooperation. True enough, Beijing and Moscow signed a Road Map for Military Cooperation to guide collaboration from 2021 to 2025.[46] Beijing and Tehran signed a 25-year agreement in 2021 to increase military and other types of cooperation.[47] And Putin and Kim pledged mutual support if either country faced external 'aggression' by way of their June 2024 agreement.[48] But China appears to be wary about developing a strong multilateral arrangement with countries as volatile as North Korea and Russia.[49] Should direct military cooperation ever be required, these countries would not be well prepared to fight together, in contrast to NATO allies or the United States, Japan, South Korea and other partners in Asia. NATO alliance members plan jointly for contingencies, regularly train and exercise together, and share a command structure, all of which make joint operations in a crisis far easier. In Afghanistan, the Balkans and other areas, NATO has deployed forces, with member states working together under shared command. In Asia, US allies are less integrated, but engage in regular exercises and other forms of cooperation. While China and Russia are founding members of the Shanghai Cooperation Organisation, it is a relatively weak institution, and several of its members – such as India and Pakistan – have deeply conflicting interests.[50]

Secondly, there are periodic disagreements between the countries. Chinese leaders have expressed concerns about Russia's warming military relations with an erratic North Korea, particularly if they strengthen Pyongyang's nuclear and missile capabilities, and are concerned that Moscow will embolden North Korea and destabilise the region.[51] Beijing has been especially reluctant to help Pyongyang with its nuclear programme.[52]

Iranian leaders also expressed dismay with Russia and China for their diplomatic positions on a spat between the United Arab Emirates (UAE) and Iran over the sovereignty of three islands in the Gulf – Greater Tunb, Lesser Tunb and Abu Musa – strategically positioned along the approach to the Strait of Hormuz.[53] For energy-security reasons, Russia and China seek good relations with the UAE and Saudi Arabia, which are hostile to Tehran. In 2024, senior Iranian officials summoned the Chinese ambassador to Tehran and protested 'the repeated support of the Chinese government for the baseless claims' made by the UAE, emphasising that the three islands belonged to Iran in perpetuity.[54] In addition, China's theft of Russian technology and know-how has created friction between Beijing and Moscow. China likely stole technology from Russia's Su-33 fighter aircraft to develop the J-15 carrier-based fighter, and China has frequently breached agreements with Russian arms suppliers by reverse-engineering Russian equipment to produce its own weapons systems, copying Russia's Su-27 fighters to develop its J-11 fighter and Russia's S-300 surface-to-air missile (SAM) system to produce its HQ-9 SAM system.[55]

Thirdly, China is the only major economy of the four countries, and it has more important trading partners than North Korea, Iran and even Russia. The top ones are the United States (which accounts for 17% of China's total exports and imports), Japan (5%), South Korea (4%) and Vietnam (4%).[56] The European Union also imports over €500bn-worth of goods annually from China.[57] Western sanctions on Russia have made Moscow less sensitive to economic pressure from the United States and its allies, while Iran and North Korea, long diplomatic pariahs and heavily sanctioned by the West, have learned to endure. China, however, has a wobbly economy and an ageing population, so reducing trade and investment from the United States and its allies is politically risky.[58] For the moment, China cannot swap Russia for the United States, Japan or South Korea, let alone Europe as a whole.

Re-imagining scenarios

Notwithstanding genuine limits to cooperation, the strengthened relations among the four countries have important implications for future scenarios. When the United States anticipated a Russian invasion in the lead-up to

February 2022, it was not imagining a major Chinese role in the conflict, and Chinese involvement has made all the difference. Without China's support, Russia's economy might have collapsed, and in any event its military machine would be far less formidable. Even the more limited military aid from North Korea and Iran in the form of ammunition and drones has helped keep Russia in the fight and made the attritional war more costly for Ukraine.

In the past it was reasonable to think of each of the four countries in isolation and to assess that in a crisis each one could only draw on its own resources. Now the role of each country's partners must also be considered. While it is impossible to imagine every possible future permutation, brief consideration of two familiar contingencies suggests how the new partnerships could complicate crisis management.

If China were to try to blockade Taiwan, help from Russia would be invaluable. One Russian role might be to distract the US and especially European countries, limiting the military and financial support they could provide Taiwan. A Russian build-up on the border of Poland or a Baltic state, for example, would alarm European countries and the United States, compelling them to divert limited military resources to the defence of a fellow NATO member. More directly, Russia could provide China with advanced air-defence systems and anti-ship cruise missiles, among other weapons, and share jamming, electronic-warfare and other capabilities and techniques it has developed in the Russia–Ukraine war. If the US and its allies responded to the blockade by cutting off oil and gas sales to China, with the US Navy helping enforce restrictions, Russia's massive energy reserves could fill China's spiking energy needs. Russia, Iran and North Korea could also buy oil and gas on the global market and redirect it to China, using their existing clandestine procurement networks to help Beijing evade sanctions.

In the Strait of Hormuz, a major oil choke point, Iran would have greater freedom of action. Its mine-laying and missile capabilities already pose a threat to shipping, and the United States and its allies would struggle to decisively end the threat.[59] Iran has avoided closing the strait because it would face additional economic penalties from an outraged world as well as vastly superior opposing forces. With Chinese and Russian help, however, Iran could overcome international sanctions. Furthermore, Chinese supersonic anti-ship cruise missiles like the YJ-12 and sophisticated Russian-made air-defence systems, plus the 100,000 naval mines China has at its disposal, would shrink Iran's military disadvantage.[60]

More generally, the prospect of China economically punishing a country that confronts Russia, or Russia using its information-warfare and sabotage assets to go after China's enemies, might give a wavering nation additional reasons to avoid cooperating with the United States and its allies.

Countering this legion of doom

China, Russia, Iran and North Korea – a veritable legion of doom – pose a serious threat to the West.[61] They have violently cracked down on democratic movements and ruthlessly suppressed freedom of information and a free press. They all disdain democratic government and free markets, and directly challenge an international system that has championed these institutions since the Second World War. Moreover, they are aggressive. In addition to attacking Ukraine, Moscow regularly meddles in the former Soviet space. China regularly threatens Taiwan and bullies the Philippines in its quest to become the dominant power in its region. Iran and North Korea are unabashedly bellicose, and Iran supports an array of militant groups – the 'axis of resistance' – that threaten its neighbours in the Middle East.

Several factors raise challenges for the notional legion's adversaries. For one, Russia will probably be able to continue generating significant military capabilities for its war in Ukraine, which increasingly pits the defence-industrial bases of the United States and Europe against those of Russia, China, Iran and North Korea. Outside aid has allowed the Russian military to maintain operations in Ukraine, including offensive ones, over the course of 2024. It has kept Russia's economy afloat, bolstering domestic support for the regime. This support is unlikely to diminish and may grow. Should the shooting stop, Russia's recovery from this exhausting war could also be quicker than expected, enabling it to pose a threat to other neighbours, in addition to a renewed threat to Ukraine.

Secondly, it is increasingly difficult for Western countries to deal with the four adversaries in isolation, as there appears to be a growing overlap in their antagonistic activities. For the United States, this development has significant implications for operational plans and military doctrine, such as that embodied in the Joint Warfighting Concept 3.0, National Military Strategy, Guidance for Employment of the Force and Joint Strategic Capabilities Plan. It now seems essential to conceptualise these adversaries as a coalition of states that can provide military, dual-use and economic assistance to one another across theatres. Thus, plans for responding to Iranian action in the Middle East or Russian aggression in Eastern Europe need to account for their potential receipt of Chinese weapons, economic aid and other support. The same goes for scenarios involving the Taiwan Strait, South China Sea or East China Sea, where Beijing could receive direct or indirect support from Moscow, Tehran or Pyongyang.

Furthermore, cooperation among the four countries undermines the argument that the United States needs to focus only or predominantly on China. According to one proponent of this view, 'so long as China is our priority, the United States will be forced to withhold forces from Europe to deter or defeat Chinese aggression, even if Russia attacks NATO first'.[62] This argument wrongly assumes that the United States cannot plan to fight more than one major power at the same time, which it did during the Second World War and planned to do for much of the Cold War.[63] As part of flexible response in the 1960s, for example, US defence planners developed a two-and-one-half strategy, which involved preparing to fight two large regional wars and one limited conflict at the same time if necessary. After the collapse of the Soviet Union and the end of the Cold War, however, the US shifted away from great-power wars and towards fighting terrorist groups. But today's rise of multiple adversaries that increasingly cooperate with one another requires the development of a defence strategy that aims to deter – and fight – at least two major wars simultaneously. Taiwan, South Korea and Japan are almost certainly watching to see whether the United States stands by Ukraine; abandoning an ally to one aggressor in the name of guarding against another aggressor could merely embolden the latter.

On balance, trans-regional security competition suggests that Western countries could better leverage countries in other regions for assistance: a global coalition is necessary to fight a global coalition. Australia, Japan,

New Zealand and South Korea have contributed billions of dollars in economic assistance and weapons to help Ukraine defeat Russia. Japanese Prime Minister Kishida Fumio, South Korean President Yoon Suk-yeol and Australian Prime Minister Anthony Albanese have all visited Kyiv to demonstrate solidarity with Ukraine. The upshot is that the United States needs to better leverage capabilities across combatant commands, as a crisis in one area may implicate the interests of countries in others. The US might, for instance, request tangible European military support for the United States and its Asian partners in selected confrontations with China. Washington also might examine scenarios for greater cooperation in the event of an escalating crisis in Europe, whereby allies and partners in other theatres, such as the Indo-Pacific, could provide weapons, spare parts and other support.

While trade between Europe and China will – and should – continue, Western states need to limit vulnerabilities in case of escalating tension with China. Some may need to dial back their partnerships with China. In April 2024, German Chancellor Olaf Scholz spent three days in China, where he visited a German factory in Chongqing, lectured at Tongji University in Shanghai, and met with Xi and other officials. Scholz brought along three cabinet members, as well as the CEOs of 12 major German companies, including BMW, Mercedes, BASF, Merck and ThyssenKrupp. China has invested in key European infrastructure, such as ports. In Greece, the Chinese shipping company COSCO owns a majority stake in terminals in the port of Piraeus.[64] Governments should encourage companies to limit their reliance on trade with China, de-risk and diversify their supply chains, and consider relocating their regional headquarters from China to countries such as Singapore. They should also make clear that, should the security climate worsen, trade and investment will be in jeopardy because governments will prioritise security over economics. Germany learned this the hard way from its reliance on Russian gas before Russia's full-scale invasion of Ukraine.

Finally, the United States and Europe must find alternatives to certain Chinese supplies. Western countries already have significant vulnerabilities with some rare-earth metals, on which China has a near monopoly, that are critical for manufacturing various missiles and munitions.[65] China dominates the advanced-battery supply chain across the globe.[66] It is the global leader in cast products, producing more than the next nine countries combined and more than five times what the United States makes.[67] In fact, the Pentagon depends on foreign governments, including China, for large cast and forged products.[68]

*   *   *

Although increased cooperation among adversaries is concerning, there is room for hope. The West has numerous advantages over China, Russia, Iran and North Korea. If it can effectively leverage them, they could be decisive. The Western model of freedom, notwithstanding its flaws and limits, remains compelling to at least some countries, and Western economies are still strong overall. Western security institutions are far more extensive, far larger in economic and military might, and far deeper politically than what exists between China, Russia, Iran and North Korea. For all the challenges that allies pose, Winston Churchill may have said it best: 'There is at least one thing worse than fighting with allies, and that is to fight without them.'

Notes

1   See Ministry of Foreign Affairs of the People's Republic of China, 'President Xi Jinping Holds Small-group Talks with Russian President Vladimir Putin at Zhongnanhai', 17 May 2024, https://www.mfa.gov.cn/eng/zxxx_662805/202405/t20240517_11306328.html; and Max Seddon, Joe Leahy and Wenjie Ding, 'Putin to Visit China as Beijing Plays Key Role in Supporting Russia', *Financial Times*, 14 May 2024.

2   President of Russia, 'Joint Statement of the Russian Federation and the People's Republic of China on the International Relations Entering a New Era and the Global Sustainable Development', 4 February 2022, http://www.en.kremlin.ru/supplement/5770.

3   See, for example, Daniel R. DePetris, 'There Is No Axis of Autocracies', *Newsweek*, 18 November 2022; and Daniel Larison, 'Hawks Pushing for "Axis of Evil" Reunion Tour', Responsible Statecraft, 22 March 2024, https://responsiblestatecraft.org/axis-of-evil/.

4   Clara Fong and Lindsay Maizland, 'China and Russia: Exploring Ties Between Two Authoritarian Powers', Council on Foreign Relations, 20 March 2024, https://www.cfr.org/backgrounder/china-russia-relationship-xi-putin-taiwan-ukraine.

5   Michelle Ye Hee Lee and Pei-Lin Wu, 'Putin Hails Russia's Ties with China as "Stabilizing" Force in the World', *Washington Post*, 16 May 2024.

6   Lucas Winter, Jemima Baar and Jason Warner, 'The Axis Off-kilter: Why an Iran–Russia–China "Axis" Is Shakier than Meets the Eye', *War on the Rocks*, 19 April 2024, https://warontherocks.com/2024/04/the-axis-off-kilter-why-an-iran-russia-china-axis-is-shakier-than-meets-the-eye/.

7   See, for example, Emma Ashford, Joshua R. Itzkowitz Shifrinson and Stephen Wertheim, 'Europe Must Step Up', *Foreign Affairs*, 22 May 2023; Elbridge Colby, 'America Must Face Reality and Prioritise China over Europe', *Financial Times*, 23 May 2024; Elbridge A. Colby and Alexander Velez-Green, 'To Avert War with China, the US Must Prioritize Taiwan over Ukraine', *Washington Post*, 18 May 2023; and Alex Velez-Green, 'The Rise of Republican National Security Prioritizers', Heritage Foundation, 28 September 2023, https://www.heritage.org/defense/commentary/the-rise-republican-national-security-prioritizers. The broader debate on Asia versus Europe, or China versus Russia, also often includes debates about supporting Taiwan or Ukraine.

8   See Ruonan Liu and Songpo Yang, 'China and the Liberal International Order: A Pragmatic and Dynamic Approach', *International Affairs*, vol. 99, no. 4, July 2023, pp. 1,383–1,400; and Andrew Radin and Clint Reach, 'Russian Views of the International Order', RAND Corporation, 18 May 2017, https://www.rand.org/pubs/research_reports/RR1826.html.

9   Philip Zelikow, 'Confronting Another Axis? History, Humility, and Wishful Thinking', *Texas National Security Review*, vol. 7, no. 3, Summer 2024, https://tnsr.org/2024/05/confronting-another-axis-history-humility-and-wishful-thinking/.

10 President of Russia, 'Meeting with Young Entrepreneurs, Engineers, and Scientists', transcript of remarks by Vladimir Putin, 9 June 2022, https://en.kremlin.ru/events/president/news/68606.

11 See Christy Lee, 'Despite Faltering Economy, China Unlikely to Disrupt Aid to North Korea', VOA News, 8 August 2023, https://www.voanews.com/a/despite-faltering-economy-china-unlikely-to-disrupt-aid-to-north-korea/7217382.html; and 'Why China Is Unlikely to Restrain Iran', *The Economist*, 25 April 2024, https://www.economist.com/china/2024/04/25/why-china-is-unlikely-to-restrain-iran.

12 See Office of the Director of National Intelligence, 'Support Provided by the People's Republic of China to Russia', July 2023, https://democrats-intelligence.house.gov/uploadedfiles/odni_report_on_chinese_support_to_russia.pdf.

13 Office of the Director of National Intelligence, 'Annual Threat Assessment of the U.S. Intelligence Community', 5 February 2024, p. 8 (emphasis added), https://www.armed-services.senate.gov/imo/media/doc/2024_intelligence_community_annual_threat_assessment.pdf.

14 See, for example, Steve Holland and Susan Heavey, 'US Says China Is Boosting Russia's War Machine in Ukraine', Reuters, 15 April 2024, https://www.reuters.com/world/us-says-china-is-boosting-russias-war-machine-ukraine-2024-04-12/; and Ministry of Foreign Affairs the People's Republic of China,

'Qin Gang: China Resolutely Opposes Unilateral Sanctions', 10 May 2023, https://www.mfa.gov.cn/eng/zxxx_662805/202305/t20230510_11074402.html.

15 Quoted in Andrew Macaskill, 'UK Defence Minister Says China Working to Supply Lethal Aid to Russia', Reuters, 23 May 2024, https://www.reuters.com/world/uk-defence-minister-says-china-working-supply-lethal-aid-russia-2024-05-22/.

16 See, for example, Karen Gilchrist, 'How Surging Trade with China Is Boosting Russia's War', CNBC, 28 September 2023, https://www.cnbc.com/2023/09/28/how-surging-trade-with-china-is-boosting-russias-war.html; Sam Cranny-Evans and Thomas Withington, 'Russian Comms in Ukraine: A World of Hertz', RUSI, 9 March 2022, https://rusi.org/explore-our-research/publications/commentary/russian-comms-ukraine-world-hertz; Holland and Heavey, 'US Says China Is Boosting Russia's War Machine in Ukraine'; Roman Kolodii, Giangiuseppe Pili and Jack Crawford, 'Hi-tech, High Risk? Russo-Chinese Cooperation on Emerging Technologies', RUSI, 1 March 2024, https://www.rusi.org/explore-our-research/publications/commentary/hi-tech-high-risk-russo-chinese-cooperation-emerging-technologies; Paul Mozur, Aaron Krolik and Keith Bradsher, 'As War in Ukraine Grinds On, China Helps Refill Russian Drone Supplies', New York Times, 21 March 2023; Office of the Director of National Intelligence, 'Support Provided by the People's Republic of China to Russia'; Austin Ramzy and Jason Douglas, 'Booming Trade with China Helps Boost Russia's War Effort', Wall Street Journal, 21 August 2023; Nathaniel Sher, 'Behind the Scenes: China's Increasing Role in Russia's Defense Industry', Carnegie Politika, 6 May 2024, https://carnegieendowment.org/russia-eurasia/politika/2024/05/behind-the-scenes-chinas-increasing-role-in-russias-defense-industry?lang=en; and US Department of the Treasury, 'U.S. Continues to Degrade Russia's Military-industrial Base and Target Third-country Support with Nearly 300 New Sanctions', 1 May 2024, https://home.treasury.gov/news/press-releases/jy2318.

17 See Sher, 'Behind the Scenes'; and US Department of the Treasury, 'U.S. Continues to Degrade Russia's Military-industrial Base and Target Third-country Support with Nearly 300 New Sanctions'.

18 See Holland and Heavey, 'US Says China Is Boosting Russia's War Machine in Ukraine'.

19 See US Department of the Treasury, 'U.S. Continues to Degrade Russia's Military-industrial Base and Target Third-country Support with Nearly 300 New Sanctions'.

20 See, for example, Aamer Madhani, 'US Intelligence Finding Shows China Surging Equipment Sales to Russia to Help War Effort in Ukraine', Associated Press, 19 April 2024, https://apnews.com/article/united-states-china-russia-ukraine-war-265df843be030b7183c95b6f3afca8ec; and Kelly Ng and Yi Ma, 'How Is China Supporting Russia After It Was Sanctioned for Ukraine War', BBC, 17 May 2024, https://www.bbc.com/news/60571253.

21 Author interviews with US government officials, 2024; and Office of the Director of National Intelligence, 'Support Provided by the People's Republic of China to Russia'. Several Chinese-based companies, such as Poly Technologies, Fujian Baofeng Electronic Company, China Taly Aviation Technologies Corporation, Juhang Aviation Technology Shenzhen, Finder Technology Limited, Tulun International Holding Limited and many others have likely exported items used for military purposes to Russia. US Department of the Treasury, 'U.S. Continues to Degrade Russia's Military-industrial Base and Target Third-country Support with Nearly 300 New Sanctions'. Although vital to Russia, some of the Chinese material, such as chips, are of low quality compared with more advanced chips from the United States, Europe, Japan, South Korea and Taiwan.

22 See Brian Hart et al., 'How Deep Are China–Russia Military Ties?', Center for Strategic and International Studies, 4 August 2022, https://chinapower.csis.org/china-russia-military-cooperation-arms-sales-exercises/.

23 See, for example, Seong Hyeon Choi, 'China Cuts Arms Imports to Rely More on Its Own Weapons Tech but Russia Still Biggest Overseas Supplier: SIPRI', South China Morning Post, 11 March 2024; National Air and Space Intelligence Center, Competing in Space, 2nd ed. (Washington DC: US Air Force, December 2023); and Kevin Pollpeter et al., China–Russia Space Cooperation: The Strategic, Military, Diplomatic, and Economic Implications of a Growing Relationship (Montgomery, AL: China Aerospace Studies Institute, 2023).

24 Danny Citrinowicz, 'Iran Is on Its Way to Replacing Russia as a Leading Arms Exporter', Atlantic Council, 2 February 2024, https://www.atlanticcouncil.org/blogs/iransource/iran-drone-uavs-russia/; Defense Intelligence Agency, 'DIA Releases Updated Report on Russia's Use of Lethal Iranian Unmanned Aerial Vehicles (UAVs) in Ukraine', 24 August 2023, https://www.dia.mil/News-Features/Articles/Article-View/Article/3504948/dia-releases-updated-report-on-russias-use-of-lethal-iranian-unmanned-aerial-ve/; Michael Gordon, 'Russia Moves Forward with Plans to Buy Iranian Ballistic Missiles', Wall Street Journal, 4 January 2024; and Parisa Hafezi et al., 'Exclusive: Iran Sends Russia Hundreds of Ballistic Missiles', Reuters, 21 February 2024, https://www.reuters.com/world/iran-sends-russia-hundreds-ballistic-missiles-sources-say-2024-02-21/.

25 See Dalton Bennett and Mary Ilyushina, 'Inside the Russian Effort to Build 6,000 Attack Drones with Iran's Help', Washington Post, 17 August 2023.

26 See Defense Intelligence Agency, 'DIA Releases Updated Report on Russia's Use of Lethal Iranian Unmanned Aerial Vehicles (UAVs) in Ukraine'; Deborah Haynes, '"Explosive" New Attack Drone Developed by Iran for Russia's War in Ukraine', Sky News, 10 January 2024, https://news.sky.com/story/explosive-new-attack-drone-developed-by-iran-for-russias-war-in-ukraine-13045093; and 'Iran Develops New High Tech Attack Drone for Russia', Jerusalem Post, 10 January 2024.

27 See Paul Iddon, 'Iran Might Receive Its First Su-35 Flanker Fighters from Russia Next Week', *Forbes*, 20 April 2024; 'The Iran–Russia Military Axis', *Wall Street Journal*, 3 November 2023; 'Russia Says It's Working on Major New Agreement with Iran', Reuters, 12 December 2023, https://www.reuters.com/world/russia-says-its-working-major-new-agreement-with-iran-2023-12-12/; and Natasha Turak, 'Iran Has the Largest Ballistic Missile Arsenal in the Middle East', CNBC, 23 February 2024, https://www.cnbc.com/2024/02/23/iran-reportedly-sends-hundreds-of-ballistic-missiles-to-russia.html.

28 See Conflict Armament Research, *North Korean Missile Relies on Recent Electronic Components* (London: Conflict Armament Research, February 2024), https://storymaps.arcgis.com/stories/0814c6868bbd45a98b15693a31bd0e7f; Defense Intelligence Agency, *North Korea: Enabling Russian Missile Strikes Against Ukraine* (Washington DC: Defense Intelligence Agency, 2024), https://www.dia.mil/Portals/110/Documents/News/Military_Power_Publications/DPRK_Russia_NK_Enabling_Russian_Missile_Strikes_Against_Ukraine.pdf; Micah McCartney, 'Russia Could Soon Receive More Weapons from North Korea, Analysts Say', *Newsweek*, 12 March 2024; and Choe Sang-Hun, 'North Korea Launches Rocket with Its First Spy Satellite', *New York Times*, 21 November 2023.

29 See David Sanger, 'Putin Once Tried to Curb North Korea's Nuclear Program. That's Now Over', *New York Times*, 19 June 2024.

30 See Defense Intelligence Agency, 'North Korea: Enabling Russian Missile Strikes Against Ukraine', p. 1; and John Feng, 'Half of Russia's North Korea-made Artillery Shells Don't Work: Ukraine', *Newsweek*, 27 February 2024.

31 See Victor Cha and Ellen Kim, 'A Renewed Axis: Growing Military Cooperation Between North Korea and Russia', Center for Strategic and International Studies, 6 September 2023, https://beyondparallel.csis.org/a-renewed-axis-growing-military-cooperation-between-north-korea-and-russia/.

32 *Ibid.*

33 See Defense Intelligence Agency, 'North Korea: Enabling Russian Missile Strikes Against Ukraine', p. 1.

34 See Sang-Hun, 'North Korea Launches Rocket with Its First Spy Satellite'.

35 See Natasha Bertrand, 'Report: North Korean Missile Fired by Russia Against Ukraine Contained US and European Components', CNN, 20 February 2024, https://www.cnn.com/2024/02/20/politics/north-korean-missile-russia-ukraine-components/index.html; Sam Fossum and Kevin Liptak, 'Russia and North Korea "Actively Advancing" in Arms Deal Negotiations, Says US', CNN, 31 August 2023, https://www.cnn.com/2023/08/30/europe/russia-north-korea-advancing-arms-deal-intl/index.html; and Edward Wong and Julian Barnes, 'Kim Jong-un and Putin Plan to Meet in Russia to Discuss Weapons', *New York Times*, 4 September 2023.

36 See Warren P. Strobel and Michael R. Gordon, 'How Putin Rebuilt Russia's War Machine with Help from U.S. Adversaries', *Wall Street Journal*, 19 June 2024.

37   Quoted in Paul Sonne, 'Putin
     Threatens to Arm North Korea,
     Escalating Tension over Ukraine', *New
     York Times*, 20 June 2024.

38   See Clara Fong and Eleanor
     Albert, 'The China–North Korea
     Relationship', Council on Foreign
     Relations, 7 March 2024, https://
     www.cfr.org/backgrounder/
     china-north-korea-relationship.

39   See United States Institute of Peace,
     'Iran and China: Military Ties',
     28 June 2023, https://iranprimer.
     usip.org/blog/2023/jun/28/
     iran-china-military-ties.

40   See President of Russia, 'Joint
     Statement of the Russian Federation
     and the People's Republic of China
     on the International Relations
     Entering a New Era and the Global
     Sustainable Development'.

41   See 'China Tells Iran Cooperation
     Will Last After Attack on Israel',
     Bloomberg News, 15 April 2024,
     https://www.bloomberg.com/news/
     articles/2024-04-16/china-tells-iran-coop
     eration-will-last-after-attack-on-israel.

42   See, for example, Kourosh Ziabari,
     'Why Iran Won't Cross China on the
     Uighurs', *Asia Times*, 21 February 2021.

43   See Thomas Kohlmann, 'Why Iran and
     Russia Can Dodge Western Sanctions',
     DW.com, 26 April 2024, https://www.
     dw.com/en/why-iran-and-russia-can-
     dodge-western-sanctions/a-68928255.

44   Ng and Ma, 'How Is China
     Supporting Russia After It Was
     Sanctioned for Ukraine War'.

45   Author interview with senior European
     military officials, 19 March 2024.

46   See Ricardo Barrios and Andrew S.
     Bowen, 'China–Russia Relations',
     Congressional Research Service, 13

     September 2023, p. 1, https://crs
     reports.congress.gov/product/pdf/IF/
     IF12100.

47   See Farnaz Fassihi and Steven Lee
     Myers, 'China, with $400 Billion Iran
     Deal, Could Deepen Influence in
     Mideast', *New York Times*, 29 March
     2021; and 'Iran and China Sign 25-year
     Cooperation Agreement', Reuters, 29
     March 2021, https://www.reuters.com/
     article/idUSKBN2BJ0HG/.

48   See Kim Tong-Hyung and Aniruddha
     Ghosal, 'Russia and North Korea
     Sign Partnership Deal that Appears
     to Be the Strongest Since the Cold
     War', Associated Press, 19 June
     2024, https://apnews.com/article/
     vladimir-putin-kim-jong-un-russia-
     north-korea-summit-ukraine-
     a6b8d2c12de7ee2ab6716d4747c9850e.

49   See Lingling Wei, Ann M. Simmons
     and Timothy W. Martin, 'Behind
     Putin Visit, Unease in Beijing over His
     Potential Next Stop: North Korea',
     Wall Street Journal, 19 May 2024.

50   The Shanghai Cooperation Organisation
     was formed in 1996 by China, Russia,
     Kazakhstan, Kyrgyzstan and Tajikistan.
     Uzbekistan joined in 2001, India and
     Pakistan in 2017, and Iran in 2023.

51   See Christy Lee, 'Analysts: Russia–North
     Korea Military Ties Pose Dilemma
     for China', VOA News, 1 February
     2024, https://www.voanews.com/a/
     analysts-russia-north-korea-military-
     ties-pose-dilemma-for-china/7467749.
     html; and Wei, Simmons and Martin,
     'Behind Putin Visit, Unease in Beijing
     over His Potential Next Stop'.

52   See Bruce W. Bennett, 'North Korea
     and China Aren't the Allies You Think
     They Are', RAND Corporation, 26
     September 2023, https://www.rand.

org/pubs/commentary/2023/09/ north-korea-and-china-arent-the-allies-you-think-they.html.

53 See 'China Maintains Stance on Disputed Gulf Islands Despite Iran's Anger', Reuters, 3 June 2024, https://www.reuters.com/world/ china-maintains-stance-disputed-gulf-islands-despite-irans-anger-2024-06-03/; 'Iran Summons Russian Envoy over Statement on Persian Gulf Disputed Islands', Reuters, 24 December 2023, https://www.voanews.com/a/ iran-summons-russian-envoy-over-statement-on-persian-gulf-disputed-islands-/7410524.html; and Tala Taslimi, 'Iran Grows Wary of Russia Amid Moscow's Support for UAE in Island Spat', Nikkei Asia, 23 July 2023, https://asia.nikkei.com/Politics/ International-relations/Iran-grows-wary-of-Russia-amid-Moscow-s-support-for-UAE-in-island-spat.

54 Islamic Republic of Iran Ministry of Foreign Affairs, 'Chinese Ambassador Summoned to Iran Foreign Ministry', 2 June 2024, https:// en.mfa.ir/portal/newsview/746841/ Chinese-ambassador-summoned-to-Iran-Foreign-Ministry.

55 See Mark Ashby et al., *Defense Acquisition in Russia and China* (Santa Monica, CA: RAND, 2021); and Cortney Weinbaum et al., *Assessing Systemic Strengths and Vulnerabilities of China's Defense Industrial Base* (Santa Monica, CA: RAND Corporation, 2022).

56 World Integrated Trade Solution (WITS), 'China Trade', accessed 14 June 2024, https://wits.worldbank.org/ countrysnapshot/en/CHN.

57 Eurostat, 'China–EU – International Trade in Goods Statistics', February 2024, https://ec.europa.eu/euro stat/statistics-explained/index. php?title=China-EU_-_international_ trade_in_goods_statistics.

58 See Anne Stevenson-Yang, 'China's Dead-end Economy Is Bad News for Everyone', *New York Times*, 11 May 2024.

59 See Caitlin Talmadge, 'Closing Time: Assessing the Iranian Threat to the Strait of Hormuz', *International Security*, vol. 33, no. 1, Summer 2008, pp. 82–117.

60 See April Brady, 'Russia Completes S-300 Delivery to Iran', *Arms Control Today*, December 2016, https:// www.armscontrol.org/act/2016-11/ news-briefs/russia-completes-s-300-delivery-iran; and A.J. Douglas, 'Get Serious About Countering China's Mine Warfare Advantage', *US Naval Institute Proceedings*, June 2023, https://www. usni.org/magazines/proceedings/2023/ june/get-serious-about-countering-chinas-mine-warfare-advantage.

61 The Legion of Doom is a team of supervillains in the DC comics universe. Usually led by arch-fiend Lex Luthor, the legion opposes the Justice League and the Superfriends. For more details, see 'Legion of Doom', https://comicvine.gamespot.com/ legion-of-doom/4060-43922/.

62 Velez-Green, 'The Rise of Republican National Security Prioritizers'.

63 See Jim Mitre, 'A Eulogy for the Two-war Construct', *Washington Quarterly*, vol. 41, no. 4, Winter 2019, pp. 7–30.

64 See Karin Smit Jacobs, *Chinese Strategic Interests in European Ports* (Brussels: European Parliamentary Research Service, February 2023), https://www.europarl.europa.eu/ RegData/etudes/ATAG/2023/739367/ EPRS_ATA(2023)739367_EN.pdf.

65 See, for example, Joe Gould, 'Pentagon Legislation Aims to End Dependence on China for Rare Earth Minerals', *Defense News*, 18 May 2020, https://www.defensenews.com/congress/2020/05/18/pentagon-legislation-aims-to-end-dependence-on-china-for-rare-earth-minerals/; and Norbert Neumann, 'Securing the Rare Earth Supply Chain Is Crucial for Defence', *Airforce Technology*, 23 March 2022, https://www.airforce-technology.com/analysis/ securing-the-rare-earth-supply-chain-is-crucial-for-defence/.

66 See US Department of Defense, *Securing Defense-critical Supply Chains* (Washington DC: US Department of Defense, February 2022), p. 19.

67 See Statista, 'Volume of Global Casting Production from 2018 to 2020, by Country', 26 April 2022, https://www.statista.com/statistics/237526/casting-production-worldwide-by-country/.

68 See US Department of Defense, *Securing Defense-critical Supply Chains*, p. 27.

Making Net Assessment Work: Evaluating Great-power Competition

Nicholas Kitchen

Great-power competition, we are told, has returned. A preoccupation with the nature, implications and sustainability of American unipolarity in the aftermath of the Cold War has given way to the view that international affairs is fundamentally characterised by strategic competition between great powers. How best to conceptualise and respond to this emerging international contest is a matter of some debate.[1] States compete over many things, and not always in zero-sum ways. In the United States at least, where great-power competition has attained acronym status as 'GPC' in security-policy circles, the dominance of this rhetorical frame increasingly risks conflating an assessment of systemic conditions with a strategic goal.[2] Moreover, analysts disagree about what today's strategic competition is really *about*: does it pit political systems against each other, in a contest between democracy and autocracy?[3] Or is it fundamentally about a power transition, and China's strategy to replace the US as the global superpower?[4] Is Russia's military assertiveness a function of either of these systemic contests, or a different, more limited struggle for a sphere of influence? Should we understand the rollback of globalisation and liberal multilateralism in favour of more autarkic national policies as a series of domestic political choices, or as a more fundamental reconfiguring of a liberal-international order that is no longer fit for purpose?

Nicholas Kitchen is Director of the Centre for the Study of Global Power Competition (CGPC) and Senior Lecturer in International Relations at the University of Surrey.

Survival | vol. 66 no. 4 | August–September 2024 | pp. 51–70   https://doi.org/10.1080/00396338.2024.2380196

Whatever great powers may be competing over, it is clear that intensifying systemic competition concerns major powers, middle powers and small states alike. The United States bases its National Security Strategy on the assessment that 'we are in the midst of a strategic competition to shape the future of the international order'.[5] The United Kingdom set its 2023 Integrated Review Refresh against the 'backdrop of a more volatile and contested world' requiring the country to 'out-cooperate and out-compete those that are driving instability'.[6] For Thailand, 'the politics of global powers and formations of international blocs remain the main factors affecting the context of global security'; and the Philippines concurs that 'heightened rivalries among the major powers are contributing to a more tense geopolitical landscape'.[7] Even Vanuatu, a nation of just 300,000 people, sees 'strains in the rules-based order' and 'rivalry between the major powers' as central to its security environment.[8]

The security strategies of states across the spectrum of national power therefore recognise, whether they are competing to shape international order or caught up in the turbulence, that as great-power competition intensifies, it will increasingly impact their security and prosperity. And if states are operating in an era of great-power competition, it is incumbent on them to know who is *winning*.

The need for net assessment

'Are we winning?' is a question that programmes of net assessment may seek to answer. In recent years, as the political salience of competitive international dynamics has grown, interest in net assessment has revived.[9] The retirement of Andrew Marshall after 40 years as director of the US Department of Defense's Office of Net Assessment in 2015, and his death four years later, spurred a resurgence of curiosity about this almost-mythologised activity.[10] In this period, calls for the UK to establish its own net-assessment function were predicated on a 'darkening strategic picture' of great-power competition, and explicitly modelled on the United States' institutional set-up.[11] While clearly a part of post-Brexit efforts to reimagine the UK as a globally active, independent power following its departure from the European Union, the result, first established in 2018 and then formalised in 2020 as the Secretary of State's Office for Net Assessment and Challenge (SONAC) in the Ministry of Defence, is a substantive initiative, having been designed to 'short-circuit' departmental bureaucracy.[12] The decision to appoint as its first director a relative outsider to the defence bureaucracy – Rob Johnson from Oxford University's Changing Character of War programme, who was, significantly, appointed at two-star level – reinforced that initial sense of independence.

Slightly confusingly, the UK had long had an Assessments Staff within the Cabinet Office, reporting to the Joint Intelligence Committee, so it is important to distinguish between strategic net assessment and intelligence assessment. Intelligence assessment is primarily focused on what is known about situations of concern, such as a terrorist threat. The Assessments Staff evaluates diverse sources of information, including secret intelligence, to provide decision-makers with the best possible assessment of issues in which national interests are seriously engaged. Such assessments may involve some 'netting', to the extent that they may evaluate the UK's own interests and resources against an adversary's capabilities and intentions, but they lack the scope for wider reflection.

Net assessment, on the other hand, is primarily concerned with making assessments net of the other side. Its principal benefit is its reflexiveness: the willingness – conditioned by a degree of bureaucratic independence – to conduct self-analysis free of optimism bias. Such assessments may operate at various levels, from the operational to the grand strategic, and the diagnosis they provide should shed light on where strategic advantage lies – that is, which side holds an advantage in terms of power. But establishing a net-assessment function is not the same thing as understanding the task of net assessment, and making it work in practice.

The challenges of power assessment

Deciding that it's important to know the current status of a competition is one thing; working out how to evaluate that status is quite another. Wars can clarify the issue by determining whose preferences should prevail. As Daniel Frei put it, the reason peaceful conflict settlement is so difficult is that we lack a consensus on the concept and measurement of power;

if such a consensus could be found, establishing and maintaining peace would not be a problem.[13] Winston Churchill said something similar, in pithier fashion: 'Always remember, however sure you are that you can easily win, that there would not be a war if the other man did not think he also had a chance.'[14]

Yet victories in war – which provide confirmed data points by which power analysts might calibrate their instruments – are increasingly rare. The 75-year absence of a major war between great powers reflects the discarding of the *ultima ratio* of competition as a serious policy option. Thus, power assessments have become largely subjective; it is not the 'facts' of power, but actors' understandings of each other's power, that matters. Assessments of power must therefore establish as best they can not just the material factors that may be brought to bear, but also how they might be understood and responded to. Net assessments must do this dynamically, applying equally dispassionate analytical rigour both to the adversary, and – often more problematically – to oneself.

Working out 'what counts' as power is clearly fundamental to this task. But what power is, how it operates, and how to identify and measure it is the subject of intense debate. Every major study of the concept notes that the question of how to conceive of and define power – and other, similar terms such as influence, control, authority, persuasion and coercion – is one on which agreement has so far proven elusive.[15] As a result, there are myriad forms and associations of power. It is said to have three dimensions and four faces; to be hard, soft, sharp, sticky, social, relational, structural, discursive, reciprocal, compulsory, productive, active, inactive, intentional, unintentional, extensive, intensive, disciplinary, authoritative, direct, indirect, potential, actual, distributive, zero-sum, institutional, diffused, symbolic, visible, invisible, hidden, public, private, ubiquitous, normative, civilian, useable, protean, latent and agenda-setting; and to have an architecture, networks, communities, elements, levels, spaces, capillaries, boundaries, balances and imbalances. This conceptual complexity must be continually wrestled with when undertaking a power assessment. It is therefore worth setting out a few of the basic conceptual propositions that are needed to underpin programmes of net assessment.

Power is a social relationship

Robert Dahl's classic definition describes power as the ability of actor A to make actor B do what the latter would otherwise not do. This captures a basic truth and the underpinning rationale for *net* assessments of power: that power is a relationship between actors.[16] It is therefore necessary to define the nature of that relationship prior to assessing the relative power of the actors within it.[17]

Power is not the same as outcomes

Relational concepts of power such as Dahl's can be criticised for their equation of power with power effects – the outcomes of the relationship. This poses an obvious risk of circularity, and means there can be no assessment of who *is* powerful, only who *was* powerful. Yet past performance is no guarantee of future results. Equating power with success also undermines the concept of asymmetry, and conflates power with total compliance, as opposed to the 'opportunity' to prevail. Sometimes an actor's power will produce the desired effects, and sometimes it won't. This is, after all, why we employ strategists: to increase the chances of success.[18]

Power is not the same as resources

Equating power with power resources – the 'bases' of power, or more often, 'capabilities' – has been political scientists' go-to method for avoiding the difficulties of equating power with outcomes. This 'national power' approach assumes that power resources produce power outcomes: more sophisticated dispositional treatments may suggest that *under certain conditions* power resources are *likely* to produce power.[19] Still, a detailed understanding of the circumstances – the social relationship between actors – is needed to identify the likely effects of such a disposition with any clarity. Power 'emerges' through the effects of the resources that produce it when it shapes the capacity of others to determine their fate.[20] How and when it can be identified remains a deeply probabilistic exercise.

Power resources are difficult to measure

Identifying power with resources becomes even more problematic when we consider how to go about measuring those resources. Certainly, some things can be definitively assessed. 'Bean-counting' approaches can establish quantities of particular types of weaponry or derive findings about research and development capacity. However, such approaches can lack rigour, lumping distinct capabilities together or, worse, using proxy measures such as military spending or GDP.[21] Even with an accurate picture of the relevant resources under the control of a designated actor, one must take into account the processes by which those resources might be brought to bear. The ability to convert latent resources, such as the productive capacity of the economy, into what Stanley Hoffman has called 'usable power' may be limited by the administrative capacity of the state, political authority or public trust.[22]

Power is not fungible and cannot be aggregated
Academic treatments of power analysis recognise that power is multidimensional – that is, it can operate across multiple pathways. Authors have characterised these dimensions in different ways: by form – as decision-making power, non-decision-making power and ideological power; by structures – as security, knowledge, production, finance; and by means of operation – as hard and soft power.[23] Others equate the dimensions of power with the resources used to produce that power – military, economic, diplomatic, cultural.

Regardless of how the dimensions of power are distinguished, strategic advantage lies in understanding which combination is likely to be effective in overcoming resistance in any given interaction. Aggregating power – either by adding together evaluations of incommensurable resources, or by combining multiple relationship- or dimension-specific assessments – is impossible, since neither the resources used to produce power nor the causal pathways by which it operates can be reduced to a single denominator. Power resources lack fungibility: they are not easily converted into or substituted for another resource.[24]

This is not to say that power resources exhibit *no* fungibility – indeed, questions of fungibility may be addressed at the level of strategy, through the reallocation of resources or the linking of strategic problems.[25] But it is to suggest that notions of polarity or rankings of powers are misleading: in the absence of either a single dominant issue or deep fungibility of power resources, analyses that suggest a single international power structure are 'virtually meaningless'.[26] Despite this, analysts have continued to develop quantitative assessments of power balances, drawing on differing metrics of power, and aggregating them with varying degrees of complexity.[27] If taken too seriously by decision-makers, such efforts empower their makers with the capacity to define the balance of power itself.

'Victory' is elusive

A recognition among analysts that there is no form of power that is 'basic to all the others' would seem to contradict an axiom of realist thought that the *ultima ratio* of power in international relations is victory in war.[28] Military power is certainly *important*, but in general, strategic advantage does not rest on the resort to violence, and indeed, 'victories' are rarely clear and unambiguous.[29] Military power is almost always used in concert with other resources: just as the threat of force can lend weight to diplomacy, warfare without the actual or potential support of diplomacy is 'merely butchery'.[30]

Indeed, the contemporary absence of great powers that make full use of their military capabilities generates important questions for power analysis, particularly in relation to escalation. Simply put, if the *ultima ratio* is not used, of what use is it? In what way is it relevant for assessments of power? This is not to dismiss the utility of unused military forces – the very fact they have not been used may demonstrate their value as a deterrent – but to point out that the cause of non-use is a legitimate object of a power assessment. If, as some suggest, the existence of nuclear weapons and the serious costs of great-power conflict have rendered major war obsolete, fundamental questions of force purpose, dispute management and escalation, the most appropriate tools of power, and what it means to 'win' must be revisited.[31]

Conducting assessments of global power competitions

From the preceding analysis one thing should be clear: seeking to produce a single, aggregate assessment of the status of a power competition at any given moment is a fool's errand. At the same time, ongoing power assessment is clearly crucial in allowing strategic net assessments to inform decisions around strategy and investment in capabilities. How, then, to go about such an apparently Sisyphean task?

The question of what exactly a net assessment should study is another source of debate. Narrow definitions focus on questions of military strength. For example, Eliot A. Cohen, who served as a military assistant to Marshall for a time in the 1980s, sees net assessment as the military balance: a quantitative and qualitative appraisal of two or more military forces.[32] Stephen Rosen sees 'national security establishments' as the object of analysis, which is slightly broader, but retains the narrow focus on military competition.[33] In this sense, publicly available quantitative assessments such as the International Institute for Strategic Studies' *Military Balance* are examples of net assessment.[34]

For Marshall, 'mere tabulations' of this kind were an 'evasion of the problem'.[35] Cohen was similarly critical of bean-counting approaches to net assessment, warning against the seductiveness of modelling and simulations, and arguing instead that political factors should 'begin, end, and pervade' the analysis.[36] He thus distinguished *strategic* net assessment as the weighing of *politico*-military balances.[37] Cohen is rare in making this useful distinction: the conflation of the two terms pervades the literature, as much, one suspects, for linguistic convenience as for anything else. Upholding the distinction points to the idea that strategic net assessment should be a more expansive and holistic effort at the level of grand strategy, as opposed to simply an exercise in net-assessing military forces.

To make the point, we can usefully contrast different forms of net power assessment (see Table 1). Strategic net assessment may draw on studies of military effectiveness,[38] but a broader conception of strategic effectiveness should integrate the whole range of resources on which multiple actors may draw, and the differing types of strategies they could employ to achieve their ends. Strategic net assessment's scope, and its longer time horizon, therefore entails broad, multidisciplinary analyses. This kind of inclusive, holistic exercise exists to provide a long-term diagnosis of the total enterprise of strategic competition, one that integrates whatever factors may be relevant.[39] It is in this sense that Rosen emphasises the importance of elevating intellectual flexibility over restrictive parameters when establishing what strategic net assessment is and does. 'Good net assessment', he says, 'requires self-conscious rejection of a fixed definition of net assessment'.[40]

Eschewing definitions means that good assessment is probably easier to envisage in theory than implement in practice; it is notable that strategic net assessment is often discussed in terms of what it is *not*, rather than what it is. When operationalised by officials, holism and flexibility must give way to the requirement to define, prioritise, plan and deliver specific tasks and activities, and to collate the results of those activities into some bureaucratic 'product'. During the Cold War, both the United States and the Soviet Union developed their own net-assessment concepts and methodologies. A consideration of how and why these historic approaches differed can shed some light on how net assessment might best be constructed and used by states under conditions of great-power competition today.

Strategic net assessment in the United States

In the United States, military–strategic assessment has long been primarily an empirical and problem-orientated exercise. This methodological predisposition reflects the way the discipline of International Relations developed as a sub-discipline of political science in the United States in the aftermath of the two world wars. (In Europe, International Relations remained more closely tied to history and philosophy.) The political demand for some form of strategic net assessment grew out of the RAND Corporation's studies of the strategic balance in the 1950s and 1960s, and reflected the prevailing 'Chicago School' in the social sciences that saw the social world as fundamentally knowable, and therefore manageable.[41]

It was no coincidence that Marshall had joined RAND from the University of Chicago as a statistician, working alongside other mathematicians, engineers, physicists and technical economists.[42] Marshall's distinctiveness,

Table 1: **Forms of net assessment**

Form of analysis	Scope	Analytical focus	Consumer	Methodology	Time horizon
Estimate of the situation	Tactical or operational	Immediate military effort	Military officers	Formulaic	Days, weeks, months
Systems analysis	Campaign	Tangible questions of effectiveness (how much is enough?)	Decision-makers facing immediate policy choices	Single, formal, deductive	Months, years
Strategic net assessment	Grand strategic	Broad competition; first-order intangible questions (what is the nature of the problem?)	Long-term planners, senior political decision-makers	Flexible, eclectic, inductive	Decades

however, lay in the fact that although he was educated very much within this tradition, he largely rejected the idea that states were analogous to rational, value-maximising individuals, highlighting instead how strategy formation and implementation were regularly irrational and suboptimal as a result of non-strategic factors such as formative experiences, cultural inclinations and organisational–bureaucratic dynamics.[43]

While RAND may have been dominated by positivism and rational choice in its systems-analysis approach to strategic issues, Marshall preferred theoretical and methodological pluralism, and embraced multiple disciplinary perspectives. He described quantitative-estimating procedures as 'vague and impressionistic at one level' and 'mechanical at another', and focused on the conceptual problems of assessments.[44] Frustrated that RAND's political scientists 'absolutely refused, as far as we could tell, to look at what the Soviets actually did', Marshall developed a more intellectually curious Office of Net Assessment.[45] He repeatedly emphasised that strategic net assessment was intended to be diagnostic, highlighting problems, opportunities, and areas of comparative advantage and disadvantage. This would illuminate the nature of major national-security problems in their broadest sense – political, economic and technological, as well as military – rather than providing policy recommendations.[46]

Marshall brought insights from organisational behaviour, bounded rationality, business strategy, evolutionary–biological and psycho-cultural approaches to the task of strategic net assessment. But it was an interest in broader systemic and non-linear questions – rather than anything specific about the methodologies used to address them – that set Marshall's vision apart.[47] As one of his former staffers put it, any method that offers 'analytic manageability … purchases intellectual ease at the price of a deceptive and unwarranted certainty'.[48]

While Marshall had originally proposed that his office report directly to the president or the White House's national security advisor, the responsibility for commissioning net assessments was ultimately given to the secretary of defense. Situated in the Pentagon, the Office of Net Assessment became a sort of internal think tank, and research suggests that its influence varied depending on its relationship with Pentagon leaders.[49] Despite its professed commitment to intellectual pluralism, the rules and values of the analyses it prepared for the Pentagon's use were always likely to be conditioned by that bureaucratic setting. As one observer put it, if the principal 'customer of a net assessment is the U.S. Secretary of Defense, and you, as the new director of net assessment, call a bloated bureaucracy like the Pentagon your home, chances are that your analysis is much more heavily influenced by your environment than it is by actual developments in the world'.[50]

Strategic net assessment in the Soviet Union

The difficulty of assessing power without being influenced by bureaucratic or intellectual paradigms is made clear by the Soviet Union's own version of strategic net assessment, the 'correlation of forces'.[51] Correlation of forces is a concept and methodological tool that is used to evaluate the balance in a conflictual relationship, and encompasses a wide range of factors, only one of which is military. Its integrates two levels of assessment: a general, worldwide level that is assessed largely qualitatively and intuitively, and more specific individual- or regional-level assessments.[52]

There has been a tendency to view the Soviet concept of correlation of forces as a tool of policy rather than a scientific undertaking, and to dismiss it as a 'cognitive deception' designed to make up for military weakness by including 'exotic', non-military elements.[53] In part, this stems from a Western preoccupation with quantitative analysis that translates into a willingness to ignore variables that can only be evaluated qualitatively or whose influence is uncertain and cannot be predetermined, features that correlation-of-forces analysis regarded as important.[54] Western rejection of the approach also reflects the concept's ideological character. Correlation of forces is explicitly Marxist–Leninist, proceeding from the idea that the ultimate endpoint of any force competition is the correlation of class forces in the worldwide system of international politics.[55]

Correlation of forces, so conceived, was therefore rooted in the Soviet world view. Yet as an approach to strategic net assessment, stripped of its ideological priors, its integration of the power of transnational social systems alongside the power of individual states allows it to grasp the systemic character of power competition in a way that balance of power cannot.

It recognises that competition between states takes place within a continuously transforming global system of socio-political ideas and norms, which may advantage or disadvantage particular protagonists at particular times.

In practice, the Soviet Union's use of the correlation of forces was ideologically predisposed to stress the decisive character of social, revolutionary and progressive movements in the overall equation, 'forces' that were assumed to be inevitable, irreversible and fundamentally favourable to the Soviet side.[56] A similar critique might be made, however, of the less explicit assumptions underpinning Western liberal analysis of world historical forces following the end of the Cold War.[57]

The return of strategic net assessment

These histories may provide a sense of how and why the Cold War ended as it did, and why neither side was successful in foreseeing it.[58] While the Soviet Union may have believed in principle in the possibility of a single, comprehensive, strategic net assessment, the non-fungibility of power and doubts about the reliability of ideological teleology undermine this stance, and it is not clear that the Soviets ever really adopted it in practice. One suspects Soviet assessors would have had at least as healthy a scepticism as their American counterparts of contemporary advocates of systems analysis, who argue that advanced computational models can add 'rigour' to net assessment.[59]

In the Cold War, both the United States and the Soviet Union were clear about the nature of the competition they were involved in. For each, it was an existential contest in which mutually assured destruction constituted a defence dilemma that prevented either side from resorting to 'hot' war.[60] Such clarity is more elusive today, yet legitimate questions about a state's ability to understand how and where to invest, in what resources, in support of which dimensions of power are regularly posed in a way that presumes we understand both the nature and parameters of contemporary strategic competition as plainly as we did during the Cold War. This error is compounded by approaches that view 'national power' as a property that can be created, as opposed to a series of context-specific descriptions of power relationships and structures.[61] To repeat one of the basic conceptual principles discussed earlier, measuring 'national power' in the abstract or aggregate is to misunderstand the concept of power.

The question of what is being assessed, of the existence and nature of power competition, should be both the starting point and an enduring principle of contemporary strategic net assessment. This would help prevent particular assumptions or modes of thought becoming axiomatic, mitigating against groupthink and the tendency of bureaucracies to make stronger claims for their assessments than is warranted.[62] In originally recommending the development of a new framework for American strategic analysis, Marshall made clear that the first task of committing to an extended strategic competition was to assess the nature of that competition – 'in part to see if … assumptions [about it] are valid'.[63]

Marshall's office was soon convinced that existing assumptions about the Soviet Union were valid, and turned its attention to determining how to prevail in the US–Soviet competition. It eventually diagnosed the underlying weakness of the Soviet economy, which produced a strategy of provoking the Soviet Union into bankrupting itself.[64] The ultimate success of this strategy should not blind us, however, to the difficulties of carrying out net assessments. Assessing how contemporary trends may play out over time is an exercise laden with contingency, dependent on the nature of the trend being evaluated, the time frame over which the assessment seeks to run, and the extent to which uncertain trends may interact with one another. Some trends – such as programmes to replace existing equipment – may be known entities, subject to uncertainties around political choice, but, as a matter of technical delivery, predictable within a relatively small margin of error. Others may be more uncertain, such as the evolution of political attitudes over time. New innovations or emerging trends are inherently more likely to diverge from predictions, as are trends unfolding over longer periods, since small variations will have longer for their effects to play out. Unexpected technological breakthroughs, institutional transformations, the emergence of new actors, or seismic political reconfigurations within or between states may be disruptive across a range of assessments. The nature of the competition itself may change, especially if there is uncertainty about how to interpret it in the first place.

Some have argued that strategic net assessment should explicitly understand itself as a predictive tool, because policymakers see it as such.[65] Yet this notion runs counter to good long-term analysis. It is certainly true that diagnostic analysis – understanding the nature of the system and specific interactions within it – will tend to suggest that particular courses of action are more desirable than others, or that a particular actor is better adapted to the tasks at hand. Some form of prognosis is therefore an inevitable outcome of diagnostic efforts, pointing to the likely outcomes of prevailing policies. Thus, it would be odd if strategic net assessment did not offer a view on current strategy.

However, if strategic net assessment becomes an exercise in prognosis, one that is primarily concerned with providing policy recommendations or cures for the problems about which it has offered diagnoses, then it will necessarily make predictions about the likely benefits of those interventions. Conceived in such a way, its ability to make future diagnoses may be prejudiced by its own and others' judgements of the success of its strategic proposals. Treating strategic net assessment as a predictive tool, or insisting that it provide proxy hypotheses for the contingencies it identifies,[66] is not necessary to evaluate whether its outputs are rigorous and worthwhile.

*   *   *

If competition for power between states has re-emerged as the driving force of national policies, then understanding the nature of that competition will be a crucial task. The UK's net-assessment function has so far taken care to ground its work in the conceptual propositions around power discussed earlier, and to focus on understanding power relationships in context and thinking broadly about the sources of strategic advantage, rather than engaging in the bean-counting of capabilities. Even so, its institutional siting within the Ministry of Defence, and its necessary bureaucratic focus on Russia and China, may serve to straitjacket its thinking about what sort of strategic competition we are in, and what dimensions of power may be most important.

Making net assessment work – that is, conducting net assessment in a conceptually robust, empirically thorough and intellectually open way – is of enormous importance. Conducting it with attention to the complexities of the concept of power will not provide simple or clear answers to the questions of great-power competition. But it should facilitate a deeper understanding of strategic problems that will enable effective decision-making.

Notes

1   See Michael J. Mazarr, 'Understanding Competition: Great Power Rivalry in a Changing International Order – Concepts and Theories', RAND Corporation, 2022.

2   See Daniel Nexon, 'Against Great Power Competition: The U.S. Should Not Confuse Means for Ends', *Foreign Affairs*, 15 February 2021.

3   See Matthew Kroenig, *The Return of Great Power Rivalry: Democracy Versus Autocracy from the Ancient World to the U.S. and China* (New York: Oxford University Press, 2020), p. xiii.

4   See Michael Pillsbury, *The Hundred-year Marathon: China's Secret Strategy to Replace America as the Global Superpower*, 1st ed. (New York: Henry Holt and Company, 2015).

5   White House, 'National Security Strategy', October 2022, https://www.whitehouse.gov/wp-content/uploads/2022/10/Biden-Harris-Administrations-National-Security-Strategy-10.2022.pdf.

6   HM Government, 'Integrated Review Refresh 2023: Responding to a More Contested and Volatile World', pp. 2–3, https://assets.publishing.service.gov.uk/media/641d72f45155a2000c6ad5d5/11857435_NS_IR_Refresh_2023_Supply_AllPages_Revision_7_WEB_PDF.pdf.

7   Office of the National Security Council, Thailand, 'Executive Summary: National Security Policy and Plan B.E. 2566–2570 (2023–2027)', p. 15, https://www.nsc.go.th/wp-content/uploads/2024/01/ExcutiveSummary.pdf; and National Security Council, Philippines, 'National Security Policy 2023–2028', p. 12, https://nsc.gov.ph/images/NSS_NSP/National_Security_Policy_Manual_FINAL_E-COPY_with_WATERMARK_140823.pdf.

8   Government of Vanuatu, 'Vanuatu National Security Strategy: Secure and Resilient', 2019, p. 16, https://www.gov.vu/images/publications/Vanuatu_National_Security_Strategy.pdf.

9   See Gabriel Elefteriu, 'A Question of Power: Towards Better UK Strategy Through Net Assessment', Policy Exchange, November 2018, https://policyexchange.org.uk/wp-content/uploads/2018/11/A-Question-of-Power-Net-Assessment-Gabriel-Elefteriu-Policy-Exchange-November-2018.pdf.

10 See Jeffrey S. McKitrick and Robert G. Angevine (eds), *Reflections on Net Assessment* (Jaffrey, NH, and Alexandria, VA: Andrew W. Marshall Foundation and Institute for Defense Analyses, 2022).

11 Elefteriu, 'A Question of Power', p. 5.

12 Gabriel Elefteriu, 'The MoD's Newly Independent "Net Assessment" Capability Can Make a Huge Difference', Policy

Exchange, 18 January 2022, https://policyexchange.org.uk/blogs/the-mods-newly-independent-net-assessment-capability-can-make-a-huge-difference/.

13 Daniel Frei, 'Vom Mass der Macht', *Schweizer Monatshefte*, vol. 49, no. 7, 1969, p. 646. I am grateful to Vera Linke for her assiduous translation of Frei's work.

14 Winston Churchill, *My Early Life: A Roving Commission* (London: Thornton Butterworth, 1930), p. 246.

15 See David A. Baldwin, *Power and International Relations: A Conceptual Approach* (Princeton, NJ: Princeton University Press, 2016); Robert A. Dahl, 'The Concept of Power', *Behavioral Science*, vol. 2, no. 3, 1957; Harold Lasswell and Abraham Kaplan, *Power and Society: A Framework for Political Inquiry* (New Haven, CT: Yale University Press, 1950); and Steven Lukes, *Power: A Radical View*, 2nd ed. (Basingstoke and New York: Palgrave Macmillan, 2005).

16 See Dahl, 'The Concept of Power'.

17 See Baldwin, *Power and International Relations*.

18 See Kenneth Waltz, *Theory of International Politics* (Reading, MA: Addison-Wesley, 1979), pp. 191–3.

19 See Peter Morriss, *Power: A Philosophical Analysis*, 2nd ed. (Manchester: Manchester University Press, 2002).

20 See Michael Barnett and Raymond Duvall, 'Power in International Politics', *International Organization*, vol. 59, no. 1, 2005.

21 In 2014, a statistical 're-basing' of GDP statistics saw Nigeria's GDP grow by 89% overnight. See Diane Coyle, *GDP: A Brief but Affectionate History* (Princeton, NJ: Princeton University Press, 2015).

22 Stanley Hoffmann, 'Notes on the Elusiveness of Modern Power', *International Journal*, vol. 30, no. 2, 1975. See also Jeffrey W. Taliaferro, 'State Building for Future Wars: Neoclassical Realism and the Resource-extractive State', *Security Studies*, vol. 15, no. 3, July–September 2006, pp. 464–95.

23 For more on characterising power by form, see Lukes, *Power*. For more on characterising it by structures, see Susan Strange, *States and Markets* (London: Bloomsbury, 2015). For more on characterising it by means of operation, see Joseph S. Nye, Jr, *Soft Power: The Means to Success in World Politics*, 1st ed. (New York: PublicAffairs, 2004).

24 See Stefano Guzzini, 'Fungibility of Power Resources', in Keith Dowding (ed.), *Encyclopedia of Power* (London: SAGE Publications Ltd, 2011), pp. 266–7.

25 See Robert J. Art, 'Force and Fungibility Reconsidered', *Security Studies*, vol. 8, no. 4, Summer 1999, pp. 183–9.

26 See David A. Baldwin, *Paradoxes of Power* (New York: Basil Blackwell, 1989), p. 167.

27 A 2001 RAND Corporation study notes that 'it is not always clear which resources are appropriate as measures of real power, or whether the resources nominally possessed in any given instance are actually usable by the actor in question'. 'Despite these difficulties', the report continues, 'the concept of power as resources has remained attractive enough and will not be easily discarded'. Ashley J. Tellis et al., 'Measuring National

Power in the Postindustrial Age',
RAND Corporation, 2000, p. 14.

28 The point that there is no form of
power that is 'basic to all the others' is
made in Lasswell and Kaplan, *Power
and Society*, p. 94. For more on realist
perspectives, see Edward Hallett Carr
and Michael Cox, *The Twenty Years'
Crisis, 1919–1939* (New York: Palgrave,
2001); Robert Gilpin, *War and Change in
World Politics* (Cambridge: Cambridge
University Press, 1981); and Waltz,
Theory of International Politics.

29 See Dominic D.P. Johnson and
Dominic Tierney, *Failing to Win:
Perceptions of Victory and Defeat in
International Politics* (Cambridge, MA:
Harvard University Press, 2006).

30 David A. Baldwin, 'Force, Fungibility,
and Influence', *Security Studies*, vol. 8,
no. 4, Summer 1999, p. 175.

31 See Carl Kaysen, 'Is War Obsolete? A
Review Essay', *International Security*, vol.
14, no. 4, Spring 1990, pp. 42–64; Michael
Mandelbaum, 'Is Major War Obsolete?',
Survival, vol. 40, no. 4, Winter 1998–
99, pp. 20–38; John Mueller, 'The
Obsolescence of Major War', *Bulletin
of Peace Proposals*, vol. 21, no. 3, 1990,
pp. 321–8; and Nina Tannenwald, 'The
Nuclear Taboo: The United States and
the Normative Basis of Nuclear Non-
use', *International Organization*, vol. 53,
no. 3, Summer 1999, pp. 433–68.

32 Eliot A. Cohen, 'Net Assessment: An
American Approach', Jaffee Center for
Strategic Studies, 1990, p. 4.

33 Stephen Peter Rosen, 'Net Assessment
as an Analytical Concept', in Andrew
W. Marshall, J.J. Martin and Henry
S. Rowen (eds), *On Not Confusing
Ourselves: Essays on National Security
Strategy in Honor of Albert & Roberta
Wohlstetter* (Boulder, CO: Westview,
1991), p. 290.

34 See International Institute for Strategic
Studies, 'The Military Balance',
https://www.iiss.org/publications/
the-military-balance/.

35 Andrew W. Marshall, 'Problems of
Estimating Military Power', RAND
Corporation, August 1966, p. 2.

36 Eliot A. Cohen, 'Toward Better
Net Assessment: Rethinking the
European Conventional Balance',
International Security, vol. 13, no. 1,
Summer 1988, p. 85.

37 Cohen, 'Net Assessment: An American
Approach', p. 4.

38 Allan Millett and Williamson
Murray's three-volume history
of military effectiveness was
commissioned by Andrew Marshall
for the Office of Net Assessment,
and deals with both world wars
and the interwar period. See Allan
R. Millett and Williamson Murray,
*Military Effectiveness: Volume 1, The
First World War*, new ed. (Cambridge:
Cambridge University Press, 2010);
Allan R. Millett and Williamson
Murray, *Military Effectiveness: Volume
2, The Interwar Period* (Cambridge:
Cambridge University Press, 2010);
and Allan R. Millett and Williamson
Murray, *Military Effectiveness: Volume
3, The Second World War* (Cambridge:
Cambridge University Press, 2010).
The question of the sources of military
effectiveness is fundamental to the
classics of strategic studies, as well
as being the animating concern of
military-operations research, and
a wealth of work in sociology and
political science that considers the
vast array of social and political

variables that may underpin a state's capacity to translate basic resources into military power. Stephen Biddle, 'Military Effectiveness', in *Oxford Research Encyclopedia of International Studies* (Oxford: Wiley-Blackwell, 2010), https://oxfordre.com/internationalstudies/display/10.1093/acrefore/9780190846626.001.0001/acrefore-9780190846626-e-35.

[39] See George E. Pickett, James G. Roche and Barry D. Watts, 'Net Assessment: A Historical Review', in Marshall, Martin and Rowen (eds), *On Not Confusing Ourselves*, p. 177.

[40] Rosen, 'Net Assessment as an Analytical Concept', p. 284.

[41] This conceit often obscured some of the more subtle insights of the Chicago School's leading lights. Frank Knight, for example, highlighted the importance of *both* risk – where probabilities could be determined – *and* uncertainty – where probabilities could not be known. Frank Hyneman Knight, *Risk, Uncertainty and Profit* (Boston, MA: Houghton Mifflin, 1921).

[42] See Andrew F. Krepinevich and Barry D. Watts, *The Last Warrior: Andrew Marshall and the Shaping of Modern American Defense Strategy* (New York: Basic Books, 2015), pp. 13–15.

[43] See Dmitry Adamsky, 'The Art of Net Assessment and Uncovering Foreign Military Innovations: Learning from Andrew W. Marshall's Legacy', *Journal of Strategic Studies*, vol. 43, no. 5, 2020.

[44] Marshall, 'Problems of Estimating Military Power', p. 9.

[45] Quoted in Mie Augier, 'Thinking About War and Peace: Andrew Marshall and the Early Development of the Intellectual Foundations for Net Assessment', *Comparative Strategy*, vol. 32, no. 1, 2013, p. 6.

[46] See United States National Security Council, 'Memorandum for Record: National Net Assessment', 10 April 1973.

[47] See Stephen Peter Rosen, 'The Impact of the Office of Net Assessment on the American Military in the Matter of the Revolution in Military Affairs', *Journal of Strategic Studies*, vol. 33, no. 4, August 2010, pp. 469–82.

[48] Cohen, 'Toward Better Net Assessment', p. 89.

[49] Thomas Skypek, 'Evaluating Military Balances Through the Lens of Net Assessment: History and Application', *Journal of Military and Strategic Studies*, vol. 12, no. 2, Winter 2010, pp. 20–1.

[50] Franz-Stefan Gady, 'Is the Pentagon's Andrew Marshall the Leo Strauss of Military Analysis?', *Diplomat*, 14 January 2015, https://thediplomat.com/2015/01/is-the-pentagons-andrew-marshall-the-leo-strauss-of-military-analysis/.

[51] The Russian term *sootnosheniye sil* has been variously translated as 'correlation', 'alignment', 'ratio' and 'relationship of forces'. While some US translators opted for 'balance of power', Soviet translations avoided this term since the balance of power was anathema to progressive class struggle. Instead, they drew a clear conceptual distinction between the terms. Michael J. Deane, 'The Soviet Concept of the "Correlation of Forces"', Stanford Research Institute Strategic Studies Center, May 1976, pp. 43–5.

[52] See *ibid.*, p. iv.

[53] See Julian Lider, 'The Correlation of World Forces: The Soviet Concept', *Journal of Peace Research*, vol. 17, no. 2, June 1980, p. 151; and Vernon V.

Aspaturian, 'Soviet Global Power and the Correlation of Forces', *Problems of Communism*, vol. 29, May–June 1980, pp. 9–10.

54 See Deane, 'The Soviet Concept of the "Correlation of Forces"', pp. 23–4.

55 See A. Sergiyev, 'Leninism as a Factor of International Relations', *International Affairs (Moscow)*, May 1975, p. 101.

56 See Aspaturian, 'Soviet Global Power and the Correlation of Forces', p. 10.

57 See Francis Fukuyama, *The End of History and the Last Man* (London: Hamish Hamilton, 1992); and Nicholas Kitchen and Michael Cox, 'Just Another Liberal War? Western Interventionism and the Iraq War', in Amitav Acharya and Hiro Katsumata (eds), *Beyond Iraq: The Future of World Order* (Singapore: World Scientific, 2011), pp. 65–84.

58 The authors of a 2017 study on 'protean power' cite Mary Sarotte's description of the historical accident that led to the fall of the Berlin Wall as an example of how radical uncertainty pervades inter-national politics. See Mary Elise Sarotte, *The Collapse: The Accidental Opening of the Berlin Wall* (New York: Basic Books, 2014), cited in Peter J. Katzenstein and Lucia A. Seybert, *Protean Power: Exploring the Uncertain and Unexpected in World Politics* (Cambridge: Cambridge University Press, 2017), p. 5.

59 Aaron B. Frank, 'Toward Computational Net Assessment', *Journal of Defense Modeling and Simulation*, vol. 14, no. 1, 2017.

60 See Barry Buzan, 'A New Cold War? The Case for a General Concept', *International Politics*, vol. 61, no. 2, March 2024, pp. 1–19.

61 See John Clark, 'Left in the Dark: How a Lack of Understanding of National Power Generation Threatens Our Way of Life', Policy Exchange, July 2019, https://policyexchange.org.uk/wp-content/uploads/2019/07/Left-in-the-dark.pdf.

62 Observing how US intelligence assessed the Soviet Union's early nuclear-weapons programme, David Lilienthal, then chair of the US Atomic Energy Commission, wrote: 'The thing that rather chills one's blood is to observe what is nothing less than lack of integrity in the way the intelligence agencies deal with the meagre stuff they have. It is chiefly a matter of reasoning from our own American experience, guessing from that how much longer it will take Russia using our methods and based upon our own problems of achieving weapons. But when this is put into a report, the reader, e.g., Congressional committee, is given the impression, and deliberately, that behind the estimates lies specific knowledge, knowledge so important and delicate that its nature and sources cannot be disclosed or hinted at.' David Eli Lilienthal, *The Journals of David E. Lilienthal, Volume 2: The Atomic Energy Years, 1945–1950* (New York: Harper & Row, 1964), p. 376.

63 Andrew W. Marshall, 'Long-term Competition with the Soviets: A Framework for Strategic Analysis', RAND Corporation, April 1972, p. v.

64 See Krepinevich and Watts, *The Last Warrior*, pp. 153–92.

65 Peter Roberts and Sidharth Kaushal, 'Strategic Net Assessment: Opportunities and Pitfalls', *RUSI Journal*, vol. 163, no. 6, 2018, p. 70.

66 *Ibid.*, p. 74.

NATO and Ukraine: The Peril of Indecision

Liana Fix

At the North Atlantic Treaty Organization (NATO) summit in Washington, celebrating the Alliance's 75th birthday in July 2024, Ukraine's future within NATO was nominally reaffirmed. Despite the unprecedented level of cooperation and support behind defending Ukraine, however, no criteria or timeline for Ukraine's accession were established. The far shore of the 'bridge' to Ukraine's NATO membership is not in sight.[1] The summit offered little more than 'Bucharest+', reprising the ambiguity of the infamous 2008 NATO summit at which the Alliance nebulously and unseriously declared that Ukraine and Georgia would eventually become NATO members.[2] Meanwhile, the actual window for Ukraine's accession may be closing. Risk-averse NATO member states fear that the prospect of Ukraine's membership will only intensify Russia's expansionist inclinations. And potential leadership changes in Europe and the United States could erode the strong transatlantic consensus on support for Ukraine and the already weaker consensus about bringing it into NATO.

At the 2023 NATO summit in Vilnius, the NATO–Ukraine Council was inaugurated, enhancing cooperation between Ukraine and NATO, and promising Ukraine that it would become a NATO member when 'conditions are met' and 'allies agree', a tautological statement that provided little guidance.[3] NATO allies did reassure Ukraine that it could bypass the burdensome Membership Action Plan, NATO's standard instrument for accession,

Liana Fix is a fellow for Europe at the Council on Foreign Relations.

Survival | vol. 66 no. 4 | August–September 2024 | pp. 71–76   https://doi.org/10.1080/00396338.2024.2380197

and proceed to membership on an expedited basis, as Finland and Sweden have. But the vagueness about when that would happen produced discontent in the Ukrainian delegation. While it was clear that membership could not be extended when war was ongoing for fear of immediately triggering the Article 5 obligation to directly confront Russia militarily on Ukraine's behalf, it was unclear how stable an armistice would have to be to afford Alliance members the requisite degree of comfort for Ukraine to become a member.[4] In Washington this July, the US administration sought to avoid another rift by displaying unity above all else. While understandable, this approach left little room for honest, open and creative debate.

Two arguments

The conversation about Ukraine's membership in NATO has been dominated by two arguments. The first is that NATO cannot offer a specific time for accession – such as the end of the war or the point at which front lines become stabilised – since this would discourage Russian President Vladimir Putin from agreeing to terminate the war. The underlying assumption is that Putin is actually interested in ending the war short of abject Ukrainian capitulation, yet he has repeatedly stated the opposite. He may also be convinced that, even if no timeline is explicitly specified in an official NATO communiqué, Ukraine would become a NATO member sooner or later in the absence of complete Russian victory. Indeed, this fatalistic logic seems consistent with his justification for pre-emptively starting the war in the first place. But before Russia invaded Ukraine in 2022, NATO members had argued they could not offer Ukraine a timeline for accession since that would provoke Putin and invite aggression. Thus, timeline phobia appears to have paralysed NATO. Establishing what sequence of developments would make membership ripe would at least restore NATO's control over the process.

The second argument is that the timeline and membership criteria should remain unspecified because as such they will be useful bargaining chips in peace negotiations and could enable Ukrainian President Volodymyr Zelenskyy to sweeten Ukrainians on potentially crucial territorial concessions. The implicit premise of this argument is, of course, that NATO's formal commitment to Ukraine's membership is entirely reversible and depends mainly on political circumstances.

The Israel and West Germany models, once widely entertained, did not surface in 2024 summit discussions.[5] The consensus has settled on Ukraine relying on bilateral security agreements that offer neither a clear pathway nor a satisfactory alternative to membership. Even if placed under the umbrella of a security compact, such arrangements add nothing to what was already agreed at the G7 in 2023. The prevailing view contemplates merely a substantial role for NATO in support of Ukraine, including coordination, security-sector support and financial commitments. Given the salient possibility that the quasi-isolationist, anti-NATO Donald Trump could be elected US president in November, the 2024 summit's central preoccupation was not advancing Ukraine's NATO membership. It was rather to Trump-proof support for Ukraine by bringing support structures under the NATO umbrella. While Washington oversold the outcome of the summit with deceptive 'bridge' rhetoric, Ukraine did emerge from it institutionally closer to NATO than virtually any non-member of that Alliance has ever been. The eventual effect of this dispensation could be a two-tier NATO: one for members protected by Article 5, and the other for those not so protected. Although defence alliances are not mainly about justice, it would be difficult to avoid creating the perception that NATO was a free-rider, unjustly benefiting from Ukraine's sacrifice for NATO's security without fully reciprocating.

An alternative approach
Instead of voluntarily taking Ukraine's NATO membership off the table by eliding when and how it could happen, NATO could explicitly frame the membership option as integral to ending the war and bringing security and stability to the region. For this to be credible, senior officials would need to present a clear account of how and under what assumptions Ukraine's membership in NATO could come about.[6] The most plausible scenario is a variation of the West Germany model, laid out by François Heisbourg in these pages a year ago.[7] A key aspect of the West German case potentially fits the current situation in Ukraine: while

the West German government refrained from relinquishing its goal of reunification with East Germany, it accepted the temporary division of the country and abjured the use of force to undo it in return for Western security guarantees and NATO membership.

Other features, of course, are different. Unlike Russian-occupied territories of Ukraine, East Germany had its own state, albeit one dominated by the Soviet Union, and had not faced attempted annexations. There also was no active warfare along the territorial divide. But the larger lesson for Ukraine seems applicable. Once the front lines in the war are substantially stabilised – for example, when Russia pauses its onslaught due to exhaustion or an agreed ceasefire or armistice – it would be strategically feasible for NATO to invite Ukraine to join the Alliance provided Kyiv accepted existing territorial allocations as the status quo and agreed to postpone the liberation of occupied territory pending political developments that could make it possible. In line with French President Emmanuel Macron's proposal, a small deployment of NATO troops could then be stationed in Ukraine as a 'tripwire', as they have been in the Baltic states since 2014, to deter resumed Russian military aggression.

Admittedly, this option would not be easy to digest or implement. It would require resolve and courage on the part of both Ukraine and NATO members, especially the United States. But peace and security for Ukraine appears unsustainable without NATO membership, and there is no comfortable non-binary solution to Ukraine's predicament, a two-tiered NATO being flagrantly problematic. And, though Putin will blanch at the West Germany model, it may be relatively palatable to future Russian leaders. Outside NATO, Ukraine has had the leeway to launch strikes across the Russian border in response to air and missile attacks and ground assaults staged from Russia, as it has consistently demonstrated. As a member of NATO, however, Ukraine would be constrained from attacking Russian territory owing to concerns about NATO–Russia escalation underpinned by Article 5. Thus, NATO membership for Ukraine could well increase security for both Ukraine and Russia, and enhance regional stability.

*   *   *

With no timeline or membership criteria, Ukraine's NATO accession is in effect postponed until an unspecified time at which a Russian leader is in power who either does not resent and feel threatened by Ukraine's membership or does not have the military means to contest it. These are improbable eventualities. Furthermore, on the Western side, the convergence that has occurred since the Russian invasion between a devotedly Atlanticist US president and a Europe collectively awakened to Russia's revanchist threat is unlikely to tighten further, at least in the near term. Indeed, the Biden administration's reluctance to articulate a timeline or set of membership criteria suggests that even if Joe Biden or a like-minded alternative Democratic nominee wins the election, he may be inclined to kick the membership question down the road. Should Trump be elected, Ukraine's membership in NATO is almost unimaginable. Once closed, the window is unlikely to be reopened. If it does close, and a new Trump administration ends American support, Ukraine would be compelled to depend wholly on whatever European support was still forthcoming, give up the fight altogether or go it alone. In such circumstances, outlandish and risky scenarios, including a Ukrainian nuclear option, could arise. Ukraine and Europe more broadly would, in any event, face a dark and uncertain future.

Notes

1   North Atlantic Treaty Organization, 'Washington Summit Declaration', 10 July 2024, https://www.nato.int/cps/en/natohq/official_texts_227678.htm.

2   See North Atlantic Treaty Organization, 'Bucharest Summit Declaration', 3 April 2008 (updated 5 July 2022), https://www.nato.int/cps/en/natolive/official_texts_8443.htm.

3   North Atlantic Treaty Organization, 'Vilnius Summit Communiqué', 11 June 2023 (updated 19 June 2023), https://www.nato.int/cps/en/natohq/official_texts_217320.htm.

4   See Liana Fix, 'The Future Is Now: Security Guarantees for Ukraine', *Survival*, vol. 65, no. 3, June–July 2023, pp. 67–72.

5   Under the Israel model, Western allies would bilaterally provide major arms, military equipment and training to Ukraine on a long-term basis without establishing a formal alliance relationship, which would resemble the United States' security arrangement with Israel. The West Germany model would call for Ukraine to be admitted to NATO without relinquishing its sovereign claim on Russian-occupied Ukrainian territory but forswearing

the use of force against Russia, which would remain a de facto occupying power in parts of Ukraine, recalling the terms of West Germany's admission to NATO in 1955. See Eliot A. Cohen, 'The "Israel Model" Won't Work for Ukraine', *Atlantic*, 13 July 2023, https://www.theatlantic. com/ideas/archive/2023/07/israel-model-ukraine/674683/; and François

Heisbourg, 'How to End a War: Some Historical Lessons for Ukraine', *Survival*, vol. 65, no. 4, August–September 2023, pp. 7–24.

6   See Ivo Daalder and Karen Donfried, 'What Ukraine Needs From NATO', *Foreign Affairs*, 26 March 2024, https://www.foreignaffairs.com/ukraine/what-ukraine-needs-nato.

7   See Heisbourg, 'How to End a War'.

Winning the US–China Technology Race

David C. Gompert

The last time America faced an opposing superpower, the Cold War arms race framed its strategy. The Soviet Union failed to keep pace technologically with the United States and lost the Cold War essentially because its closed economy, society and state went bust. This is unlikely to happen to China, which is the second-largest economy in the world and well integrated into the global economic system. The United States' current rivalry with China should be seen through the prism of a technology race, in which the ability to imagine, discover and apply innovations will decide who wins.

In the new race, the United States is competing with a technological rival that eschews free enterprise in favour of state control. The US should avoid complacency about the inherent advantage of the democratic-capitalist system in scientific discovery. The US government may need to dedicate more resources and devise more effective mechanisms for stimulating free enterprise to compete in military technology.[1]

Starting now, the United States should increase investment in defence technology with an eye to denying China military superiority in the Pacific. Yet today's crises are diverting Pentagon funding from such investment, and, even with ample funding, it now takes too long for American civilian innovation to yield improved forces. Two policies could shrink or eliminate these disadvantages: reducing funding for current strategic confrontations; and accelerating the military output of private innovation. Each policy is

David C. Gompert is former acting US Director of National Intelligence.

Survival | vol. 66 no. 4 | August–September 2024 | pp. 77–84   https://doi.org/10.1080/00396338.2024.2380198

necessary, but neither alone is sufficient. Each challenge is difficult, but neither is insurmountable.

Fighting today's fires

Like most large enterprises, the US Department of Defense must strike the right balance between meeting immediate demands and anticipating future ones – in business parlance, operations versus investment. At present, it is getting that balance wrong. Ledgers tell the story. US defence spending rose sharply following Russia's 2022 invasion of Ukraine. Since then, an annual increase of $50 billion or so has been baked into annual Pentagon spending, which will reach $850bn judging by its 2025 budget request. This increase over three years is going almost entirely to support operations in Europe, the Western Pacific and the Middle East.[2]

Given the prominence of Russian aggression, the Gaza war and related instability, and China's threat to Taiwan, expanded funding to support operations comes as no shock. But it masks the insufficiency in investment in military research and development (R&D), which has flattened out at roughly $140bn per year over the past three years.[3] A shrinking fraction of the US defence budget is going to the technology race with the opposing superpower. Operating needs are taking precedence over strategic ones, with no sign of change.

US alliances – which the Biden administration has strengthened – could help enable the United States to channel more resources into technologically outcompeting China without neglecting current defence needs. Europe is a case in point. America's NATO allies spend $380bn on defence[4] – roughly three times what Russia does. Russia's ground, air and naval forces, as well as its command and control of them, have performed badly in Ukraine and would be overmatched in a war with a determined NATO. Not counting US forces committed to NATO, the Alliance's arsenal exceeds Russia's by wide margins in combat aircraft, active and reserve personnel, special-operations forces and naval combatants.[5] The accession of Finland and Sweden has significantly augmented the numbers and quality of NATO forces.

Whatever happens on the ground in Ukraine, Russia probably lacks the material capacity to correct these imbalances. The European Union's gross domestic product of $17 trillion is roughly eight times Russia's. Although oil and gas sales have stabilised the Russian economy at $2trn, the demands of the war for soldiers and roubles are afflicting Russia with rising inflation and sagging productivity. Just 1% of its GDP goes to R&D.[6]

Fears of Russia's forces trampling NATO's after defeating Ukraine's appear unrealistic. The Russian military has been unable to seize more than the Russian-speaking fifth of Ukraine. European members of NATO can do much more to improve the quality of their military capabilities. Accordingly, there is scope for the United States to pare the cost of its European obligations without weakening NATO's security or America's commitment to it.

Even though Russia lacks the means to seize NATO territory, it is important that the United States, for now, not depend solely on its European allies to provide Ukraine with the means to defeat Russian aggression. At present, American weapons for Ukraine are indispensable and compensate for inadequacies in European supplies. That said, it is essential that US assistance to Ukraine not come at the expense of US investment in military R&D needed to outcompete China technologically. In due course, European allies will – at least, should – expand their ability to outmatch Russian capabilities qualitatively and quantitatively.

European allies also have top-notch special-operations and naval capabilities, including modern aircraft carriers, which can bolster US efforts to counter Iran and its proxies. The recent US-choreographed response to Iranian threats to the Middle East suggests that Europe, Gulf Arab states and Israel itself can reduce demands on American forces. As for the Western Pacific, the United States can expect greater defence contributions from Japan, which is mounting a major military upgrade and pledging to help contain China in the region.[7]

Emerging military technology

While sound investment calls for a long view, short-term timing is critical. A wave of new technologies of enormous military potency – artificial intelligence (AI), quantum computing, chip and battery design, revolutionary space networks – is cresting. These technologies can improve Chinese targeting of US forces. AI can operate uncrewed aircraft and ships, multiply the quality of intelligence and foster flexible decision-making. Quantum computing can accelerate data processing and improve cyber security. Better, smaller chips and batteries can revolutionise microelectronic and energy performance. And a large network of satellites is a force multiplier in all battlefield domains and across vast geographical areas.

The Chinese now have extended-range surveillance systems that can track US ships and observe US bases throughout the Western Pacific. They also possess ballistic, cruise and hypersonic missiles with sufficient accuracy and range to exploit such surveillance and strike exposed US forces across the region. Facing these threats, the US military is already developing and deploying less vulnerable forces by way of dispersed strike platforms with longer-range weapons, submarines, uncrewed platforms and space-based command and control. But America's military R&D is still in lower gear than China's. Simply put, although the United States outspends China in military investment, including R&D, China's state-centred system enables it to transform funding and talent into deployed capabilities faster than the United States' private-enterprise-centred system.

America's R&D is in lower gear than China's

While the central state has principal responsibility in China for generating new technology, private enterprise is the locomotive of American invention. Aggregate US spending on R&D comes to 2.5% of its $25trn economy, whereas China's is 2% of an $18trn economy.[8] However, Beijing is able to shovel money and talent directly into the People's Liberation Army for quick results, while it takes years for the US government to marshal private investment for the benefit of US national defence. For instance, it took the better part of the 1980s for data networking to migrate from public to US military capabilities.

To compete with China in military technology, the US government could increase defence spending to levels that meet both present operational needs and sustained investment increases – say, by $50bn. But this could imply a Pentagon budget of over $1trn, which would dwarf that of China, Russia and all other US adversaries combined, and could swell the $1.5trn federal-budget deficit and interest obligations. We know from Cold War experience that such profligate American military spending can produce severe inflation. From this perspective, money freed from increased allied support for current operations would best be used to stimulate private-sector innovation.

For purposes of illustration, it is not unreasonable that, say, $25bn a year be spared from current US operational demands and earmarked for the race in military technology. But, unlike the Chinese state, the US government cannot simply plow massive additional funds directly into military R&D. While scientific innovation is rising in the US high-tech industry, the Defense Department and other government agencies could make their markets more inviting. Even though Pentagon business reform has become more focused, it still takes roughly five years for promising private-sector innovations to translate into actual military capabilities.

One of the most serious impediments to private firms seeking to develop military capabilities is the lag between fruitful R&D and steady revenue streams from production. Such firms must absorb the full costs of management, marketing and technical staff for several years. For start-ups, which are often the source of innovation, those costs are prohibitive, and it is unrealistic to expect venture capitalists to bear them without the prospect of timely earnings. The effect of this disincentive is at best delay in exploiting innovative technology for military applications, at worst outright discouragement of private innovation for defence applications. The Pentagon's so-called 'valley of death' – shades of Monty Python – is where many start-ups go to die.

The Defense Department could mitigate this problem by investing funds to defray costs before production can begin and steady revenue can flow. Ideally, investment from the prospective military client and from the Pentagon itself would attract private capital at this critical stage.[9] Of course, the US military cannot supply funds willy-nilly to whatever private start-up needs them. Of critical importance, then, is a mechanism to screen applicants for their potential to deliver important military capabilities and become self-sustaining.

The US Air Force has established such an option for small businesses.[10] Start-ups whose labs have demonstrated promising innovations can apply for service-client and departmental funding to match external capital. The prospect of matching government funding encourages private entities to invest. While individual cases may be small, the total can reach billions of dollars. All military services and defence-intelligence agencies should offer such a facility. In effect, the Pentagon would become an investor, drawing and matching private capital, before it becomes a regular buyer. Done properly, the $25bn or so liberated from operations could be put to strategic use to stimulate and accelerate the transfer of private-sector technology for military advantage, especially for competition with China.

*   *   *

It is possible for the United States to take a firm lead in the race with China for superior military technology by calling on allies and private innovators to facilitate selective but substantial investment in critical defence technologies. Private entrepreneurs would no longer be discouraged from pursuing business with the armed services, and the time from laboratory to battlefield could be greatly shortened. To this end, Washington needs to rally the imagination, the determination, the trust and the confidence of allies and entrepreneurs.

Notes

1   See David C. Gompert, 'Spin-on: How the US Can Meet China's Technological Challenge', *Survival*, vol. 62, no. 3, June–July 2020, pp. 115–30.

2   See Office of the Under Secretary of Defense (Comptroller)/Chief Financial Officer, 'Defense Budget Overview – Fiscal Year 2025 Budget Request', US Department of Defense, March 2024 (revised 4 April 2024), https://comptroller.defense.gov/Portals/45/Documents/defbudget/FY2025/FY2025_Bud.get_Request_Overview_Book.pdf.

3   See Courtney Albon and Colin Demarest, 'Pentagon Trims Tech Research Funding Request; AI, Networking Flat', C4ISRNet, 12 March 2024, https://www.c4isrnet.com/battlefield-tech/2024/03/12/pentagon-trims-tech-research-funding-request-ai-networking-flat/.

4   See North Atlantic Treaty Organization, 'Secretary General Welcomes Unprecedented Rise in NATO Defence Spending', 14 February 2024, https://www.nato.int/cps/en/natohq/news_222664.htm.

5   See Barry Posen, 'Europe Can Defend Itself', *Survival*, vol. 62, no. 6, December 2020–January 2021, pp. 7–34.

6   See Statista, 'R&D Expenditure as a GDP Share in Russia 2001–2020', 20 March 2024, https://www.statista.com/statistics/461754/share-of-gdp-expenditure-on-research-and-development-russia/.

7   See Lotje Boswinkel, 'Forever Bound? Japan's Road to Self-defence and the US Alliance', *Survival*, vol. 66, no. 3, June–July 2024, pp. 105–28.

8   David Matthews, 'US Holds Off China Challenge in Global R&D Spending Race', *Science/Business*, 14 March 2024, https://sciencebusiness.net/news/international-news/us-holds-china-challenge-global-rd-spending-race.

9   See Gompert, 'Spin-on'.

10 See AFWERX, 'STRATFI/TACFI', afwerx.com/divisions/afventures/stratfi-tacfi.

A Bridge No More? Turkiye's Geopolitical Significance in the Twenty-first Century

Çağdaş Üngör

Turkiye's geopolitical significance was in little doubt during the Cold War. The country joined the US-led NATO alliance in 1952 and shared a border with the Soviet Union, placing it at the centre of this ideological confrontation.[1] The conviction that Turkiye's geographical location continues to confer unique strategic leverage lingers in Ankara today.[2] The Turkish Straits are seen to embody the country's ongoing status as a 'bridge' between Europe and Asia at a time when China's economic rise, growing Sino-US rivalry, and technological shifts brought about by the Fourth Industrial Revolution and global decarbonisation efforts appear to be ushering in an 'Asia-Pacific century'.[3] Although Turkiye is still a NATO member and partner to the United States, it is questionable whether the country's physical geography is enough to shore up its leverage in a new cold war between China and the US.

A bridge no more?

Ankara is not particularly close to either China or the US. This is true both in the geographical sense and in terms of the norms and values these countries espouse. Disagreements over regional and global issues between Washington and Ankara in the last decade have created substantial divisions between them. Unlike during the Cold War, Turkiye and the US do not

Çağdaş Üngör is a professor in the Department of Political Science and International Relations at Marmara University in Istanbul. She declares that she has no known competing financial interests or personal relationships that could have appeared to influence the work reported in this paper. A longer version of this article will be published by the *Turkish Studies* journal in summer 2024 under the heading 'A Bridge Pushed to the Periphery?: Turkey's Geopolitical Significance in the Asia-Pacific Century'.

Survival | vol. 66 no. 4 | August–September 2024 | pp. 85–90   https://doi.org/10.1080/00396338.2024.2380199

necessarily view the same countries as either friends or foes. Most notably, the Turkish government does not view China as a threat, a fact that leaves no room for Turkiye in the US-led Indo-Pacific strategy that has been promoted by the Trump and Biden administrations. This can be seen, for example, in Turkiye's absence from the Washington-backed India–Middle East–Europe Economic Corridor (IMEC), which was announced at the G20 summit in New Delhi in 2023.[4]

It does not follow, however, that Turkiye's distance from the US means it enjoys closer ties with China. Although Sino-Turkish relations have become friendlier since the 2010s, China has not emerged as a direct substitute for Turkiye's souring relations with the West.[5] Turkiye's NATO membership still limits its ability to develop strong ties with Beijing through institutional mechanisms such as the Shanghai Cooperation Organisation (SCO). This is especially true since NATO revealed its most recent strategic concept at the Madrid Summit in 2022, which painted China as a rival to the Alliance. At an SCO summit in November 2023, Turkiye was excluded from an agreement envisaging a transport corridor linking China, Pakistan, Afghanistan, Kazakhstan, Russia and Belarus.[6] China–Turkiye relations have also been impeded by the domestically sensitive Uyghur issue. Although Ankara has lowered its voice on China's human-rights violations in Xinjiang in recent years, Turkiye still ranks lower than several other Middle Eastern countries in Beijing's hierarchy of diplomatic partnerships.

Turkiye and the US do not view the same countries as foes

The Turkish Straits may still provide Ankara with substantial leverage over real and perceived enemies (while serving as an important maritime choke point, particularly for Russian oil shipments), but the Malacca Strait and Suez Canal are far more important in terms of Asia–Europe trade flows. Likewise, no Turkish locations are listed among the world's busiest maritime ports, many of which are found in the Asia-Pacific.[7] Turkiye's relatively insignificant role in China's land-based Belt and Road Initiative (BRI) casts further doubt on its bridge status.[8] Despite the popularity of token projects such as the Ankara–Istanbul high-speed railway or Kumport container terminal, China's BRI has so far delivered little in the way of life-changing development to Turkiye.[9] It is possible that the Middle Corridor (also known as the Trans-Caspian International Transport Route), which aims to connect China and Europe through Central Asia, the Caspian Sea, the Caucasus and Turkiye, may revive Turkiye's bridge status in the future. This initiative has gained new appeal in Western countries seeking alternatives to the Northern Corridor and the Russian Trans-Siberian Railway in the wake of the war in Ukraine.[10] Substantial financial investment and overall policy coordination for the corridor are still lacking, however.[11]

Another major transformation that is likely to lessen Turkiye's geo-political significance is the global push to achieve zero carbon. Turkish governments have long taken pride in the country's ability to physically connect the energy-rich Central Asian countries with European markets. Previous pipeline projects in Turkiye, such as the Baku–Tbilisi–Erzurum (BTE) pipeline, TurkStream or the Trans Anatolian Natural Gas Pipeline Project (TANAP), have facilitated this role. But the European Union's net-zero outlook, goal of becoming the first climate-neutral continent by 2050 and declining demand for fossil fuels may take a toll on Ankara's ambition to turn Turkiye into an energy hub and undermine its bridge status in the energy sector. Russia's invasion of Ukraine may have created a short-term boost in European demand for Caspian oil and gas, but Europe's green transition is expected to leave China the biggest market for these resources.[12]

Finally, Turkiye is not among the pioneering nations of the Fourth Industrial Revolution, the technological products of which are shaping global geopolitics as well as economic rivalries. Despite its considerable advances in drone technology, Turkiye has displayed little progress in key areas such as artificial intelligence (AI), robotics or quantum computing.[13] In 2023, Turkiye was ranked 39th out of 62 countries in an index measuring investment, innovation and implementation in the field of AI.[14] Scholarly works cite Turkiye's domestic political dynamics, such as the increasing politicisation of state institutions and prevalent nepotism at its research centres, among the factors impeding the country's progress in AI technologies.[15] Unlike Taiwan, Turkiye does not excel in strategically important items suited for a digitalised world, such as semiconductors. Nor does Turkiye have abundant mine and mineral resources that could be used to develop renewable technologies.[16] Similarly, Turkiye's first electric vehicle – the TOGG – is not expected to become a globally competitive brand any time soon, despite its popularity in Turkish pro-government circles.[17]

* * *

How can Turkiye remain geopolitically relevant in a world focused on technological development and the Asia-Pacific? Turkiye is not geographically close to either of the two poles in the emerging US–China rivalry, nor does it appear to enjoy a privileged relationship with Washington or Beijing. With the bulk of Asia–Europe trade flowing via maritime routes to Turkiye's south and railways to its north, the country's bridge status seems to have diminished substantially in the twenty-first century. New connectivity projects, such as the Middle Corridor or the Turkiye–Iraq Development Road, may partially remedy this problem, but their completion remains a long-term prospect. To gain geopolitical leverage, therefore, Ankara needs to invest in its human resources, key technologies and niche products. The international success of Turkish drone technology and TV productions can be replicated in other areas. This will, of course, require a fresh look at Turkiye's educational and research institutions, which are currently haemorrhaging highly skilled workers to other countries. To prevent Turkiye's further slide into the world's geopolitical periphery, solutions will be needed for the country's democratic backsliding and economic downturn. Granting autonomy to the country's universities, eliminating nepotism and rewarding merit in the scientific–technological sphere will also be crucial in reversing Turkiye's brain drain and restoring its creative spirit.

Notes

1 See Ian O. Lesser, 'Turkey, the United States and the Delusion of Geopolitics', *Survival*, vol. 48, no. 3, Autumn 2006, pp. 83–96.

2 For a discussion of the notion that Turkiye's geographical location confers unique strategic leverage, see Pınar Bilgin, '"Only Strong States Can Survive in Turkey's Geography": The Uses of "Geographical Truths" in Turkey', *Political Geography*, vol. 26, no. 7, 2007, pp. 740–56.

3 For a discussion of how the Turkish Straits have been seen to embody

Turkiye's status as a 'bridge' between Europe and Asia, see Lerna K. Yanık, 'The Metamorphosis of Metaphors of Vision: "Bridging" Turkey's Location, Role and Identity After the End of the Cold War', *Geopolitics*, vol. 14, no. 3, 2009, pp. 531–49.

4   See Çağdaş Üngör, 'Asya ve Avrupa'yı Türkiye'siz Bağlamak', *UİK Panaroma*, 14 September 2023, https://www.uikpanorama.com/blog/2023/09/14/cu-6/; and Ragıp Soylu, 'Turkey's Erdogan Opposes India–Middle East Transport Project', *Middle East Eye*, 11 September 2023, https://www.middleeasteye.net/news/turkey-erdogan-opposes-india-middle-east-corridor.

5   See Ziya Öniş and Maimaiti Yalikun, 'Emerging Partnership in a Post-Western World? The Political Economy of China–Turkiye Relations', *Southeast European and Black Sea Studies*, vol. 21, no. 4, 2021, pp. 507–29.

6   See Dana Omirgazy, 'Kazakhstan Takes Part in First SCO Transport Forum in Tashkent', *Astana Times*, 2 November 2023, https://astanatimes.com/2023/11/kazakhstan-takes-part-in-first-sco-transport-forum-in-tashkent/.

7   World Shipping Council, 'The Top 50 Container Ports', 2021, https://www.worldshipping.org/top-50-ports.

8   See Nilgün Eliküçük Yıldırım and Gözde Yilmaz, 'Use/Misuse of Chinese BRI Investment? BRI-related Crony Capitalism in Turkey', *Southeast European and Black Sea Studies*, vol. 23, no. 2, 2023, pp. 365–83; and Christoph Nedopil Wang, 'China Belt and Road Initiative (BRI) Investment Report 2023 H1', Green Finance and Development Center,

FISF Fudan University, Shanghai, July 2023, https://greenfdc.org/china-belt-and-road-initiative-bri-investment-report-2023-h1/.

9   See Yalkun Uluyol, 'Partnership with Limits: China–Turkey Relations in the Late AKP Era', Heinrich Böll Foundation, 20 March 2024, https://tr.boell.org/en/2024/03/20/partnership-limits-china-turkey-relations-late-akp-era.

10 See European Bank for Reconstruction and Development, 'Sustainable Transport Connections Between Europe and Central Asia', June 2023, https://www.ebrd.com/news/publications/special-reports/sustainable-transport-connections-between-europe-and-central-asia.html.

11 See Tuba Eldem, 'Russia's War on Ukraine and the Rise of the Middle Corridor as a Third Vector of Eurasian Connectivity: Connecting Europe and Asia via Central Asia, the Caucasus, and Turkey', SWP, 28 October 2022, https://www.swp-berlin.org/10.18449/2022C64/; and Suat Beylur et al., *Tarihi İpek Yolunun Yeniden Canlandırılmasında Orta Koridor: Mevcut Durum, Potansiyel, Güncel Meseleler* (Ankara: Hoca Ahmet Yesevi Uluslararası Türk-Kazak Üniversitesi, 2022).

12 See Gabriele Cassetti et al., 'Reinforcing the Paris Agreement: Ambitious Scenarios for the Decarbonisation of the Central Asian and Caspian Region', *Renewable and Sustainable Energy Transition*, vol. 3, August 2023, p. 10; and Morgan Bazilian et al., 'Four Scenarios of the Energy Transition: Drivers, Consequences, and Implications for Geopolitics',

Wiley Interdisciplinary Reviews: Climate Change, vol. 11, no. 2, 2020.

13 See Francis Fukuyama, 'Droning On in the Middle East', *American Purpose*, 5 April 2021, https://www.americanpurpose.com/blog/fukuyama/droning-on/; 'Meet the World's New Arms Dealers', *The Economist*, 19 September 2023, https://www.economist.com/international/2023/09/19/meet-the-worlds-new-arms-dealers; and Soumitra Dutta et al. (eds), 'Global Innovation Index 2022: What Is the Future of Innovation-driven Growth? 15th Edition', World Intellectual Property Organization, Geneva, https://www.wipo.int/edocs/pubdocs/en/wipo-pub-2000-2022-en-main-report-global-innovation-index-2022-15th-edition.pdf.

14 Tortoise Media, 'The Global AI Index', 28 June 2023, https://www.tortoisemedia.com/intelligence/global-ai/.

15 See, for example, Muhammed Can, 'Under the Leadership of Our President: "Potemkin AI" and the Turkish Approach to Artificial Intelligence', *Third World Quarterly*, vol. 44, no. 2, 2023, pp. 356–76.

16 See IRENA, 'Geopolitics of the Energy Transition: Critical Materials', 12 July 2023, https://www.irena.org/Digital-Report/Geopolitics-of-the-Energy-Transition-Critical-Materials.

17 See Greig Mordue and Erman Sener, 'Upgrading in the Automotive Periphery: Turkey's Battery Electric Vehicle Maker Togg', *Development and Change*, vol. 53, no. 4, 2022, pp. 760–95.

Keir Starmer's Britain: Can the Centre Hold?

Dana H. Allin

Britain in early July 2024 was cliché-soaked. Rain plagued Wimbledon. Prime minister Rishi Sunak had already gotten theatrically drenched on 22 May, standing outside 10 Downing Street to call an election that his Conservatives were sure to lose. It rained six weeks later on 5 July, the morning after polling day. On that morning, a BBC news presenter felt it necessary to explain to viewers that the crowds getting wet outside of Buckingham Palace were regular tourists waiting for the Changing of the Guard. It is possible that most did not even notice the successive motorcades that sped past them: the first containing Sunak to offer his resignation to King Charles; the second carrying Labour Party leader Keir Starmer to accept the king's invitation to form a new government.

I confess to some ambivalence about the monarchical pomp that contributed – in the past decade, with accelerating absurdity – to an English exceptionalism driving a deluded Brexit. On 5 July, however, with the gyres of democracy spinning out of control across the Atlantic in America and, so it seemed at the time, across the English Channel in France, Britain's constitutional rituals were not just comforting; they framed a political succession of banal – and therefore somehow bracing – conservatism.

Dana H. Allin is an IISS Senior Fellow and the Editor of *Survival*, and an adjunct professor at the Johns Hopkins School of Advanced International Studies (SAIS–Europe) in Bologna, Italy.

Survival | vol. 66 no. 4 | August–September 2024 | pp. 91–97   https://doi.org/10.1080/00396338.2024.2380200

You say you want a revolution ...

I am hardly the first to observe that Britain since its 2016 referendum threw away one of its enduring, intangible assets – small-c conservatism. In pursuit of the chimeric, sunlit uplands of Brexit, the Tory populist revolution devoured its children: five prime ministers in eight years, each one more ideologically frivolous than the last, until Sunak tried to calm things down with a degree of technocratic normality. Yet even Sunak was driven by the populist furies to the grotesque stunt of trying to deport asylum seekers to Rwanda.

For one post-Brexit phase, this circus was mirrored in the Jeremy Corbyn-led Labour Party, with its own ideological caprice including a sinister streak of anti-Semitism. Starmer was Corbyn's deputy leader. A human-rights lawyer and then state prosecutor who only entered politics in his 50s, Starmer performed a balancing act that was both conventionally political and forthrightly humane. He stood by the left-wing Corbyn but at the same time gave voice to outrage at the anti-Semitism that Corbyn tolerated, if not encouraged.[1] Cognitive dissonance must sometimes be managed, and Starmer managed it well. Soon after taking the helm, he expelled Corbyn from the party.[2]

Labour had spent much of the late twentieth century battling Trotskyites and other radicals in its midst while producing mainly serious-minded leaders and prime ministers. Neil Kinnock, Labour's leader from 1983–92, won that battle against the 'militant tendency' decisively enough to pave the way for Tony Blair's New Labour and, by extension, Starmer's solemn manifesto centring on 'national renewal' and 'mission-driven government'.[3] Whatever else happens, Labour turned itself into a plausible party of government. The astonishing speed of passage from Corbyn's epic defeat by Boris Johnson in 2019 to Starmer's landslide victory in 2024 attests to that accomplishment.

Starmer's conservatism is most evident in his current position on Britain and the European Union. While Corbyn's ambivalence about EU membership – an artifact of leftist attitudes from the 1970s – was arguably a significant factor in the referendum result, Starmer was an unambivalent Remainer. Yet in the recent campaign he stated that the United Kingdom would not rejoin even the European Single Market in his lifetime.[4] He has, to be sure, promised to negotiate closer trading relations and much closer cooperation with the EU in the context of countering Russian aggression across many domains. The caution is nonetheless striking and perhaps odd. Britain's government finances are dire, its social and physical infrastructure decayed. The new government has promised continued fiscal conservatism, relying on economic growth to pull the country out of its hole. In these circumstances, rejoining the single market would seem to be akin to picking up a 20-pound note off the floor. Polls show, moreover, that over 60% of Britons now believe that Brexit was a mistake.[5] So Labour's current position looks, on one level, unimaginative and even cowardly. On another, Starmer may simply see wisdom in the judgement of Tory grandee Kenneth Clarke, a committed europhile who nevertheless concluded during the endless parliamentary turmoil after 2016 that there was no stable future for Britain inside the EU. Clarke for this reason opposed holding a second referendum. By this reasoning, for all the harm inflicted by the Brexit revolution, counter-revolution would inflict more harm.

The organisation of choice

The Conservative Party's Brexit obsession damaged Britain immensely: in the first instance by raising barriers with its nearest and largest economic partners, but also by ripping apart an organic, semi-constitutional relationship, which also encompassed foreign and security policy.[6] For at least a decade, moreover, Brexit has been the central polarising issue of British politics and culture, animating a version of the culture wars that have so sharply divided America. It is ominous indeed to hear the feckless former prime minister Liz Truss echoing Trumpian language of a 'deep state' that conspired to wreck her record-short term of office.[7] Perhaps, though, Starmer conservatism can also calm this bitterness. While it would be too much to say that Britain feels comfortable in its multi-ethnic skin, it was genuinely moving to hear Sunak, in his resignation speech, relate with pride the remarkable cultural milestone of his daughters lighting Diwali candles at Downing Street. So far, the UK culture wars have not seriously threatened Britain's own constitutional norms or the rule of law. As UK journalist Nick Cohen noted, writing in his Substack column, this distinguishes British Conservatives from American Republicans:

> however much there is to say against the British Conservative party – and
> I have said most of it – it is not an anti-democratic movement. We had
> the blessing of a peaceful handover of power on Friday morning. Rishi
> Sunak did not follow Donald Trump and deny the results of a legitimate
> election. His supporters did not storm Parliament. The Conservatives are
> right wing while the Republicans are far-right wing. I do not use that label
> out of leftish rhetorical excess. It is a simple statement of fact to describe
> as 'far right' extreme conservatives who do not accept democratic rules.[8]

Brexit Britain fell pretty deeply into the turmoil of twenty-first-century populism, yet it could be said in summer 2024 that the centre was holding. This appeared even more impressively true in France, where Marine Le Pen's seemingly ascendent Rassemblement National (National Rally in English) came first in the first round of snap parliamentary elections called by President Emmanuel Macron, but then fell to third behind a leftist alliance and Macron's own centrist formation in the second round. That second round occurred three days after Britain's election, so Europe in the course of a week had the happy experience of political establishments in two leading countries managing to organise a choice that offered its voters real democracy while walling off extremism. In the French case, this was accomplished through a somewhat haphazard version of an old tradition: a 'Republican Front' against what are still deemed off-limits strains of fascism. France's drama isn't over, as Catherine Fieschi details elsewhere in these pages.[9] Both countries face severe difficulties. But they have been or should be able to form governments on the basis of a liberal consensus and – critically at this juncture – a determination to defend liberal values against Russia in Ukraine and elsewhere.

America's cold civil war

This brings us to America, magnitudes more important for that defence. The American paradox is of a country more comfortably multi-ethnic than Britain, with a stronger economy and the unquestionable wherewithal to help defend Ukraine for as long as it takes, yet paralysed by a cold civil war.

On 12 July, at a Donald Trump rally in Butler, Pennsylvania, a 20-year-old gunman shot at and came very close to assassinating the former president.

The attempt did not, in and of itself, fit easily into that narrative of civil conflict. The attack by a registered Republican did not seem overtly political or ideological, except insofar as lonely young men immersed in gun culture form a recognisable and perhaps faintly ideological subculture with menacing and – in endless mass killings – deadly implications. Yet the June 1968 assassination of Robert Kennedy by an angry Palestinian, the April 1968 assassination of Martin Luther King, Jr, by a white racist, and even the November 1963 assassination of John F. Kennedy by a US Marine Corps veteran who had spent time in the Soviet Union all seemed more clearly political. Moreover, as the *New York Times* historian-columnist Jamelle Bouie and others have observed, the current moment is hardly among the most politically violent periods in even recent American history.[10]

As Bouie also says, however, that comparison does not capture the febrile fear and sense of impending political doom on both sides of an angrily polarised America. The cold civil war is a consequence of near-even electoral division and the firm conviction on both sides that electoral outcomes are existential. Trump's ferality and a MAGA movement that has swallowed the Republican Party leads Robert Kagan, a prominent past neo-conservative who is now firmly anti-Republican, to warn against a pre-emptive submission to an already forming Trumpian dictatorship.[11] From the opposite direction, in ways that I admittedly find hard to fathom or explain, Republicans echo the warning of Michael Anton, a National Security Council staffer in the Trump administration. Anton wrote in 2016 that the prospective election of Hillary Clinton represented a threat to America comparable to that of the 9/11 hijackers on United Airlines Flight 93 – so dire that the only option was to storm the cockpit, even if it meant death for everyone on board.[12]

Three days after the attempt on his life, Trump chose as his running mate Ohio Senator J.D. Vance, who had just claimed that the Biden campaign's anti-Trump rhetoric had incited the attack.[13] *Financial Times* columnist Ed Luce noted the irony that between Vance and Biden, only Vance had once directly compared Trump to Adolf Hitler.[14] But Vance has since developed into an articulate voice of MAGA radicalism at home and Trumpian neo-isolationism abroad, particularly critical of Biden's support for Ukraine and NATO.[15]

Whatever Trump is offering, abroad and at home, is not conservative. In this he is an authentic avatar of the American Right. On 1 July, the US Supreme Court, shaped critically by the three justices Trump appointed, decided that presidents have 'presumptive immunity' for all official acts, though prosecutors can overcome that presumption if they can show that charges related to official acts would not intrude on the 'authority and functions of the executive branch'.[16] They remanded the US Department of Justice's case against Trump to the trial court to weed out those 'official acts' before proceeding to try him on charges – if there are any left – related to his attempt to reverse the results of the 2020 election. It is difficult to avoid the conclusion that this Supreme Court is a political actor determined to re-empower a former president whom juries have found civilly liable for sexual abuse and defamation and criminally liable for campaign-finance fraud, and whom common sense indicates is guilty of trying to overthrow the American republic. In the same week that the court seemed to validate a lawless presidency, it also appeared intent on uprooting entrenched stand-ards of early twentieth-century Progressivism and mid-twentieth-century New Dealism, coded by MAGA as the 'administrative state'.

As in Britain, the conservative alternative in the United States comes from the centre left. As I write, however, the Democratic Party is in crisis because of the ineluctable, and hardly unforeseen, reality that its presump-tive nominee, President Joe Biden, is old and getting older. An abysmal Biden debate performance – the performance of an old man – has sparked panic among Democrats and Trump-fearing foreign allies. Yet there is a clear anti-MAGA plurality, if not majority, in the United States. Perhaps the stolid determination of Keir Starmer is a model to which American elites could turn to frame the choice that their centrist country seems to want.

Notes

1   See, for example, Charlie Cooper, 'Keir Starmer: Labour's Anti-Semitism "Day of Shame"', *Politico*, 29 October 2020, https://www.politico.eu/article/ keir-starmer-labours-anti-semitism-day-of-shame/.

2   See, for instance, Chas Geiger, 'Jeremy Corbyn Won't Be Labour Candidate at Next Election, Says Starmer', BBC

News, 15 February 2023, https://www.
bbc.com/news/uk-politics-64640069.

3 See Labour Party, 'Change: Labour
Party Manifesto 2024', https://labour.
org.uk/wp-content/uploads/2024/06/
Change-Labour-Party-Manifesto-2024-
large-print.pdf.

4 See Kiran Stacey, 'Britain Will
Not Rejoin EU in My Lifetime,
Says Starmer', *Guardian*, 3 July
2024, https://www.theguardian.
com/politics/article/2024/jul/03/
britain-will-not-rejoin-eu-in-
my-lifetime-says-starmer.

5 See, for example, Max Colchester,
David Luhnow and Josh Mitchell,
'Brexit Backlash: Brits Now Regret
Their Populist Revolt', *Wall Street
Journal*, 28 June 2024, https://www.wsj.
com/world/uk/brexit-british-regret-
uk-election-837cbf4c.

6 See Christopher Hill, *The Future of
British Foreign Policy: Security and
Diplomacy in a World After Brexit*
(London: Polity Press, 2019).

7 Quoted in Sam Blewett, 'Liz Truss'
Journey from Downing Street to
"Deep State" Conspiracist', *Politico*,
12 March 2024, https://www.politico.
eu/article/liz-truss-unlikely-journey-
from-downing-street-chief-to-deep-
state-conspiracist/.

8 Nick Cohen, 'Lessons from the
UK for America's Fight Against
Trump', Substack, 7 July 2024,
https://nickcohen.substack.com/p/
lessons-from-the-uk-for-americas.

9 Catherine Fieschi, 'France's Political
Crisis', *Survival*, vol. 66, no. 4, August–
September 2024, pp. 115–126.

10 Jamelle Bouie, 'How Does Trump's
Violent Rhetoric End?', *New York
Times*, 26 April 2024, https://www.
nytimes.com/2024/04/26/opinion/
trump-political-violence-civil-war.
html?showTranscript=1.

11 Robert Kagan, 'A Trump Dictatorship
Is Increasingly Inevitable. We Should
Stop Pretending', *Washington Post*,
20 November 2023, https://www.
washingtonpost.com/opinions/
2023/11/30/trump-dictator-2024-
election-robert-kagan/.

12 Michael Anton, 'The Flight 93
Election', *Claremont Review of Books*, 5
September 2016, https://claremont
reviewofbooks.com/digital/
the-flight-93-election/.

13 J.D. Vance (@JDVance1), post to X, 14
July 2024, https://x.com/JDVance1/
status/1812280973628965109.

14 Edward Luce, 'With Vance,
Trump Is Doubling Down on
Maga', *Financial Times*, 15 July
2024, https://www.ft.com/content/
eaeb2c10-8495-45fb-94c5-396546c638ba.

15 See 'J.D. Vance's Opposition to U.S.
Support for Ukraine: In His Own
Words', *New York Times*, 15 July 2024,
https://www.nytimes.com/2024/07/15/
world/europe/ukraine-jd-vance.html;
and Judith Evans, '"The Election Was
Stolen": JD Vance in Quotes', *Financial
Times*, 16 July 2024, https://www.
ft.com/content/90ab5a8a-507b-428e-
8ea9-c5cd2c62ef96.

16 Supreme Court of the United States,
Trump v. United States, No. 23-939, 1
July 2024, https://www.supremecourt.
gov/opinions/23pdf/23-939_e2pg.pdf.

Noteworthy

A world at the polls

'The people have sent us a message. They have decided we have to work together.'

African National Congress leader Cyril Ramaphosa reflects on the need to enter a coalition with other parties to form a government after his party failed to retain its majority in the South African parliament on 10 June 2024.[1]

'I will become the first female president of Mexico. And as I have said on other occasions, I do not arrive alone.'

Claudia Sheinbaum delivers a speech on 3 June after being elected the first female president of Mexico on 2 June.[2]

'To run the government, a majority is necessary. But to run the nation, a consensus is necessary. The people want us to deliver better than before.'

Indian Prime Minister Narendra Modi speaks to members of the coalition assembled after his party lost its parliamentary majority in June.[3]

'Today power will change hands in a peaceful and orderly manner, with good will on all sides. That is something that should give us all confidence in our country's stability and future. The British people have delivered a sobering verdict tonight. There is much to learn and reflect on and I take responsibility for the loss.'

Rishi Sunak concedes defeat in the United Kingdom's parliamentary election on 4 July.[4]

'The tide is rising. It did not rise high enough this time, but it continues to rise and our victory has simply been deferred.'

Marine Le Pen reacts to the worse-than-expected performance of her National Rally party in the second round of France's parliamentary elections on 7 July.[5]

2024 Shangri-La Dialogue

'Together with others, we put forward the archipelagic doctrine which regards all archipelagic states as a single unit, with the waters around, between and connecting the islands irrespective of their breadth and dimension forming part of their internal waters. This doctrine has since been enshrined in the 1982 United Nations Convention on the Law of the Sea, or UNCLOS … Our efforts stand in stark contrast to assertive actors who aim to propagate excessive and baseless claims through force, intimidation and deception.'

President Ferdinand R. Marcos, Jr, of the Philippines delivers the keynote address at the IISS Shangri-La Dialogue in Singapore on 31 May 2024.[6]

'I know you have followed closely the South China Sea issue. Thanks to concerted efforts made by countries in the region, the South China Sea has seen overall stability. However, a certain country, emboldened by outside powers, has broken bilateral agreements and its own promises, made premeditated provocations and created false scenarios to mislead the public. Moreover, it has ignored the overall interests of our region and violated the ASEAN Charter by allowing an outside country to deploy a mid-range missile system. This act will endanger the security and stability of our region, and it will eventually backfire. I am sure that the international community is clear-eyed about this.'

Admiral Dong Jun, China's minister of national defense, speaks at the Shangri-La Dialogue on 2 June.[7]

Putin visits Pyongyang

'Today, as before, Russia and the Democratic People's Republic of Korea are actively advancing their multifaceted partnership. We highly appreciate the DPRK's unwavering support for Russia's special military operation in Ukraine, their solidarity with us on key international matters and willingness to defend our common priorities and views within the United Nations. Pyongyang has always been our committed and like-minded supporter, ready to confront the ambition of the collective West to prevent the emergence of a multipolar world order based on justice, mutual respect for sovereignty and consideration of each other's interests.'

Russian President Vladimir Putin contributes an article to North Korea's Rodong Sinmun *newspaper to mark his visit to Pyongyang on 18 June 2024.[8]*

'Relations between our countries have risen to a new high level of alliance. A legal basis has been laid, making it possible to fulfil the ambitious plan of the leadership of the two countries and the age-old aspiration of our peoples to reliably protect peace and security in the region and in the world and to build strong states in line with the common interests of the Democratic People's Republic of Korea and the Russian Federation.'

North Korean leader Kim Jong-un speaks at a joint press conference in Pyongyang with Putin on 19 June.[9]

'The United States, ROK [Republic of Korea], and Japan condemn in the strongest possible terms deepening military cooperation between the DPRK and Russia, including continued arms transfers from the DPRK to Russia that prolong the suffering of the Ukrainian people, violate multiple United Nations Security Council Resolutions, and threaten stability in both Northeast Asia and Europe.'

Senior officials from Japan, South Korea and the United States release a joint statement on 25 June on the signing of a 'Treaty on Comprehensive Strategic Partnership' between Russia and North Korea.[10]

Donald Trump, felon

'Guilty.'

On 30 May 2024, the jury foreman announces the verdict in the trial of former US president Donald Trump on 34 counts of falsifying records to cover up a sex scandal.[11]

'Today's verdict does not change the fact that the American people face a simple reality. There is still only one way to keep Donald Trump out of the Oval Office: at the ballot box. Convicted felon or not, Trump will be the Republican nominee for president.'

Michael Tyler, communications director for the Biden campaign.[12]

'I'm a very innocent man, and it's okay, I'm fighting for our country. I'm fighting for our Constitution. Our whole country is being rigged right now.'

Trump releases a statement on 30 May.[13]

'The justice system should be respected, and we should never allow anyone to tear it down. It's as simple as that.'

US President Joe Biden.[14]

'We conclude that under our constitutional structure of separated powers, the nature of Presidential power requires that a former President have some immunity from criminal prosecution for official acts during his tenure in office. At least with respect to the President's exercise of his core constitutional powers, this immunity must be absolute. As for his remaining official actions, he is also entitled to immunity.'

The US Supreme Court rules that US presidents have legal immunity for their 'official acts' in a decision released on 1 July.[15]

No debate?

'The mission for Joe Biden in the presidential debate held in Atlanta on June 27th was clear: to prove his critics wrong, by showing that he was mentally fit and thereby reverse the polling deficit that makes Donald Trump the favourite to win the American election in 2024. Unfortunately, his performance was an unmitigated disaster – perhaps the worst of any presidential candidate in modern history. The president, who is 81 (and would be 86 by the end of a second term in office), stammered indecipherably, struggled to complete his lines of attack and proved his doubters completely correct. Although Mr Trump was in his typical form – meandering, mendacious, vindictive – he somehow appeared the more coherent and lucid of the pair. Mr Biden's decision to seek re-election rather than standing aside for a younger standard-bearer now looks like a reckless endangerment of the democracy he claims to want to protect.'

The Economist *analyses the debate between US presidential candidates Joe Biden and Donald Trump that took place on 27 June 2024.*[16]

Sources

1 Gideon Rachman, 'Ramaphosa and South Africa on the Edge', *Financial Times*, 10 June 2024, https://www.ft.com/content/af4cd921-7c55-4458-926c-0293712e17f7?emailId=88fd62de-a331-420c-9097-5dc53cec057a&segmentId=22011ee7-896a-8c4c-22a0-7603348b7f22.

2 Natalie Kitroeff, Simon Romero and Emiliano Rodríguez Mega, 'Claudia Sheinbaum Makes History as First Woman Elected to Lead Mexico', *New York Times*, 3 June 2024, https://www.nytimes.com/2024/06/02/world/americas/mexico-election.html.

3 Mujib Mashal and Hari Kumar, 'Modi, Striking a Modest Tone, Is Sworn In for a Third Term', *New York Times*, 9 June 2024, https://www.nytimes.com/2024/06/09/world/asia/india-changed-modi-swearing-in.html.

4 Kevin Schofield, "Labour Has Won": Rishi Sunak Concedes Defeat as Tories Suffer Humiliating Loss', *HuffPost UK*, 5 July 2024, https://uk.news.yahoo.com/labour-won-rishi-sunak-concedes-040155580.html.

5 Angelique Chrisafis, 'France Election: Surprise Win for Leftwing Alliance Keeps Le Pen's Far Right from Power', *Guardian*, 7 July 2024, https://www.theguardian.com/world/article/2024/jul/07/exit-poll-shows-surprise-win-for-left-wing-alliance-in-french-election.

6 IISS, 'President of the Philippines Ferdinand R Marcos, Jr Delivers Keynote Address', 31 May 2024, https://www.iiss.org/events/shangri-la-dialogue/shangri-la-dialogue-2024/plenary-sessions/keynote-address/.

7 IISS, 'China's Approach to Global Security', 2 June 2024, https://www.iiss.org/events/shangri-la-dialogue/shangri-la-dialogue-2024/plenary-sessions/fifth-plenary/.

8 President of Russia, 'Article by Vladimir Putin in Rodong Sinmun Newspaper, Russia and the DPRK: Traditions of Friendship and Cooperation Through the Years', 18 June 2024, http://en.kremlin.ru/events/president/news/74317.

9 President of Russia, 'Press Statement Following Russia–DPRK Talks', 19 June 2024, http://en.kremlin.ru/events/president/transcripts/74334.

10 US Embassy and Consulates in Russia, 'Joint Statement by Senior Officials of the United States, the Republic of Korea (ROK) and Japan on DPRK–Russia Cooperation', 25 June 2024, https://ru.usembassy.gov/joint-statement-by-senior-officials-of-the-united-states-the-republic-of-korea-rok-and-japan-on-dprk-russia-cooperation/.

11 Ben Protess et al., 'Trump Convicted on All Counts to Become America's First Felon President', *New York Times*, 30 May 2024, https://www.nytimes.com/2024/05/30/nyregion/trump-convicted-hush-money-trial.html.

12 Joan E. Greve and Nick Robins-Early, 'Trump Conviction in Hush-money Case Sparks Sharply Divergent Reactions', *Guardian*, 31 May 2024, https://www.theguardian.com/us-news/article/2024/may/30/trump-guilty-hush-money-republicans-democrats-reaction.

13 'Trump: "I'm a Very Innocent Man"', *Politico*, 30 May 2024, https://www.politico.com/live-updates/2024/05/30/trump-hush-money-criminal-trial/trump-remarks-after-the-verdict-00160819.

14 White House, 'Remarks by President Biden on the Middle East', 31 May 2024, https://www.whitehouse.gov/briefing-room/speeches-remarks/2024/05/31/remarks-by-president-biden-on-the-middle-east-2/.

15 Supreme Court of the United States, *Trump v. United States*, no. 23–939, 1 July 2024, p. 6, https://www.supremecourt.gov/opinions/23pdf/23-939_e2pg.pdf.

16 'Joe Biden's Horrific Debate Performance Casts His Entire Candidacy into Doubt', *The Economist*, 28 June 2024, https://www.economist.com/united-states/2024/06/28/joe-bidens-horrific-debate-performance-casts-his-entire-candidacy-into-doubt.

The Geopolitics of EU Enlargement: From Club to Commons

Veronica Anghel and Erik Jones

Among the European Union's responses to Russia's full-scale invasion of Ukraine were promises to bring in new member states from Eastern Europe and the Western Balkans. Ukraine and Moldova are the most prominent candidates or prospective candidates, but Albania, Bosnia, Georgia, Kosovo, Montenegro, North Macedonia and Serbia are also on the list. Even Turkiye, which the EU identified as a candidate in 2005, is still in the queue for accession. Not all these countries may join, of course; even if they all do, some, like Georgia or Turkiye, may take a very long time. What is important is that the EU has shown credible signs of commitment to enlargement with the creation of a €50 billion Ukraine Facility and a €6bn Growth Plan for the Western Balkans.[1] Enlargement is now firmly on the agenda.

The reason is not immediately obvious, particularly in the context of Russia's war against Ukraine. Joining the EU is a long and complicated process for candidate countries, which must reform their economic and political institutions to make them consistent with European norms. It is also politically and administratively challenging for the EU itself, which needs to adapt the European Commission, European Council, European Parliament and budget to accommodate a larger number of increasingly diverse members. This, more than anything else, explains why the countries

Veronica Anghel is an assistant professor at the Robert Schuman Centre for Advanced Studies at the European University Institute. **Erik Jones** is Director of the Schuman Centre.

Survival | vol. 66 no. 4 | August–September 2024 | pp. 101–114 https://doi.org/10.1080/00396338.2024.2380203

of the Western Balkans have spent decades waiting for accession, and why Turkish membership remains a distant prospect. The 'Eastern Three', as Georgia, Moldova and Ukraine are called in Brussels, could face similar disappointment.[2] Russia's aggression may have spurred the Ukrainians into heroic action, but it has not changed the basic requirements for accession or enlargement.

The new enthusiasm for enlargement stems from geopolitics. The accession of Turkiye and the Western Balkan countries was never viewed as essential to protecting the single market, the single currency or the single financial space – the main shared 'goods', or 'commons', that the EU provides for its members. In fact, these countries were widely viewed as a threat to EU coherence, which is why French President Emmanuel Macron rejected efforts to open negotiations with North Macedonia in October 2019 and called for a fundamental reconsideration of the enlargement process.[3] Now, however, Russia's aggression against Ukraine, the military threat it poses to Moldova and Georgia, and its efforts to destabilise the Western Balkans are jeopardising the European project.

The threat Russia and other hostile third countries pose is more than just military. Governments in many EU member states that border Russia, Ukraine and the Baltic Sea express concern, of course, that Russian aggression will not stop if Ukraine falls. But a Russian victory would also be important owing to its disruption of European supply chains, energy and agricultural markets, its impact on population movements, the inflation it would create, and the financial speculation and instability it would encourage. Similar concerns arise from the prospect that other third countries, like China, will exploit instability on the frontiers of Europe to sow division within the EU.

Accordingly, the EU has changed the way Europeans think about enlargement. As Macron explained in a speech delivered at the Sorbonne on 24 April 2024:

> We have begun to rethink our geography within the limits of our neighbourhood. Europe now sees itself as a coherent whole in the wake of Russia's aggression, affirming that Ukraine and Moldova are part of our

European family and are destined to join the Union when the time comes, as are the Western Balkans.[4]

The presumption is that the people, firms, civil-society groups and other organisations within those bordering countries already have access to the EU through personal ties, business dealings, supply chains, association agreements, customs unions, and deep and comprehensive trading arrangements. Those existing ties are substantially what makes the EU attractive to the outside world and competitive in world markets. They are also a source of vulnerability to conflict and instability. This explains why Macron spent much of his Sorbonne speech on migration, disinformation and economic security in addition to Russian aggression. Formal EU enlargement is not the only way for the EU to address such concerns. The EU has a very different strategy for working with governments in the Southern Mediterranean. But enlargement is the most powerful instrument the EU has to stabilise countries on its periphery and to establish a strong boundary between those countries and the world outside them.

Historical precedent

The European project started for geopolitical reasons.[5] French foreign minister Robert Schuman proposed the creation of the European Coal and Steel Community in 1950 as a vehicle for stabilising occupied West Germany and integrating it into Europe. British foreign minister Ernest Bevin proposed the creation of a Western European Union in 1954 to extend formal security guarantees to West Germany and manage the process of German rearmament. Both proposals were responses to the threat posed by the Soviet Union, and both organisations have since been absorbed into the EU.

NATO, of course, arguably played a more important role than the EU-predecessor organisations in responding to the Soviet threat.[6] But EU enlargement has also been used to address internal security concerns, such as the reconciliation of historical enemies like France and Germany, and Germany and Poland; the treatment of cross-border ethnic minorities like Hungarians in Romania or Slovakia and Russians in the Baltic states; and the resolution of border disputes such as the one between Germany and its eastern neighbours, or between Slovenia and Croatia. Through enlargement and other measures, the EU helped stabilise relations between Greece and Turkiye in the 1980s and 1990s, and strengthen Cyprus vis-à-vis Turkiye in the 2000s and 2010s.[7] Ireland used its membership in the European Community to gain greater parity with Great Britain in the 1970s and 1980s; it used its membership in the European Union to help broker peace in Northern Ireland in the 1990s; and it has continued to use its EU membership to stabilise relations with Northern Ireland since Brexit.[8]

Enlargement has also played a role in shaping the EU's international identity. The United Kingdom's accession, though it had a significant economic dimension, followed a geopolitical logic. France accepted the UK's third application in the early 1970s at a time of increased transatlantic tension. As former British permanent representative to the EU Stephen Wall observed, British prime minister Edward Heath believed that 'European countries could not hope to exercise influence unless they were united, with an economic base comparable in size to that of the United States or the Soviet Union'.[9] Now Brexit has hindered both Britain and the EU in the conduct of foreign and security policy.[10]

Geopolitical enlargement came at a high cost

This geopolitical logic has an economic dimension. Each step in the expansion of the European project has brought economic advantages. Each step has also required important adaptations for both the new member states and the European project. This first enlargement of the European Community raised challenges of adjustment for new member states, and of adaptation for European institutions and financial arrangements that stretched well into the 1980s. The British budgetary rebate was only agreed in 1984 and the Single European Act in 1987. The British and Danish governments insisted on unprecedented opt-outs along the way, and that pattern continued through the Maastricht and Amsterdam treaty negotiations in the 1990s.[11] Thus, geopolitical enlargement came at a high cost in terms of institutional coherence and ease of decision-making within the EU.

Each enlargement has involved security as well as economic considerations. The accession of Greece in 1981, and Spain and Portugal in 1986, stabilised their respective transitions from authoritarianism to democracy. Enlargement to Austria, Finland and Sweden – three traditionally neutral countries – occurred after the Cold War had ended, when their formal neutrality no longer clashed with the EU's foreign and security policy. At each step, both new member states and European institutions have had to adapt – mostly after rather than before formal expansion of membership.

The historic enlargement of the EU with the countries of Central and Eastern Europe in 2004 and 2007 started slowly, as existing member states expressed concern about the economic and political readiness of potential candidates and the EU's 'absorption capacity' – that is, the ability of its institutions and the budget to accommodate a wider and more diverse membership.[12] The process accelerated at the end of the 1990s in the shadow of disruption in the Western Balkans and out of concern that it might spread to other post-communist countries.[13]

This acceleration of the accession process meant that the EU would have to adapt its budget and institutions to a wider and more diverse membership only after enlargement took place. Having agreed on the Nice Treaty in 2001, and reached a budget deal in 2002, member states launched the European Convention, inviting the candidate countries to participate in the negotiation of the European Constitutional Treaty.[14] A faster enlargement also created risks that countries would be brought into the EU without having established the kind of resilient economic and political institutions required for member states to function effectively. Hungary and Poland joined in 2004 only to reveal significant shortcomings in the performance of their democracies. Bulgaria and Romania joined late, in 2007, with special permission to tackle issues related to corruption and the rule of law after becoming member states. Almost 20 years later, those efforts are ongoing. Nevertheless, European leaders agreed that such risks were worth accepting as the price of bringing stability.[15] That gamble paid off in terms of both economic growth and political stability, but it has been challenging in terms of relations between East and West within the EU and the functionality of the institutions themselves.[16]

The lesson from that experience is not that the EU should do anything possible to avoid bringing in more countries like Hungary and Poland or Bulgaria and Romania. Enlargement to Central and Eastern Europe without those countries would not have made sense. Instead, the lesson is that the EU needs to learn how to manage such risks better, both during and after the accession process. Moreover, the sheer diversity of these precedents suggests that there are few strong red lines to exclude potential candidates for membership. Countries have joined despite having frozen conflicts or active secessionist, including terrorist, movements within their borders (Britain and Spain); parts of the country occupied by foreign powers (Germany and Cyprus); relatively weak juridical institutions and deep corruption (Bulgaria and Romania); excessive political power held by oligarchs (Bulgaria and the Czech Republic); contentious neighbours that seek or already have EU membership (Slovenia and Italy; Croatia and Slovenia); and large domestic minorities that share ethnicity with a hostile third power (the Baltic states). Many candidate countries have such problematic security-related or geopolitical characteristics. That should be no reason to deny membership, but it does signal how difficult it will be to make new enlargement successful.

A delicate balancing act

Prospective new member states must join quickly enough to sustain political momentum behind reform efforts necessary to qualify for membership but slowly enough to absorb the costs of adjustment. Getting the balance right is hard for any government. Opt-outs for the UK and Denmark enabled accession and avoided later conflicts by putting off or eliminating the need for unpopular reforms, but they also created important status differences for both countries that sapped enthusiasm for the European project – critically in the UK.[17] Theirs is a story of lost momentum. The situation in Hungary and Poland reflects the failure to absorb adjustment costs.[18] Having pushed hard to undertake the reforms necessary to qualify for membership, the left-wing government that brought Poland into the EU collapsed almost as soon as accession was completed, yielding to a right-wing, eurosceptical government in 2005.[19] The left's sway in Hungary lasted longer, but tensions between a democratic left and an illiberal right were deeply embedded and the latter prevailed after the left-wing prime minister was caught on tape admitting that the scale of economic reforms – including austerity measures – required to comply with EU standards had been misrepresented.[20]

The East German and Czech cases reflect the elusiveness of any one formula for success.[21] West Germany quickly absorbed the five East German *Länder* in 1990. The German government pushed hard to privatise state-owned enterprises, liberalise market institutions and extend welfare-state provisions. But it did little to integrate the East German workforce into the wider German economy. As a result, the costs of adjustment fell dispropor-tionately on East German workers and households in ways that financial transfers could only partially offset. East German voters expressed their discontent by moving first to the extreme left and then to the extreme right. In the 2024 European elections, the far right came first in each of the five regions, capturing between 27% and 31% of the vote.[22]

Successive Czech governments moved more slowly with privatisation and reform efforts after the fall of communism and managed to keep much of the workforce employed. This pacing smoothed the adjustment process but created tensions between the Czech government and European institu-tions, which some Czech politicians, like prime minister and later president Václav Klaus, were quick to exploit for political gain. The Czech Republic joined the EU but opted out of the single currency, and the Czech people developed a broad sense of euroscepticism.[23]

The East Germans and the Czechs were not alone in Central and Eastern Europe in embracing political extremism alongside sceptical attitudes towards the EU. Given the scale of the adjustments required to make the transition from central planning to market-based economies, and authoritar-ian to democratic governments, it would be surprising if political backlash did not arise – particularly from those who lost out economically or politi-cally along the way.[24] That national politicians would lay responsibility for this suffering on the EU as a 'foreign influence' is also unsurprising.[25] The point to note is that similar adjustments necessarily took place in countries that did not join the EU. Often, those countries experienced backlashes against liberal market economies and democratic politics that were stronger than those in EU countries because they were unmuted by the benefits and obligations of EU membership. In this sense, the alternative to accession is worse. North Macedonia offers a good example of what can go wrong when authoritarian rulers get access to unrestricted Chinese lending for infra- structural development. Quickly, the politics and economics of the country began to revolve around access to Chinese lending and the government con- tracts that flowed alongside the infrastructure projects, even though many of the projects were never completed and the government had no hope of ever being able to pay the money back.[26]

The EU was aware of the risks associated with the political and eco- nomic transition from communism. That is the main explanation for why the enlargement process to Central and Eastern Europe started so slowly. The threats to the rule of law were obvious from the outset. So were the dangers that economic adjustment would fuel political extremism. Only after European politicians accepted that the alternative of leaving countries outside the EU would be worse did they ask the European Commission to find a way to bring those countries into the EU without doing excessive damage to the European project.[27] Part of the solution was procedural. The European Commission changed the rules for negotiating entry so that can- didates would race one another in completing the negotiation process. This procedural change was made very publicly in order to accelerate the pace of accession while at the same time adding political momentum to engage in necessary reforms.[28]

To ease the accession process, European officials also experimented with financial instruments, propping up key industries, channelling investment into new sectors or working with national and international development banks to co-finance other kinds of support programmes. This made it easier for national governments to match the faster pace of negotiations, but it was difficult for European Commission officials to manage politically, given the possibility that existing member states would complain about paying too much in transfers to candidate countries and accuse the commission of bending the rules instead of making sure those rules were adopted. Nevertheless, commission officials recognised that such support was neces- sary for membership to be viable over the longer term.[29]

The most recent push for enlargement builds on this experience. The European Commission is working closely with national and international development banks across Europe to channel secure forms of lending and to attract private capital to finance infrastructural development and industrial transformation – including towards green and digital technologies.[30] The challenges of adaptation may be greater for current EU candidates than they were for past ones, but they are better understood and the resources for facilitating them more substantial.

From club to commons

Greater understanding and greater resources do not remove the risk that the EU will bring in new member states before they are ready for membership or the risk that governments will turn away from democracy and the rule of law at some point after they join. Nor do they make it any easier for European institutions or European finances to accommodate the requirements of a larger and more diverse membership. So it is tempting to believe that the greatest challenge to European enlargement comes from the EU itself. But enlargement is not the source of the challenge. Any difficulty the EU faces comes from the changed geopolitical environment that makes enlargement imperative. The accession of new countries to the EU is part of the solution to that geopolitical problem and not the cause of the problem itself.

This insight comes from the economics literature on selective membership organisations – like clubs – and is central to understanding the geopolitics of enlargement. Economists refer to clubs as selective groups where it is easy to keep non-members out and where the advantages that come from membership – the club's goods – stem directly from efforts to hold the number of members down. This is not how the EU works. The EU is a selective membership organisation, but the goods that it produces – like the single market, the single currency and the single financial space – are open and not exclusive.[31] There are rules for access, but those rules are meant to ensure that the single market is a place for competition and innovation in production and exchange; that the single currency works effectively as a unit of account, store of value and medium of exchange; and that the single financial space works efficiently to connect savers with investment opportunities while at the same time facilitating trade and payments.

Any individual, firm or other organisation that abides by the rules can access the EU and benefit from what the EU produces – including those coming from countries that are not member states. In turn, EU institutions work together with member-state governments to ensure that such access is regulated consistently across different national boundaries or other points of entry; that everyone benefiting from that access continues to abide by the rules without seeking unfair advantage in the market, undermining the currency or destabilising the financial system; and that there are sufficient resources available – people as well as money – to update and enforce the rules.

The EU is not a club in the sense that economists use the term; it is the kind of selective membership organisation that governs what they call 'common resource pools' or 'commons'.[32] The EU's goal is not to wall off the goods that it produces. It is rather to ensure that the EU can continue to produce those goods sustainably so that as many people, firms and organisations as possible can benefit from accessing them – again, including those from outside existing member states. The EU wants to ensure that the single market remains dynamic and competitive, that the single currency combines wide circulation with price stability, and that the single financial space draws in as much capital as it can to finance productive investments. The report on the single market provided by former Italian prime minister Enrico Letta sets these goals out clearly.[33] The report on 'competitiveness' to be produced by former Italian prime minister Mario Draghi should be expected to do the same.

The changed geopolitical environment threatens these goals. Russia's invasion of Ukraine disrupted the functioning of the internal market by jeopardising access to energy resources and critical raw materials, by cutting off and then rerouting the flow of agricultural products from Ukraine, by displacing millions of Ukrainian citizens, and by precipitating sanctions and counter-sanctions. The collapse of Ukraine in the face of Russian aggression would only make matters worse, as would any expansion of the conflict to Moldova or Georgia. Meanwhile, Russian and Chinese involvement in the Western Balkans creates other challenges. The experience of North Macedonia is not just a cautionary tale. It is an ongoing problem across the

Western Balkans that the EU can most easily address through the leverage provided by accession negotiations and eventual EU membership.

To achieve its goals, Letta argues, the EU will not only have to project its influence beyond the single market and into the wider geopolitical context, but it will also have to enlarge its membership while cushioning the impact of that enlargement on existing member states and preparing the institutions for a wider and more diverse membership.[34] This framing is important because it makes it clear that enlargement is not a challenge to the functioning of the single market or the EU. Rather, enlargement is one instrument among many for strengthening the single market and the EU in a changed geopolitical context where economic and physical security are major sources of concern. Enlargement is risky. The EU could bring in countries before they are ready to join or that turn away from democracy and the rule of law at a later date, but those are precisely the risks that need to be managed if the EU is to protect the single market, the single currency and the single financial space from the threat posed by Russian aggression in Ukraine or the activities of Russia and other third countries in the Western Balkans.

Issues of economic and physical security have arisen in each enlargement of the EU and its predecessor organisations. That explains why enlargement tends to take place before adaptation of the EU's institutions and budgets – because the choice for enlargement and the need for adaptation flow from the same geopolitical influences. It also explains why Macron and Letta place so much emphasis on common European values in sketching their visions for the future of Europe. Their argument is not that only Europeans share those values – it is that only those who share the values that underpin the EU's single market, the single currency and the single financial space should enjoy access to them. Letta makes it clear that support for the rule of law plays a critical role in the protection of other values and that mutual trust is indispensable for the success of the European project.[35] These commitments are what binds Europeans together in the more hostile geopolitical environment. They provide the coherence Macron identified in Europe after Russia invaded Ukraine.

*   *   *

The EU's push for enlargement in response to Russian aggression is a geopolitical decision that poses significant challenges. The candidates have to reform to meet the requirements for membership, the EU has to adapt its institutions and finances, and existing member states have to learn to tolerate a wider and more diverse community. The decision to expand also poses significant risks. The EU might grant membership to countries before they are ready, it might overload its own institutions and finances, and it might sour relations with existing member states – much as the historic enlargement to Central and Eastern Europe contributed to Brexit. Even so, enlargement remains the best tool for protecting the single market, the single currency and the single financial space from the consequences of Russian aggression in Europe. That is the geopolitical calculus. And this is not the first time the EU or its predecessor organisations have reasoned this way. The EU is not a club from which it is easy to exclude members; it is a commons in which the focus is on finding the best way to regulate access – not just for candidate countries but, more importantly, for the individuals, firms and other organisations within them. Enlargement poses risks for the sustainability of the European project, but, in the current geopolitical climate, the alternatives are worse.

Notes

[1] See European Commission, 'The Ukraine Facility', https://eu-solidarity-ukraine.ec.europa.eu/eu-assistance-ukraine/ukraine-facility_en; and European Commission, 'New Growth Plan for the Western Balkans', https://neighbourhood-enlargement.ec.europa.eu/enlargement-policy/new-growth-plan-western-balkans_en.

[2] For an early expression of this concern, see Veronica Anghel and Erik Jones, 'Broken Promises Diplomacy: The Russia–Ukraine War and the End of Enlargement as We Know It', in Jelena Džankić, Simonida Kacarska and Soeren Keil (eds), *A Year Later:* *War in Ukraine and Western Balkan (Geo)Politics* (San Domenico di Fiesole: European University Institute, 2023), pp. 6–14. See also Richard Youngs, *Geoliberal Europe and the Test of War* (London: Agenda Publishing, 2024), pp. 83–102.

[3] See République française, 'Conférence de presse de M. Emmanuel Macron, président de la République, sur le Brexit, la construction européenne, l'offensive turque en Syrie et l'élargissement de l'Union européenne, à Bruxelles le 18 octobre 2019', 18 October 2019, https://www.vie-publique.fr/

discours/271370-emmanuel-macron-18102019-union-europeenne.

4   'Emmanuel Macron: Europe – It Can Die. A New Paradigm at the Sorbonne', Groupe d'Études Géopolitiques, 26 April 2024, https://geopolitique.eu/en/2024/04/26/macron-europe-it-can-die-a-new-paradigm-at-the-sorbonne/.

5   For two classic versions of this argument, see Alan Milward, *The European Rescue of the Nation-state*, 2nd ed. (London: Routledge, 2000); and F. Roy Willis, *France, Germany and the New Europe, 1945–1967* (Stanford, CA: Stanford University Press, 1968).

6   See A.W. DePorte, *Europe Between the Superpowers: The Enduring Balance*, 2nd ed. (New Haven, CT: Yale University Press, 1986); and Geir Lundestad, *The United States and Western Europe Since 1945* (Oxford: Oxford University Press, 2003).

7   See Alexis Heraclides, *The Greek–Turkish Conflict in the Aegean: Imagined Enemies* (London: Palgrave Macmillan, 2010); and Erik Siegl, 'Greek–Turkish Relations – Continuity or Change?', *Perspectives*, no. 18, Summer 2002, pp. 40–52.

8   See Mary C. Murphy, *Europe and Northern Ireland's Future: Negotiating Brexit's Unique Case* (London: Agenda Publishing, 2018).

9   Quoted in Stephen Wall, *Reluctant European: Britain and the European Union from 1945 to Brexit* (Oxford: Oxford University Press, 2020), p. 99.

10 See Christopher Hill, *The Future of British Foreign Policy: Security and Diplomacy in a World After Brexit* (Cambridge: Polity, 2019).

11 See Rebecca Adler-Nissen, *Opting Out of the European Union: Diplomacy, Sovereignty and European Integration* (Cambridge: Cambridge University Press, 2014).

12 See Veronica Anghel and Erik Jones, 'Failing Forward in Eastern Enlargement: Problem Solving Through Problem Making', *Journal of European Public Policy*, vol. 29, no. 7, 2022, pp. 1,092–1,111.

13 See Paolo Cecchini, Erik Jones and Jochen Lorentzen, 'Europe and the Concept of Enlargement', *Survival*, vol. 43, no. 1, Spring 2001, pp. 155–65.

14 See Erik Jones, 'The Politics of Europe 2002: Flexibility and Adjustment', *Industrial Relations Journal*, vol. 34, no. 5, December 2003, pp. 363–78.

15 See Merje Kuus, *Geopolitics Reframed: Security and Identity in Europe's Eastern Enlargement* (London: Palgrave Macmillan, 2007).

16 See Veronica Anghel, 'Together or Apart? The European Union's East–West Divide', *Survival*, vol. 62, no. 3, June–July 2020, pp. 179–202.

17 See Adler-Nissen, *Opting Out of the European Union*.

18 See Philipp Ther, *Europe Since 1989: A History* (Princeton, NJ: Princeton University Press, 2016), p. 157.

19 See Stuart Shields, 'Poland and the Global Political Economy: From Neoliberalism to Populism (and Back Again)', in Gareth Dale (ed.), *First the Transition, Then the Crash: Eastern Europe in the 2000s* (London: Pluto Press, 2011), pp. 169–86.

20 See Veronica Anghel and Erik Jones, 'What Went Wrong in Hungary', *Journal of Democracy*, vol. 35, no. 2, April 2024, pp. 52–64; and Zsuzsanna Szelényi, *Tainted Democracy: Viktor Orbán and the Subversion of Hungary* (London: C. Hurst and Co., 2022).

21 This comparison is developed in Till Hilmar, *Deserved: Economic Memories After the Fall of the Iron Curtain* (New York: Columbia University Press, 2023).

22 See Die Bundeswahlleiterin, 'Europawahl 2024', https://www.bundeswahlleiterin.de/europawahlen/2024/ergebnisse.html.

23 See Hilmar, *Deserved*.

24 See Lenka Bustikova, *Extreme Reactions: Radical Right Mobilization in Eastern Europe* (Cambridge: Cambridge University Press, 2020); and John A. Gould, *Fragile Dreams: Tales of Liberalism and Power in Central Europe* (Ann Arbor, MI: University of Michigan Press, 2021).

25 See László Bruszt and Visnja Vukov, 'Core–Periphery Divisions Within the EU? East–West and North–South Tensions Compared', *Journal of European Public Policy*, vol. 31, no. 3, January 2024, pp. 850–73.

26 See Fabio Mattioli, *Dark Finance: Illiquidity and Authoritarianism at the Margins of Europe* (Stanford, CA: Stanford University Press, 2020).

27 See Cecchini, Jones and Lorentzen, 'Europe and the Concept of Enlargement'.

28 See Anghel and Jones, 'Failing Forward in Eastern Enlargement', pp. 1,105–6.

29 See László Bruszt and Julia Langbein, 'Development by Stealth: Governing Market Integration in the Eastern Peripheries of the European Union', *MAXCAP Working Paper Series*, no. 17, November 2015, https://userpage.fu-berlin.de/kfgeu/maxcap/system/files/maxcap_wp_17.pdf.

30 Matthias Thiemann, Dan Mocanu and Dora Piroska, 'The European Investment State and the Modalities of European Integration in Ukraine: Development Banks, Investment Frameworks and the Role of Local Actors', unpublished manuscript, 2024.

31 See Veronica Anghel and Erik Jones, 'The Enlargement of International Organisations', *West European Politics*, February 2024, https://doi.org/10.1080/01402382.2024.2311044.

32 See Elinor Ostrom, *Governing the Commons: The Evolution of Institutions for Collective Action* (Cambridge: Cambridge University Press, 1990). Ostrom (a political scientist) won the Nobel Memorial Prize in Economic Sciences for her study of these organisations. See Elinor Ostrom, 'Beyond Markets and States: Polycentric Governance of Complex Economic Systems', 8 December 2009, https://www.nobelprize.org/uploads/2018/06/ostrom_lecture.pdf.

33 Enrico Letta, 'Much More than a Market: Speed, Security, Solidarity – Empowering the Single Market to Deliver a Sustainable Future and Prosperity for All EU Citizens', European Council, April 2024, https://www.consilium.europa.eu/media/ny3j24sm/much-more-than-a-market-report-by-enrico-letta.pdf.

34 *Ibid.*, pp. 139–40.

35 *Ibid.*, p. 140.

France's Political Crisis

Catherine Fieschi

French President Emmanuel Macron is a disrupter. This was clear from the very manner in which he entered the political race for the presidency on the eve of the 2017 elections: starting from scratch, with his own movement, storming the sleepy bastions of French politics in what felt like a generational and ideological clear-out. In the run-up to the European Parliament elections on 9 June 2024, however, Macron had pledged that he would draw no conclusions. But that election saw far-right advances on much of the continent, including France, where Marine Le Pen's far-right Rassemblement National (RN, known in English as the National Rally) dominated, winning 31.4% of the vote and 30 seats.[1] In a typical swipe at convention and with characteristic swagger, 30 minutes after the results Macron took to the airwaves and dissolved the National Assembly, calling for snap parliamentary elections three weeks later.

The final results were both predictable – a hung parliament – and surprising. Despite coming resoundingly first in the elections' first round on 30 June, the RN finished last in the second round, with far fewer seats – 143 – than they and nearly everyone else had anticipated. Macron's Ensemble bloc did much better than projected, coming in second with 168 seats. Somewhat unexpectedly, the Nouveau Front Populaire (NFP), the left-wing

Catherine Fieschi is the founder and director of Counterpoint and visiting fellow at the Robert Schuman Centre of the European University Institute.

Survival | vol. 66 no. 4 | August–September 2024 | pp. 115–126   https://doi.org/10.1080/00396338.2024.2380204

alliance, emerged with the most seats, 182.[2] Despite the absence of a majority and the endless possibilities for paralysis, the results are less dramatic than they might have been. The Republican Front against the RN held, and the country did not wake up to the certainty of a far-right prime minister.

Notwithstanding some relief, these results could have tectonic consequences for the French political landscape, and for European politics in the near and medium terms. The risks of instability and policy gridlock are very real, at a moment when the government of Germany – France's key European Union partner – is also weakened and the US election threatens to upend transatlantic solidarity and force Europe to make hard and momentous security choices in the face of an aggressive Russia.

The roots of disruption

In 2017, Macron ambitiously sought to obliterate the traditional left–right divide in the French political system. His assessment was that it had not only become sterile but also contributed to polarisation, which was benefiting the far right. His strategy was to take control of the centre by wooing the left's more liberal and disenchanted voters, thus neutralising the left as a political force. In the short term, at least, it worked. After the election, the Socialist Party was decimated and bankrupt. Over the next five years, Macron successfully applied similar seduction and pressure tactics to the mainstream right, gradually attracting key political figures to his own camp and leaving the mainstream right impotent by 2022, when it won 4.78% of the vote in the French presidential election and 61 seats out of 577 in the French parliamentary elections.[3] Macron's great plan seemed to be working: he was incrementally occupying the centre and leaving only the far right intact. This allowed him to argue that he was the only thing standing between France and fascism.

But the 2022 experience also revealed the limits of Macron's plan. While he weakened the traditional left and right alignments, he was not entirely able to consolidate the centre. Most moderate left voters who had supported him in 2017 felt his government had moved too far to the right. Right-wing voters, for their part, were already increasingly attracted to the RN, which was busy sanitising its image to gain broader appeal. To make matters worse, Macron failed to invest in developing a stable and functioning political party and declined to elaborate a clear set of ideas and narratives that would anchor his centrist political vision and outlive his mandate. Whatever else happens, Macron will leave a meagre ideological legacy.

Although his government handled the COVID-19 crisis relatively well and was instrumental in securing the EU's recovery package, Macron's style of governance has been increasingly perceived as authoritarian and disconnected from ordinary voters whom he initially seemed to connect with quite well. Many would argue that his talent of persuasion is offset by a lack of empathy. However gifted, he gives the impression of someone who has never thought about walking a yard, never mind a mile, in anyone else's shoes. For example, in 2018, when a young man told him he was having no luck landing a job, Macron replied that he could find one if he merely 'crossed the street' and asked around.[4] Despite a meteoric political ascent, over time this disinterest in others' lived reality has eroded Macron's support. He has also become increasingly isolated from his circle of advisers.[5]

A costly blind spot

The 2018–19 Gilets Jaunes (yellow vests) crisis – which saw millions of workers take over roundabouts and city centres, initially to protest a rise in taxes on diesel, and evolved into almost ritualistic weekly political violence – was emblematic of this perceived indifference. It crystallised the resentment of low-waged employees in semi-rural and suburban areas of France against Parisian elites and technocrats.[6] Macron did a U-turn on the proposed taxes, kick-started a nationwide set of public conversations dubbed 'Le Grand Débat' that showcased his capacity for conversation and political theatre, and promised to 'govern and legislate differently'.[7] Yet he did not grasp the depth of the resentment and despair in vast parts of France, and his governing style and choices did not durably change. While he governed competently, his disregard for popular sentiment and public opinion seemed to intensify.

The Gilets Jaunes episode is noteworthy because despite the violence and disruption, Macron and his colleagues took it as a single bullet dodged rather than a serious warning about the depth of resentment in the country.

Though they acknowledged the grievances, addressing them came across as a box-ticking exercise. They failed to decipher the sources of the protest, in particular the sociology and the dynamic nature of the anger that was empowering the RN far more than parties of the radical left. This year's map of voting results reflects an almost complete overlap between Gilets Jaunes mobilisation and RN votes.[8] Macron's blind spot was likely a significant factor in the RN's progression from three million votes in 2017 to 10.6m in the first round of the 2024 assembly elections.

The 2022 presidential race, like the 2017 contest, produced a run-off between Macron and RN candidate Marine Le Pen. Macron was re-elected president, but the parliamentary elections firmly disavowed his policies and party, as his majority fell from 308 seats to 245, the RN's seats increased from eight to 89, and the left's seats rose from 72 to 153 thanks to the cross-party NUPES (New Ecological and Social People's Union) alliance.

Despite this shaky showing and a clearly disenchanted public, Macron governed as before – with minimal consultation and disregard for dissent. Pension reform triggered some of the most vehement protests – cross-generational and largely cross-party – since the Gilets Jaunes. The people opposed not only the unpopular substance of the reform – mainly, the gradual raising of the retirement age from 62 to 64 – but also the imperious manner in which it was imposed. Macron employed a constitutional provision, article 49.3, that allows the government to bypass the assembly. The French public concluded that their government was committed to ignoring their every expression of disagreement, even if held by a large majority. The assembly became polarised and raucous, the far right and far left increasingly vocal and frustrated. By December 2023, negotiations on a package of immigration measures further showcased the strains on Macron's shrunken majority. Several of his members refused to support it, and a few resigned. As of January 2024, despite the surprise appointment of dynamic wunderkind Gabriel Attal as prime minister, Macron was increasingly stuck. In the European Parliament election in May, Macron's party came third at 15%, the RN getting 31% and, on the left, the Social Democrats 14% and Jean-Luc Mélenchon's radical La France Insoumise (LFI) 10%.[9]

Madness without a method?

In light of these results, and hoping to catch other parties off guard, Macron abruptly dissolved the assembly and called for elections three weeks later. The French public was stunned, as were Macron's closest political allies and members of his cabinet. The RN and the far right in other parts of Europe (Germany and Italy in particular) had considerable momentum. In addition, there was pressure to secure military and financial aid for Ukraine, and the prospect of a Europhobic president being elected in the United States made the gamble seem all the more ill-judged. Macron evidently assessed that the two-round majoritarian system would work to his advantage, such that while the RN would do better than in 2022, it would be contained by ultimately forcing voters to make a moderate choice.

Macron did not foresee a ready electoral alliance on the left – another dangerous blind spot. The NUPES coalition in the National Assembly – forged in 2022 – was all but finished until the threat of an RN victory in the recent elections resuscitated it. As a result, voters were not limited to two viable choices – the RN or the presidential majority – but also now had a third: the newly minted NFP, a big tent encompassing every shade of left, including a Socialist Party fresh from an honourable showing in the European Parliament elections and the powerful radical-left LFI. Macron also held out the vain hope that the centre-right politicians would finally rally to him. Instead, most kept their distance, and a number of dissident MPs split and joined the RN. Finally, Macron underestimated the resentment in his own camp of MPs and ministers, who felt betrayed and free to run solo campaigns without any fealty to him personally. Former prime minister Édouard Philippe, whose Horizons party was in the presidential coalition, glibly announced that 'as the assembly was dissolved, so too was the coalition. Macron has killed the Presidential majority.'[10] What was supposed to be a strategic coalescence around Macron turned into the very opposite: an each-to-his-own attempt to limit damage to its agenda and exploit a fluid situation.

The gamble backfires?

The results of the first round were not particularly surprising, but they were historic in terms of the turnout (66%) and the sheer number of votes for the RN, which increased from 4.2m in the 2022 parliamentary election to 10.6m

(33%) in the first round.[11] The NFP did well (28%), though not as well as anticipated. Macron's presidential alliance reached 21%.[12] This yielded 306 three-way races in the second round, which left an opening for the RN to win big if two other candidates split the vote. It is difficult to overstate the nation's state of shock after the first round. The results, if they had been reprised a week later in the second round, would have given Macron no choice but to appoint Jordan Bardella, the RN's 28-year-old president, prime minister.

The wishful notion that snap elections would jolt voters out of some RN spell underrated the commitment of RN voters to the party. Over the past few years, Marine Le Pen has painstakingly sanitised it, even if her efforts have proven to be no more than leaflet-deep. The combination of Macron's perceived disdain of and RN's promised relief from the grind of daily life has proven an effective one, despite the government's relatively effective shielding of the French public from the energy crisis, inflation and the economic ravages of COVID.

Disaster averted

The shock of the first-round results saw non-RN French politicians resort to the customary 'Republican Front' – a cross-party arrangement whereby any candidate coming in third in a tight race with the RN in the first round would withdraw in order not to split the vote and thus allow the second-place party to prevail in the second round. Despite the established tradition, this was not without difficulty. While the left-wing NFP immediately withdrew its third-place candidates, the presidential Ensemble alliance was initially more reluctant. Having spent the entire campaign branding LFI (part of the of the NFP) as left-wing extremists, Macron initially asked voters to refrain from voting for either the RN or LFI. In the end, however, as calculations demonstrated that only a comprehensive Republican Front would block the RN's victory, Ensemble joined it. By the deadline for withdrawals, on the evening of 2 July, the initial 306 three-way races were down to 94. Some 217 candidates withdrew in order to give a better chance to any party other than the RN. Some might argue – certainly the RN did – that such horse-trading, tactical manipulation and backroom deal-making constituted exactly the sort of politics that voters were opposing.

Regardless, the Republican Front worked, and the RN went from three weeks of heady talk about governing France to a third-place finish with 143 seats – fewer than half of the required 289 seats to form an RN government.[13] It is also worth noting that the party's campaign revealed the limits, or the superficiality, of its mainstreaming: when the spotlight was directed on its candidates, many appeared to be as homophobic, xenophobic and racist as ever. Furthermore, they looked politically incompetent and unprepared to govern. Under the harsh light of high-stakes politics, it became clear that airbrushing ideology from the RN's programme in order to woo voters had not made the motivations of its leadership or rank and file any less radical or problematic than they had been.

The president's group had lost a third of its seats but made a respectable showing with 168 seats, and the NFP had come first with 182 seats. Noteworthy, in addition to the RN's shock relegation, was the fact that within the NFP, Mélenchon's LFI had largely stagnated at 71 seats, while the social-democratic Socialist Party had built on its European momentum and doubled its seats to 64.[14] This is important because it fundamentally rebalances power within the NFP: the radical LFI can no longer blithely impose its will, and there is hope for moderation under the pressure of the Greens and the Socialists. At the same time, though, it places the winning group in a more fragile situation insofar as LFI and Mélenchon are not known for compromise or a willingness to share power. Yet compromise and negotiation will be the only way forward in a situation in which there is no outright majority for any party or alliance and Macron must name a prime minister.

More uncertainty

While France escaped the grim prospect of an anti-EU, pro-Russian and profligate RN government, it grasped a seemingly unmanageable Rubik's cube of a National Assembly, in which a motley electoral alliance of left-wing parties that disagree on virtually everything except their loathing of the far right emerged as barely ahead. The RN may be third, but it has nevertheless doubled its seats. The president's centrist party is being squeezed between left and right, and it is full of resentful MPs who feel they have been unnecessarily brutalised a mere two years after having been elected.

The centre right, with 45 seats, is isolated and weakened by an exodus of personnel and voters to the RN.

The most pressing immediate issue as this journal went to press was who Macron will find to serve as prime minister. Could a grand coalition emerge, as in other European countries? In a word, is France governable?

On this score, it should be borne in mind that while the RN ran third, it did so with nearly 9m votes. A glass-half-full approach would suggest that, beyond the fact that disaster was averted for now, the election has broken the RN's momentum and has exposed the shallowness of the party's ideas and candidates, reversing Marine Le Pen's decade and a half of mainstreaming efforts in a mere three weeks. On this reading, the RN may face a glass ceiling in that a majority of French voters still consider its decisive ascendancy a red line.

A less sanguine take would be that the 10.6m votes that the RN got in the first round is one-third of the French electorate, and that the tactics employed to keep the RN out – while legal and legitimate – may further exasperate their voters, reinforce the party's claim that the system is stacked against them and, given the possibility of government instability or gridlock, make the party all the more attractive either in a year when Macron can call new assembly elections, or in 2027 in the next scheduled presidential election. In this context, speculation about the 'Melonisation' of Marine Le Pen – that is, her remaining ultra-conservative on most issues but becoming more constructive with respect to the EU once in power, in the manner of Italian Prime Minister Giorgia Meloni – seems far-fetched. Le Pen has just joined Hungarian Prime Minister Viktor Orbán's new European Parliament group Patriots for Europe, which is far from constructive with respect to the EU and is palpably pro-Putin. The RN's economic programme for the legislative elections was also based on key proposals that would have placed France in breach of a number of its EU commitments and obligations.

The deeper flaw in equating the French and Italian far right is that Italy's citizens, however bruised, are, as they have always been, overwhelmingly pro-European and feel that their very survival is tied to the EU. Meloni wants to change Europe from the inside – certainly not leave or make herself a pariah within it.[15] Le Pen, on the other hand, has led a group in the

European Parliament that is simply anti-EU, opposing all its institutions. They evince no sense of dependency on the EU, only resentment towards it. Le Pen's hatred of the EU, in particular, is visceral. Unlike Meloni, Le Pen and Bardella have done little to court foreign investors or their European partners. Meloni wants a Europe that works for Italy and in which Italy is taken seriously; Le Pen wants a Franco-centric political culture with minimal EU linkages or interference.

The RN will no doubt go through some transformations of its own, but it will likely focus on exploiting the inevitable difficulties that are plaguing French mainstream parties and politicians. As a consequence, it becomes even more important – and difficult – for the mainstream to address its voters' concerns effectively. In this vein, Macron has said he was seeking 'clarification'.[16] While certainly a swipe at the RN, this statement was mainly code for forcing a centrist coalition to finally emerge in the National Assembly. Macron was under no illusion of being able to regain a majority, but the objective, as it so often is with Macron, was to cause creative disruption that would compel stubborn political actors to change their behaviour under irresistible pressure. Disrupt he did. But the specific results – the unexpected electoral success of the left alliance, confirmation of the weakness of the centre-right – have impeded his dream of a grand centrist coalition.

Macron has said he was seeking 'clarification'

Yet without such a coalition, no law could pass without the risk of being voted down, and no prime minister could escape the constant threat of a no-confidence vote. This has prompted many to liken the current state of France's Fifth Republic to its notoriously unstable Fourth Republic between 1946 and 1958, during which there were 22 governments with an average duration of seven months. This comparison seems hasty. The Fourth Republic's instability stemmed primarily from a large contingent of post-war communist MPs agitating as the Cold War escalated. Most importantly, the 2024 election results have reinforced the Fifth Republic's parliamentary core without erasing the presidential function, which remains much stronger than it was in the Fourth Republic, involving a significant measure of control in areas beyond foreign policy.

*   *   *

Over the next year, French politics could evolve in two ways. The Fifth Republic could become a parliamentary system with a strong president that functions primarily as a referee. This would be a stiff test of an enormously plastic and accommodating constitution. Its outcome would depend substantially on Macron's capacity to fulfil such a role, which is a tenuous proposition given his pronounced tendency to meddle and control.

Another, and potentially simultaneous, development would be France's long delayed and much needed apprenticeship in the art of coalition politics in a system that has been winner-take-all to a fault. While the learning curve would be very steep and fraught, the straitjacket that Macron has wittingly or inadvertently created may force France's political elite to deliver. It is conceivable that moderates from the centre left and centre right could come together because they have no choice. Based on compatible foreign-policy views – shared support for Ukraine and the EU, common trade and industrial viewpoints – and perhaps convergence on climate and some aspects of public-service reform, such a coalition could emerge. It will ultimately depend on two factors. One is the left's willingness to compromise on government spending, which would have to be far removed from LFI's unrealistic spending programme in a country reprimanded for an excessive deficit. Otherwise, the moderates in the alliance might seek other allies and make other trade-offs. The other is the emergence of a centrist coalition. That turns on whether Macron's alliance can accept that it came in second and cannot call the shots.

Efforts to forge a coalition spanning the centre left and centre right could easily fail, especially given that some key actors are likely to have an eye on the 2027 presidential elections rather than the immediate practical demands of government. In that case, a provisional government – possibly a 'technocratic' one composed of appointed experts without formal party affiliations – will probably materialise. This would mean a much less audible France on the European stage; minimum spending that would drain material support for Ukraine and sap the momentum of reindustrialisation, including defence; and new elections in a year. The results of those elections could well be more clear-cut, but, in that case, they would also be far more authoritarian.

Notes

1   European Parliament, '2024 European Election Results', https://results.elections.europa.eu/en/index.html.

2   Ministère de l'Intérieur et des Outre-mer, 'Publication des candidatures et des résultats aux élections – Législatives 2024', 30 June and 7 July 2024, https://www.resultats-elections.interieur.gouv.fr/legislatives2024/.

3   Ministère de l'Intérieur et des Outre-mer, 'Les élections en France', 10 and 14 April 2022, https://www.archives-resultats-elections.interieur.gouv.fr/resultats/presidentielle-2022/FE.php.

4   See 'Macron Under Fire for Telling Jobseeker to "Cross the Street" to Get Work', France24, 17 September 2018, https://www.france24.com/en/20180917-macron-france-under-fire-telling-jobseeker-cross-street-get-work-unemployment.

5   See, for example, Sylvie Kauffman, 'Isolated Macron Struggles to Know What Happens Next', Financial Times, 1 July 2024, https://www.ft.com/content/33f07e00-eb00-4c6e-9dc2-31884ba77924.

6   Macron's first attempt at pension reform also triggered vast cross-sectional protests that ebbed only because of the COVID lockdown.

7   See, for example, Joseph Ataman and Elias Lemercier, 'Macron Calls for "Different" Method of Governing After Disappointing Legislative Vote', CNN, 22 June 2022, https://www.cnn.com/2022/06/22/europe/macron-deep-divisions-france-intl/index.html.

8   See Matthew Bloch et al., 'Mapping How France Voted', New York Times, 8 July 2024, https://www.nytimes.com/2024/07/08/world/europe/france-election-maps.html.

9   European Parliament, '2024 European Election Results'.

10 Quoted in Mariama Darame, 'Snap Elections: Why France Could Become Ungovernable', Le Monde, 24 June 2024, https://www.lemonde.fr/en/politics/article/2024/06/24/snap-elections-france-could-become-ungovernable_6675623_5.html.

11 Ministère de l'Intérieur et des Outre-mer, 'Publication des candidatures et des résultats aux élections – Législatives 2024'. The RN garnered 7.7m in the European Parliament elections three weeks earlier.

12 This was, at least, an improvement on its 15% in the European Parliament elections.

13 Ministère de l'Intérieur et des Outre-mer, 'Publication des candidatures et des résultats aux élections – Législatives 2024'.

14 Ibid.

15 See, for example, Rachel Donadio, 'Meloni's Cultural Revolution', New York Review of Books, 6 June 2024, https://www.nybooks.com/articles/2024/06/06/melonis-cultural-revolution-rachel-donadio/.

16 See Claire Gatinois and Nathalie Segaunes, 'French Elections: Macron Is in Search of an Elusive Coalition', Le Monde, 9 July 2024, https://www.lemonde.fr/en/politics/article/2024/07/09/french-elections-macron-is-in-search-of-an-elusive-coalition_6678793_5.html.

Sudan's Transition to War

Volker Perthes

Sudan's December 2018 revolution was a months-long series of protests that led to the overthrow, in April 2019, of the Islamist military regime of Omar al-Bashir, who had been in power since staging a coup in 1989. The Transitional Military Council that had deposed Bashir then attempted to monopolise power against wide-ranging popular protests. Eventually, the military and a broad coalition of political parties, unions and civil-society organisations known as the Forces for Freedom and Change (FFC) negotiated a civilian–military partnership and established a Political Agreement and a Constitutional Document, signed in July and August respectively.[1] A civilian government under prime minister Abdalla Hamdok and a Transitional Sovereignty Council as a collective head of state chaired by the commander-in-chief of the Sudanese Armed Forces (SAF), Lieutenant-General Abdel Fattah al-Burhan, were installed. The Political Agreement foresaw a 39-month transition period culminating in elections and a fully civilian government. Burhan was supposed to cede the chair of the Transitional Sovereignty Council to a civilian 21 months into the transition period. The 'transition calendar' was restarted following the signing of the Juba Agreement for Peace in Sudan (JPA) between the transitional government and the majority of anti-regime rebel movements in October 2020.

Volker Perthes served as the Special Representative of the United Nations Secretary-General for Sudan and Head of the UN Integrated Transition Assistance Mission in Sudan (UNITAMS) from 2021 to 2023. An expanded version of this article will be published by Stiftung Wissenschaft und Politik (SWP), the German Institute for International and Security Affairs, as an SWP Research Paper in autumn 2024.

Survival | vol. 66 no. 4 | August–September 2024 | pp. 127–148 https://doi.org/10.1080/00396338.2024.2380205

In June 2020, at the request of the Sudanese government, the United Nations Security Council had agreed to support Sudan's transition through the establishment of a political mission, the United Nations Integrated Transition Assistance Mission in Sudan (UNITAMS). The mission's mandate listed four strategic objectives: to assist the political transition towards democratic governance; to support peace processes and the implementation of peace agreements; to assist in peacebuilding, providing civilian protection and advancing rule of law; and to facilitate the mobilisation of economic and development assistance and coordinate humanitarian assistance.[2] In January 2021, I was appointed Special Representative of the Secretary-General (SRSG) for Sudan and head of UNITAMS.[3]

By 2019, Sudan, which became independent in 1956, had experienced several military coups, 59 years of military rule, and a long history of civil wars between the centre and the peripheries. In 2011, after decades of war, South Sudan separated peacefully after the so-called Comprehensive Peace Agreement of 2005 was signed and an independence referendum held. The 'other civil war' in Darfur, which had escalated in the early 2000s, led to the deployment of the African Union–United Nations Hybrid Operation in Darfur (UNAMID) peacekeeping force, whose mandate ended by 31 December 2020. The decision to draw down UNAMID was originally made in 2018, when Bashir was still in power. Conflicts in Darfur were not resolved, but they seemed to be contained; Bashir wanted to get rid of the international presence anyway; and Security Council members were eager to cut peacekeeping costs. After Bashir fell, UNAMID's mandate was briefly extended in order to give the new government time for peace talks with the main armed groups, which resulted in the JPA in 2020. The new political mission, UNITAMS, had no peacekeeping functions, but did have a political mandate to support the transition, including the implementation of the JPA.

The civilian–military partnership that saw the light in 2019 was neither the military's nor the civilians' first choice. Rather, it reflected the internal balance of power after the fall of the old regime, and was tainted by a lack of trust and often contradictory agendas. Among other things, the military controlled a major part of the national economy and effectively blocked the efforts of the civilian component to weaken the economic influence of former regime elements. Civilian politicians feared that the military leadership would refuse to relinquish the leadership of the Transitional Sovereignty Council to a civilian, while military leaders complained that the political parties were eager to prolong the transition period rather than seek a popular mandate through elections. In October 2021, the military staged a coup and ousted the civilian government under Hamdok. Divisions about the future course of the country then began to appear inside the 'military component' – between the leadership of the SAF under General Burhan and that of the Rapid Support Forces (RSF) under the leadership of General Mohamed Hamdan Dagalo, called 'Hemedti'. The RSF was a light, highly mobile group that the Bashir regime had established as an auxiliary and counter-insurgency force. Its leadership came mostly from Hemedti's own family and tribe, its core troops from Darfurian ethnic Arabs.

A year and a half after their joint coup, war broke out between the SAF and the RSF. Repeated attempts by regional and international actors to arrange a cessation of hostilities between the warring parties have thus far failed. UNITAMS was dissolved by 29 February 2024, unable to see its mandate through and support a successful completion of Sudan's transition to democracy. Instead, it witnessed a transition to war that neither local political forces nor UNITAMS and its international partners were able to prevent. This raises the question of the extent to which UNITAMS was able to exercise its good-offices function and, more generally, how UN missions could better support political transitions.

UNITAMS's tenure

UNITAMS spanned the civilian–military partnership in Sudan up to the 25 October 2021 military coup when the military ousted its civilian partners; an increasingly fractious military government up to April 2023; and the war between the SAF and the RSF. UNITAMS offered its good offices in all three phases, mainly as a facilitator, most actively in the second, post-coup phase.

UNITAMS initially set out to engage and build relationships with both the civilian and the military components of the partnership government, political and societal actors, and regional and international players. It also provided the government with technical support for the implementation of a National Plan for the Protection of Civilians, legal reform, capacity-building for women's groups and other civil-society actors, reorganising the police and the judiciary, and implementing inter-community dialogues and mine-action support. UNITAMS was neither mandated nor equipped to provide physical protection for civilians, even though many civilians, particularly in Darfur, endured outbursts of violence and forced displacement, and harboured unfounded but real expectations that UNITAMS would somehow take over the tasks of UNAMID – a more than 10,000-strong Chapter VII peacekeeping force with a $1 billion annual budget that had been able to offer limited pro- tection as well as support for peacebuilding activities. The UNITAMS staffing plan initially allowed for only 21 police advisers to work with the Sudanese Police Force in Khartoum and three locations in Darfur. Disappointment on the part of local communities may have contributed to the looting of almost all UNAMID facilities once they had been handed over to authorities and public institutions in Darfur, though the greed of some armed groups, includ- ing JPA signatories, was a larger factor.

After a failed coup attempt in September 2021, the FFC split into two blocs – the main political parties in the Hamdok cabinet and like-minded groups, referred to as FFC1 or FFC Central Committee, and the so-called FFC2, which subsequently called itself FFC National Charter and later, with the addition of other groups, FFC Democratic Bloc.[4] (Henceforth I will refer to the first coalition as FFC(CC) and the second as FFC(NC) or FFC(DB).) The latter was led by two of the JPA signatories: the Sudan Liberation Army (SLA-MM) of Minni Minawi, who had shortly before been appointed gover- nor of Darfur, and the Justice and Equality Movement under Jibril Ibrahim, who served as minister of finance. Like other armed-struggle-movement leaders who had signed the JPA, Minawi and Ibrahim saw themselves as bona fide political leaders with legitimate claims, stipulated in the JPA, to certain positions in the Transitional Sovereignty Council and government. They retained their militias, kept recruiting for them and lent some out as mercenaries to the contending parties in Libya.[5] Both movements called for the civilian government, particularly FFC politicians, to be removed in favour of the military and 'technocrats'.

In this atmosphere, the UN called for de-escalation and mediation among military leaders, the prime minister, civilian policymakers and other civilian actors, and armed-struggle-movement leaders. UNITAMS had also made direct appeals to the military leadership to refrain from any possible coup, clearly indicating that the UN and other international actors would call a coup what it was, and warning about the likely political and economic consequences of a military takeover. While public demonstrations in support of civilian rule showed impressive support, one general indicated to me that the military was about to lose patience: if UNITAMS wanted to bring the various parties together, he said, there weren't many days left. The following morning, on 25 October, Burhan and Hemedti mounted a coup.

Burhan claimed the military had moved to prevent civil war

The prime minister was taken into custody and later held under house arrest. A number of ministers and FFC leaders were detained, and internet and mobile-phone communications were cut. In a televised statement, Burhan declared a state of emergency and the dissolution of both the cabinet and the Transitional Sovereignty Council. Key provisions of the Constitutional Document, particularly those that referred to the FFC, were suspended. All undersecretaries and governors were dismissed – except, in practice, those who represented the armed groups that had signed the JPA – and more senior officials were sacked over the next few weeks. Burhan claimed that the military had moved to prevent civil war, that it would hand over power to an elected civilian government, and that he envisioned elections for summer 2023.

The UN Security Council called for a restoration of civilian government, and the African Union's (AU) Peace and Security Council (PSC) suspended Sudan's membership. Most donor countries withheld development assistance but maintained humanitarian support. On the ground, 'resistance committees' composed of activists who had helped overthrow the Bashir regime called for mass protests, which subsequently occurred several times a week in the capital and the provinces. The military and police sought to suppress these protests, often with lethal force, and at least 114 protesters had died by the end of 2022.[6] Security deteriorated throughout the country, particularly in the peripheries, as both the SAF and the RSF diverted forces from the provinces to the capital. UNITAMS gave a cautious welcome to an agreement negotiated by a number of civilian and military players, stipulating that the prime minister would form a technocratic government, but, like other international bodies, did not officially endorse it. The FFC(CC), the resistance committees and a majority of the people rejected it, and Hamdok resigned on 2 January 2022, leaving Burhan the effective head of government. Most ministries were led by officials appointed by Burhan, who increasingly came to rely on cadres from the former regime and its officially banned National Congress Party (NCP).

The coup not only ended the civilian–military partnership but also effectively aborted the 'political transition'. In turn, UNITAMS's good offices became more pertinent. In the first weeks after the coup, the mission's efforts were largely focused on having the prime minister and other detainees released and the use of excessive force against protesters curbed. In January, UNITAMS launched its own 'Consultations on a Political Process'. This was an intensive six-week process with some 110 meetings and more than 800 interlocutors in Khartoum and various provincial cities. UNITAMS made it clear before and during the process that it would not yield a definitive solution to the crisis. A summary of the discussions was published in a report that also proposed a list of priority issues for an ensuing political process, notably civilian–military relations, an accepted transitional government, legislative and oversight bodies, and more inclusive political participation.[7] In February, after some procrastination from the military, high-level delegations from the AU and the subregional Intergovernmental Authority on Development (IGAD) were able to visit Khartoum. In March, following discussions in Khartoum and at headquarters level, the AU, IGAD and UNITAMS formed what came to be called the Tripartite (sometimes, 'Trilateral') Mechanism (TM). The active involvement of the three organisations lent legitimacy to the mechanism: Sudan was a member of all three, so it was difficult to credibly denounce the trilateral efforts as a form of Western interference as hardline Islamists had done with regard to the UN.

From April 2022, the TM began to engage in various joint efforts to facilitate dialogue between military and civilian leaders. UNITAMS itself continued to engage with military, political and civil-society representatives, and to work, mostly on a technical level, with federal and state institutions, the military, police, judiciary, prosecutors and others to address human-rights, rule-of-law and protection issues, or to engage on peacebuilding efforts. UNITAMS also served as a hub for international policy discussions, notably by convening regular virtual meetings among the Friends of Sudan Group, which consisted of the representatives from the main donor countries, including France, Germany, Norway, Saudi Arabia, Sweden, the United Arab Emirates (UAE), the United Kingdom and the United States.

In June, the TM launched an unsuccessful attempt to bring the military and both pro-military and opposition politicians together for 'preparatory talks', which were boycotted by the FFC(CC) as the main opposition bloc. Parallel meetings between the FFC(CC) and the military sponsored by the US and Saudi embassies also failed to break the stalemate. Then, on 4 July, Burhan gave a televised speech in which he stated that the military would withdraw from all these talks in order to allow the civilian elements to agree among themselves on a 'government of independent national competencies'. He added that, if that happened, the military would accept such a government, the Transitional Sovereignty Council he led would be dissolved, and the SAF and RSF would form a Supreme Council of the Armed Forces that would be responsible for security and defence in agreement with the government.[8] Notwithstanding suspicions of a ruse, especially in the FFC(CC) and other opposition groups, Burhan and his fellow generals appeared to realise that they were stuck and needed a way out of the futile and increasingly dire situation that they had created.

Whatever Burhan's intentions, his announcement changed the political dynamics. The TM encouraged civilian stakeholders to treat the announcement as an opportunity to test the military's preparedness to withdraw from politics and accept a civilian government. A number of initiatives emerged, all aimed at finding consensus on a new 'transition phase' leading to government formation. The most successful one, launched by the Sudanese Bar Association (SBA), aimed at drawing up a new constitution through a month-long series of workshops and expert meetings that involved the main political parties, armed-struggle movements, civil-society representatives and jurists. UNITAMS and international non-governmental organisations provided limited expert advice during these deliberations. Despite initial scepticism, Burhan and the other generals in the Transitional Sovereignty Council eventually embraced the SBA's process as the most broad-based one, and used the Constitutional Draft it had produced as the basis for an 'amended' document of their own. On 24 October, Burhan and Hemedti presented this document to the TM and the ambassadors of the 'Quad' (Saudi Arabia, the UAE, the UK and the US), stating that it should henceforward no longer be referred to as the 'SBA draft', but as a 'National Document'.

This draft then became the basis for informal, direct negotiations between both Burhan and Hemedti and the FFC(CC) leaders, which resulted in a so-called Framework Political Agreement (FPA). It was signed on 5 December by Burhan, Hemedti and a host of political parties and groups in the FFC, others from outside the FFC, several armed-struggle movements, and civil-society organisations. The FPA stipulated a return to civilian governance with a civilian as symbolic head of state. The military would be represented in a Security and Defence Council chaired by the prime minister. The TM was asked to facilitate discussion on five critical issues on which the military and civilian negotiators of the FPA had not been able to settle, in order to achieve a Final Agreement, whereupon the military would cede authority to the new president and a government would be formed.[9] Those associated with the Bashir regime, mainly from the 'Islamic Movement' and the NCP, denounced the agreement. The leaders of the FFC(DB) declined to sign up to the agreement but they remained in discussions. Resistance committees were sceptical that the military would heed its commitments, but were prepared to give the FPA a chance. The public seemed hopeful that the agreement would lead the country out of its crisis. Violence between activists and the security forces on the streets decreased significantly.[10]

The TM now became an active convener and moderator, helping to organise broad-based discussion on the critical issues that the FPA had left open, supporting a Coordinating Committee for that process that included representatives of the SAF, the RSF and the civilian signatories of the FPA, and a Joint Secretariat for the day-to-day work. At the same time, a campaign against the FPA process became more aggressive, levelling false claims of undue interference on the part of the TM, UNITAMS or, to more personal effect, 'Volker' via media and public gatherings.

The five contentious issues were dealt with in five consecutive workshops from early January 2023, starting with a meeting on the 'Dismantlement of the Old Regime' (focusing on accountability), followed by meetings on the 'Juba Peace Agreement and the Completion of the Peace Process', 'The East' (of Sudan), 'Transitional Justice' and finally, in late March, on 'Security Sector Reform'. While modestly called workshops, these were major conferences over three or four days with between 300 and 700 participants. While the TM and the military agreed that at least 60% of the participants should come from groups other than the signatories, the strong attendance reflected the desire of groups and individuals beyond the political elite to have their voices heard.[11]

The fifth and last workshop, on security-sector reform, was the most difficult one. Sudanese society generally demanded a unified, professional army, not two or more parallel ones. The FPA had stipulated the need for 'security and military reform', and for the RSF to be integrated into the SAF, but there remained a vast gulf between the SAF leadership, who wanted the RSF under direct army command, and Hemedti, who wanted to preserve the RSF's autonomy and thereby his personal power base.

In particular, stark differences between the SAF and the RSF leaderships emerged on the timelines and modalities of an eventual integration of the RSF into a unified command structure, the composition of a unified command and its answerability to a prospective civilian head of state. Some senior SAF officials were clearly unhappy that a paper Burhan had signed, seemingly without consulting them, specified the timeline for eventual integration of the RSF as 'up to ten years'. Eventually, SAF participants withdrew from the conference. Not for the first time, the planned signing of a final political agreement was postponed.

As SRSG, I had warned the Security Council of tensions between the two military formations that had been building since the beginning of the year.[12] Later, I also urged two regional states whose influence far exceeded that of the UN to use their influence, invite the two military leaders to their capital and ask them to stand down from their confrontational course. Instead, SAF and RSF leaders built up their respective forces in the capital. The RSF brought hundreds of combat vehicles into Khartoum, while the SAF moved heavy tanks into the city. The TM continued to urge both military leaderships to de-escalate. On 14 April, the deputy commander of the RSF assured TM envoys that there would be no war between the RSF and the SAF.

War

Fighting between the SAF and the RSF broke out on the morning of 15 April, immediately engulfing Khartoum and Darfur. The UN and most diplomatic missions decided to evacuate their staff or encouraged them to move to safer regions. By the end of April, UNITAMS had relocated a core team to Port Sudan and the majority of its international staff to Nairobi, Kenya.

In Khartoum and Darfur, the RSF soon gained the upper hand, controlling most of the capital city, including the presidential palace and Burhan's residence. The RSF also occupied the Merowe airfield and detained Egyptian airmen for a few days. The SAF entrenched itself in key military installations, including the General Command compound where Burhan and his closest associates remained under siege for four months, until he was evacuated – reportedly by Ukrainian commandos[13] – and his government relocated to Port Sudan. Khartoum, together with the nearby cities Omdurman and Bahri, remained a zone of open war and devastation, while fighting continued in Darfur and spread to the Kordofan and Al Jazirah states. As of May 2024, more than 15,000 Sudanese had been killed and tens of thousands injured. The RSF controlled most of the capital, most of Darfur, parts of the Kordofan states, and the road connections between Khartoum and Darfur, as well as Al Jazirah State. The SAF controlled the eastern states, including Port Sudan and the Red Sea coast, and the north, including the border with Egypt. Both sides committed atrocities. The RSF raped women and murdered non-combatants, particularly in Khartoum and Al Jazirah State, and committed ethnically motivated massacres of the Masalit population in West Darfur.[14] It also looted UN warehouses. The SAF often used its air force and heavy artillery for indiscriminate bombing, and with allied militias committed extrajudicial killings and other human-rights violations. SAF-aligned authorities in Port Sudan frequently denied humanitarian access to RSF-controlled territories. Sudan became the largest humanitarian crisis worldwide, with more than 6.6 million people internally displaced and another 2m seeking refuge outside the country.[15] Hospitals were destroyed, health services had largely broken down and some 18m people faced acute food insecurity. Famine in large parts of the country was expected in the summer, as war curtailed planting, harvesting, transport and humanitarian access.[16]

UNITAMS encouraged ceasefires, continued to monitor violations of human rights and international humanitarian law, and tried to address them. During the first weeks of the war, first from Khartoum and then from Port Sudan, I was in regular contact with the leaders of both sides. On the second day, after several phone calls with RSF and SAF leaders, supported by personal calls from UN Secretary-General António Guterres, both sides publicly announced that they would cease the fighting for three hours in response to UN efforts – and to allow Sudanese Muslims to break the Ramadan fast. This commitment was only partly observed. The United States and Saudi Arabia gradually took over efforts to reach a ceasefire, eventually inviting military delegations from both forces to Jeddah for several rounds of negotiations.

UNITAMS's protection and political teams maintained contact with both sides, as did the UNITAMS team chairing the Darfur Permanent Ceasefire Committee and state-level ceasefire committees, which continued to hold virtual meetings with representatives of the JPA signatories as well as, initially, the SAF and RSF, and later only the SAF. These efforts occasionally secured the release of detainees or safe passage for civilians stuck between fronts. My own more or less daily contacts with the SAF and RSF leaderships continued from Port Sudan under challenging technical conditions, as phone networks had largely ceased to operate, and the internet was weak at best. I regularly raised humanitarian violations in these conversations, and both sides usually denied them. UNITAMS remained the convener of the Friends of Sudan Group, and it supported the AU's establishment of a diplomatic structure for peace efforts in Addis Ababa, involving a small Core Group of states, a larger Extended Group, and a Secretariat composed of the TM and the League of Arab States. Aside from a few preliminary meetings, this structure never became operational. Instead, a number of parallel regional ventures were launched. They included IGAD meetings, a mediation attempt by four IGAD heads of state and a summit of neighbouring states initiated by Egypt.

The US- and Saudi-sponsored talks in Jeddah constituted the only format that both warring parties accepted in principle. Washington and Riyadh initially chose to keep all other regional or international players out of these talks. Other regional efforts remained fragmented and often competitive. Even the UN's participation was limited to humanitarian coordination.[17]

The UN has continued to coordinate humanitarian aid from Port Sudan. UNITAMS's presence there has faced aggressive opposition from groups that have declared themselves pro-military. Tribesmen were bussed into the city for angry anti-UNITAMS demonstrations, accusing the mission of having triggered the war, denouncing it for not supporting the SAF, or demanding the expulsion of the SRSG. Fabricated news depicting UNITAMS as a supporter of the enemy spread through social-media networks.[18] While Burhan and the SAF distanced themselves from this kind of activity, they also tolerated it.

My own presence in Port Sudan ended rather unexpectedly. After my briefing to the Security Council in late May, when I was absent from Sudan, the secretary-general received a letter from Sudan's Permanent Mission bearing Burhan's facsimile signature requesting that I be replaced. After the secretary-general had made clear that he stood by his SRSG, Sudan's Foreign Ministry notified the UN that I had been declared *persona non grata*.[19] In line with standard practice, the UN Secretariat stated that such declarations were not applicable to UN personnel.[20] Still, the move had its effect. Having been 'PNG-ed', I was not allowed to return to Sudan, and an SRSG who resides outside the country is operationally handicapped. In any case, my PNG designation was only a first step towards ending the UN's political presence in Sudan. In November, Sudan officially requested the termination of the UNITAMS mandate. Since it had been established at the request of Sudan, the Security Council unanimously decided to end its operations by the end of February 2024. Because I could no longer do my work effectively, I resigned as SRSG in September 2023.

Why war?

It is practically impossible for any observer who wasn't involved in the actual fighting to establish who fired the first shot. The RSF was clearly better prepared for conflict, and for urban warfare, than the SAF. The SAF's unreadiness lends some credibility to the possibility that the RSF had attempted a coup, or that a third force of old-regime loyalists within the SAF but acting outside the SAF command had set off the war by attacking an RSF installation. According to civilian Sudanese observers, the initial fighting could have started by accident. What sustains wars, however, are divergent interests and conflicting fears. At bottom, growing differences between the military leaders about control over the state and its resources, and about their respective stakes if civilian rule was to be restored, produced the war.

Burhan and the SAF leadership clearly felt they were in a better political position during the weeks preceding the outbreak of hostilities. Burhan was recognised domestically and internationally as the de facto head of state and led the negotiations for the military side. When Hemedti participated, he did so as 'Number Two', as Burhan also referred to him. Burhan knew that experts from the UN, the TM and the Quad had an understanding of force integration and a unified command structure that was closer to his than to Hemedti's. Hemedti, for his part, never disputed Burhan's position as head of the Transitional Sovereignty Council, referred to him as 'president' when they appeared together, and accepted that Burhan would remain commander-in-chief of the SAF once a Final Agreement had been reached and a transfer of power to a civilian government completed. Still, he left no doubt that he wanted to change the relationship and refused to meet with the TM for several weeks because of remarks I had made to the effect that Sudan couldn't afford parallel armies. The core issue for him was the potential loss of his independent power base occasioned by his subordination to the commander-in-chief.

Against this background, it is reasonable to conclude that the UN and the international community underestimated Hemedti's willingness to defend his personal interests with military force while overestimating Burhan's and the SAF's willingness to stick to agreements they had signed. One could also ask, counterfactually, whether war would have been avoided if Hemedti had not felt heavy internal and international pressure to integrate his forces into a unified army. This is not only the story of two generals, of course. Even if Burhan had been more open to Hemedti maintaining the autonomy of his force, the SAF as an institution probably would have balked and prevented such an arrangement by way of a coup. In my judgement, Burhan would have at least grudgingly signed a Final Agreement if key demands regarding the integration of the RSF had been met. But he repeatedly failed to involve his own wider military leadership in negotiations, and to convince them of what he had agreed to on the military's behalf. Hemedti, for his part, certainly felt cornered.

Sudan's Islamic Movement and other pro-military forces have claimed that the FPA and the political process that the TM facilitated based on it had pushed the two military forces into confrontation. This claim does not make sense. Friction between the SAF and the RSF began almost immediately after they grabbed power together in October 2021 and intensified before negotiations on the FPA had even started. International players tried to transform the conflict between the two military bodies into a technical debate on security-sector reform and thereby defuse it, but it was inexorably about power and resources – that is, hard interests. Arguably, only the establishment of civilian governance and civilian oversight over the military could have checked the military power struggle. Political figures who claim that the FPA reflected an international conspiracy to push Sudan into war conveniently ignore the fact that international players were not in the room when the two Sudanese military leaders and their civilian counterparts negotiated it.

Civilian actors, as well as the armed-movements leaders who had become politicians, also perpetuated political polarisation. The TM engaged regularly and closely with the main political coalitions – the FFC(CC) and the FFC(DB) – and with individual parties and non-partisan civilian actors. But it did not work with an increasingly active third bloc, sometimes referred to as the Islamic Current, which was dominated by the Islamic Movement and the officially banned NCP, and relied on a network of groups and parties that had been allied with the Bashir regime. Arguably, UNITAMS or the

TM could have sought greater contact with this bloc even though the NCP was banned and representatives of the Islamic Movement were regarded as illegitimate in the post-revolution consensus. But it is highly unlikely that deeper engagement would have changed their steadfast stance against the political process or their uneasiness with the presence of a UN political mission. They had rejected UNITAMS from the beginning and did their best to undermine it. The Islamic Movement left no doubt that it did not want the FPA and follow-up talks between military and civilian leaders to succeed. Enhanced contacts might have improved situational awareness and toned down the anti-UNITAMS campaign a little, but it would not have quelled the Islamic Movement's interest in returning to power. Since the war began, its influence in the army and the administration has increased. By 2024, this even prompted concern among some professional SAF officers that these forces would exploit the SAF's and its allies' struggle for their own propagandistic aims.[21]

An imperfect mandate

The international approach to Sudan, including UNITAMS's mandate and resourcing, was shaped by a brief moment of revolutionary, idealistic optimism after the fall of the Bashir regime. A Security Council majority, as well as the Friends of Sudan Group and other Western and Arab donors, all agreed on supporting and stabilising the transition that the Sudanese military and its civilian counterparts had agreed on. The residual power and influence of the Islamic Movement, the NCP and their allies was under-appreciated. They supported the military's rule following the October 2021 coup because it allowed their cadres to return to positions of influence, but they left little doubt that they would make any effort, including the use of violence, to undo the FPA and prevent a civilian transition, and that they were eager to weaken or end a UN mission that supported that goal. Once war had broken out, they became the main force on the SAF side opposing a ceasefire and international efforts to end the war. One lesson here for the international community is not to underestimate the opposition to a political transition it wants to support by means of a UN mission. The other, for the UN itself, is to combine mission planning and strategic foresight. Foresight derives from historical trajectories and path dependencies, such as the frequency of civil war or military coups.

It therefore could have been useful to build military expertise into the original mandate. UNITAMS was mandated and resourced to support what looked like an unchallenged transition, driven by the civilian government and its military partners, and backed by the international community. It was not grossly under-resourced or understaffed for that purpose,[22] but the mandate did not factor in a military coup and a deteriorating political and security environment for a country with a long history of discord and war. Without military expertise going in, the mission was effectively blind on potential military developments, including the border dispute with Ethiopia and military and paramilitary movements in Darfur. In the event, the mission gained authorisation to recruit a military adviser and military observers. It was also able to bring in mediation-design expertise from headquarters when it launched the consultations in January 2022. Ideally, however, such functions would have been factored into planning for a transition-assistance mission from the beginning, when it might have been marshalled to pre-emptive effect.

Furthermore, the gap between UNITAMS's mandated tasks and resources, on the one hand, and popular expectations as to security and humanitarian matters, on the other, could have been better addressed. When the UNITAMS mandate was up for renewal in June 2022, three months into Russia's invasion of Ukraine, the Security Council was highly polarised and effectively blocked. Council members were unable to agree on new language reflecting the new political environment that the military coup had created in Sudan. They therefore simply rolled over the existing mandate rather than adapting it. This also meant that the mandate still mentioned support for the mobilisation of economic and development assistance as one of the mission's strategic objectives, even though it had become virtually impossible as donors had suspended all but humanitarian aid. Sudanese and international actors who were critical of the mission's effort to support a political process subsequently used the decrease in foreign aid as an argument against UNITAMS, accusing the mission of neglecting its humanitarian and security function in favour of 'political activities'. This, of course, is part of the broader issue of how the UN should deal with unconstitutional changes of government.[23]

International and regional support

UN good offices in general depend on support from the regional and international community. This was certainly so for UNITAMS and its TM partners. UNITAMS had been established by a unanimous vote in the Security Council, and most of the international community supported its and the TM's efforts to facilitate a political process, at least on a declaratory level. After the military takeover of October 2021, the council's exhortation to military authorities to restore the civilian-led transitional government reinforced UNITAMS's efforts to facilitate that process and probably made it easier for the mission to convince the military that it should not put obstacles in the way of the UNITAMS-led consultations. Similarly, the Security Council's statement welcoming the FPA in December 2022 lent legitimacy to the TM's efforts to facilitate a broader process on the basis of the agreement. But the general polarisation in the council also impacted deliberations on Sudan. On the ground, various actors sensed that the mission had lost the robust backing of the Security Council and could more easily be challenged.

At ground level, efforts to prevent the outbreak of armed violence would have needed higher-level involvement by international actors with more influence than the UN alone could muster. Arguably, only three states – Saudi Arabia, the UAE and the US – had the leverage to prevent a slide into war. Their respective ambassadors did support attempts at de-escalation. The US, as well as the UK, even made experts on security-sector reform available, who then closely worked with an SAF–RSF technical committee. Arguably, however, inducing military leaders to stand down from their confrontational course would have required strong pressure from at least one of the three states – or better, all of them together – and from top levels. The situation in Sudan was obviously not a priority issue for any of the capitals. US government involvement, for example, never extended beyond the level of assistant secretary of state. Sudan's war was not triggered by regional powers; nor is it a proxy war.[24] But regional powers made no visible effort to prevent it, either, and, since its outbreak, have arguably contributed to its continuation by materially supporting the warring parties.[25] The UAE has been the main supporter of the RSF; Egypt and, more recently, Iran of the SAF. Ending the war would require both an effective arms embargo and an end to gold imports from Sudan, through which both sides continue to finance their arms purchases.

*　　　*　　　*

Regarding the exercise of its good-offices function, UNITAMS was well positioned when, shortly after becoming operational in 2021, it was asked to facilitate, with South Sudan, peace negotiations between the Sudanese government and the Sudanese People's Liberation Movement–North (al-Hilu faction), a non-JPA-signatory rebel movement, both of which showed genuine interest in settling their conflict. UNITAMS brought, in addition to material support, UN values and experience into the process. Following the October 2021 coup, the mission won consent to lead a broad-based consultation process by engaging a wide spectrum of stakeholders. The mission enjoyed a high degree of credibility with civilian actors and, up to a point, the military. After the coup, when military leaders had become the only de facto authorities, they tolerated and were selectively responsive to UNITAMS's efforts to facilitate political reconciliation and promote the rule of law and human rights.[26]

UNITAMS could have been better equipped, and could have been endowed with a stronger and, particularly after the coup, more realistic mandate. And it certainly could have done some things better. That said, arguably no UN mission could have prevented two armies that were prepared to fight each other from going to war and continuing the war as long as their interests compelled them to do so and their access to resources enabled them to do so. From that perspective, UNITAMS's experience and record reinforces a hard putative truth of international relations: only major powers motivated to use their political and economic leverage decisively can change the calculations of imminent combatants.

Notes

1   See 'Sudan Political Agreement', Constitutionnet, July 2019, https://constitutionnet.org/vl/item/sudan-political-agreement; and 'Sudan Constitutional Declaration August 2019', Constitutionnet, August 2019, https://constitutionnet.org/vl/item/sudan-constitutional-declaration-august-2019.

2   See UN Security Council, 'Resolution 2524 (2020)', 3 June 2020, http://unscr.com/en/resolutions/doc/2524.

3   Among other considerations, my recollections as SRSG for Sudan inform this critical reflection of what the UN and other international actors can learn from the UNITAMS experience. I readily admit that my personal involvement may influence my analysis.

4   The FFC1 continued to refer to itself simply as FFC, but over time was generally called FFC (Central Committee). The other bloc was generally referred to as FFC2 but did not like this, since the suffix '2' signalled that it was a breakaway faction. Its composition was somewhat fluid, and it appeared under different names, but its core – Minni Minawi's Sudan Liberation Army and Jibril Ibrahim's Justice and Equality Movement – remained the same. After the war began, both blocs remained largely intact and opposed to each other. The FCC (Central Committee) became the core of the Coalition of Civil Democratic Forces (Taqaddum) formed in October 2023. In May 2024, the FFC Democratic Bloc groups and some former National Congress Party affiliates, including the notorious (and UN-sanctioned)

former Janjaweed militia leader Musa Hilal, formed a new pro-SAF political bloc under the name of Sudan Charter Forces (SCF).

5   See Gerrit Kurtz, 'The Spoilers of Darfur', SWP Comment 2022/C 53, 7 September 2022, https://www.swp-berlin.org/10.18449/2022C53/.

6   See ACLED, 'Sudan: Political Process to Form a Transitional Civilian Government and Shifting Disorder Trends', Situation Update, 14 April 2023, https://acleddata.com/2023/04/14/sudan-situation-update-april-2023-political-process-to-form-a-transitional-civilian-government-and-the-shift-in-disorder-trends/.

7   See UN Department of Political and Peacebuilding Affairs, 'Consultations on a Political Process for Sudan', February 2022, https://unitams.unmissions.org/en/consultations-political-process-sudan.

8   Quoted in 'Sudan's Military Would Abandon Power to Civilians: al-Burhan', *Sudan Tribune*, 4 July 2022, https://sudantribune.com/article261136/.

9   For an unofficial translation of the FPA, see 'Draft Political Framework Agreement', https://redress.org/wp-content/uploads/2022/12/Framework-Agreement-Final-ENG-05122022.pdf.

10   See ACLED, 'Sudan'.

11   See 'Committee to Present Draft Final Agreement to Sudan's Civil and Military Actors', Dabanga, 26 March 2023, https://www.dabangasudan.org/en/all-news/article/committee-to-

present-draft-final-agreement-to-sudans-civil-and-military-actors.

[12] See United Nations, 'Security Council Remarks – Special Representative of the Secretary-General to Sudan and Head of UNITAMS, Mr. Volker Perthes', 20 March 2023, https://unitams.unmissions.org/en/security-council-remarks-special-representative-secretary-general-sudan-and-head-unitams-mr-volker.

[13] See Ian Lovett, Nikita Nikolaienko and Nicholas Bariyo, 'Ukraine Is Now Fighting Russia in Sudan', *Wall Street Journal*, 6 March 2024, https://www.wsj.com/world/ukraine-is-now-fighting-russia-in-sudan-87caf1d8.

[14] See United Nations, 'Situation of Human Rights in Sudan: Report of the United Nations High Commissioner for Human Rights', A/HRC/55/29, 22 February 2024.

[15] See International Organization for Migration, 'Regional Sudan Crisis Response – Situation Update', 18 April 2024, https://sudan.iom.int/sites/g/files/tmzbdl1606/files/documents/2024-04/sudan-regional-crisis-response-situation-update-47.pdf.

[16] See Integrated Food Security Phase Classification, 'Sudan', IPC Acute Food Insecurity Analysis, 12 December 2023, https://www.ipcinfo.org/fileadmin/user_upload/ipcinfo/docs/IPC_Sudan_Acute_Food_Insecurity_Oct2023_Feb2024_Report.pdf; and 'Sudan: Famine Risk Is Real, FAO Warns', *UN News*, 19 April 2024, https://news.un.org/en/interview/2024/04/1148786.

[17] For an overview of regional and international diplomatic efforts to reach a ceasefire or end the war in Sudan, see International Crisis Group, 'Sudan's Calamitous Civil War: A Chance to Draw Back from the Abyss', 9 January 2024, https://www.crisisgroup.org/africa/horn-africa/sudan/sudans-calamitous-civil-war-chance-draw-back-abyss.

[18] Such fake news often reached a high degree of absurdity. One example is the 'news' that the SRSG had tried to get a UAE airplane-load of weapons for the RSF cleared by Sudanese customs.

[19] Burhan, still under siege in Khartoum, had indeed messaged me that he was unhappy with my Security Council briefing, notably with the equal distance I had displayed towards the warring parties as opposed to denouncing the RSF. The letter with his signature did not mention this point but contained a long list of allegations from the Islamist anti-UN narrative, including the claim that I had personally pushed the RSF into the war.

[20] See 'UN Says Sudan Cannot Apply Persona Non Grata to UN Envoy', Reuters, 9 June 2023, https://www.reuters.com/world/africa/un-says-sudan-cannot-apply-persona-non-grata-un-envoy-2023-06-09/.

[21] See 'Kabbashi Warns Against Political Exploitation of Sudan's Popular Resistance', *Sudan Tribune*, 28 March 2024, https://sudantribune.com/article283853/.

[22] See Daniel Forti, 'Walking a Tightrope: The Transition from UNAMID to UNITAMS', International Peace Institute, February 2021, pp. 18–21, https://www.ipinst.org/wp-content/uploads/2021/02/Walking_a_Tightrope_Sudan.pdf.

23 The UN is grappling with this issue at several levels. See, for example, Security Council Report, 'In Hindsight: The Security Council and Unconstitutional Changes of Government in Africa', 1 July 2022, https://www.securitycouncil report.org/monthly-forecast/2022-07/in-hindsight-the-security-council-and-unconstitutional-changes-of-government-in-africa.php; and United Nations Development Programme, 'Soldiers and Citizens: Military Coups and the Need for Democratic Renewal in Africa', July 2023, https://www.undp.org/africa/publications/soldiers-and-citizens.

24 See Gerrit Kurtz, 'How (Not) to Talk About the War in Sudan', SWP Megatrends Spotlight 30, 22 April 2024, https://www.swp-berlin.org/publikation/mta-spotlight-30-how-not-to-talk-about-the-war-in-sudan.

25 See 'African Union: External Support Prolongs Sudan's War', *Al Taghyeer*, 21 April 2024, https://www.altaghyeer.info/en/2024/04/21/african-union-external-support-prolongs-sudans-war/.

26 The mission was sometimes able to negotiate access for humanitarian actors or the release of individual detainees, and once even pressured one of the conflict parties to refrain from an impending attack on a city.

The Kurdish Predicament in US–Turkiye Relations

Eray Alim

In March 2024, General Michael Erik Kurilla, commander of US Central Command (CENTCOM), visited northern Syria to show support for Kurdish forces fighting the Islamic State (ISIS). Turkish officials reacted harshly.[1] Normally in a conflict situation, two allies would support each other in dealing with the threats involved. But the United States' partnerships with Syrian Kurdish groups have greatly complicated its interactions with Turkiye. The two allies have taken non-lethal military actions against each other, the US in particular having downed Turkish drones that were tracking Kurdish militants.[2] The United States is not entirely at fault. Turkiye's inconsistent policy towards Kurds both within and outside its borders has hindered its ability to present a coherent position on US–Kurdish cooperation.

Shifting interests

Turkiye could not have avoided some involvement in the Syrian crisis, given its 911-kilometre border with Syria, the inevitable pressure of war refugees and their effect on Turkiye's security. As Syria descended into conflict, Turkiye's conservative Sunni leadership sought to overthrow Bashar al-Assad's minority regime and establish a Sunni-dominated government.

Eray Alim is an associate professor in the Department of Political Science and Public Administration at Batman University in Turkiye.

Survival | vol. 66 no. 4 | August–September 2024 | pp. 149–160   https://doi.org/10.1080/00396338.2024.2380206

The coming to power of Muslim Brotherhood-inspired parties in Tunisia and Egypt during the Arab Spring fuelled the Turkish government's ambitions.[3] The United States' participation was strategically optional. But Syria is one of the few countries in the Middle East that has remained in the anti-American camp over the decades, forming the 'axis of resistance' with Iran, Hizbullah and Yemen's Houthis. The Arab Spring revolt against Assad in 2011 afforded the United States an opportunity to weaken that axis, and the US emerged as an important player in the Syrian conflict.

Early in the crisis, the United States and Turkiye worked together to remove Assad, pledging to facilitate a 'transition process' and to establish a 'new public order in Syria'.[4] The two allies also agreed to back the largely Sunni Syrian opposition that had undertaken an armed struggle against a repressive Assad regime, providing support for the big-tent armed opposition group known as the Free Syrian Army.[5]

Bilateral collaboration began to fray, however, when the Obama administration registered the disorderly nature of the Syrian opposition and, more importantly, its susceptibility to jihadist co-optation. Washington concluded that arming and training Sunni opposition forces was a flawed strategy. Al-Qaeda affiliates and other jihadists were joining the opposition and winning over previously moderate rebels, raising fears that weapons supplied to them could end up in jihadist hands.[6] Assad's regime also proved more resilient than anticipated, though it was not strong enough to withstand a multifront rebellion, which eventually resulted in a carved-up country.

By late 2013, ISIS had become the most powerful anti-Assad force in Syria, in 2014 proclaiming a 'caliphate' covering large swathes of northern Syria and western Iraq. The Turkish government did not fully appreciate the degree to which 9/11 had elevated counter-terrorism as a US strategic priority in the Middle East. Turkish leaders regarded ISIS as a secondary problem and considered the Kurdish entity known as the Democratic Union Party (PYD) and its armed wing, the People's Defence Units (YPG), which was then gaining ground in Syria, the main security threat. The PYD/YPG has close ties with the militant Kurdistan Workers' Party (PKK) in Turkiye, against which Turkiye has waged an anti-terrorist campaign since 1984. The PKK leadership based in northern Iraq's Qandil region engineered the creation of the YPG in 2011 to provide the PYD, which is the PKK's Syrian branch, with an armed group that could seize northern Syrian territories following the Syrian army's withdrawal from that region in 2012.[7] The Turkish government, however, had sent ambiguous signals to Washington, having welcomed Salih Muslim, the PYD's leader, in Ankara several times in order to persuade the Kurdish group to join what would become the Free Syrian Army.[8] The PYD turned down Turkiye's request, prompting Turkiye to regard it with suspicion and eventually declare it hostile.

The YPG's empowerment

During the early phase of the conflict, the US refrained from deploying any American soldiers in Syria despite calls to protect civilians from the Assad regime's attacks – a position informed and reinforced by the disastrous outcome of the United States' post-9/11 intervention in Iraq.[9] Even when ISIS materialised as a major player, more directly implicating US strategic interests, Washington remained determined not to dispatch large numbers of troops to Syria to defeat it. A supported proxy force made more sense. Despite Turkish objections, the US transformed YPG forces into a formidable military body by providing them with heavy machine guns, mortars, anti-tank weapons, armoured vehicles, engineering equipment and substantial training.[10] From the perspective of Turkish officials, a fortified PYD/YPG constituted 'a viable transborder Kurdish nationalist movement' that was 'the first of its kind since World War I'.[11] In 2017, the Turkish Foreign Ministry stated that 'every weapon seized by [the YPG] is a threat to Turkey'.[12]

In October 2015, the US spearheaded the creation of a new umbrella group called the Syrian Democratic Forces (SDF), which replaced the YPG as the main ground force of the US-led coalition against ISIS.[13] The idea was that incorporating fighters from other ethnic groups, such as Arabs, into the primary force would defuse Turkiye's fears of Kurdish nefariousness. However, given that the YPG was – and still is – the SDF's predominant component, this initiative failed to placate Turkiye.[14] Some Turkish officials believe that in creating the SDF, the United States was attempting to deceive and manipulate Turkiye.[15] In 2017, retired US General Raymond Thomas, who had served as commander of the US Special Operations Command when the SDF was established, lent credence to that view at the Aspen Security Forum, where he explained the rationale for rebranding the YPG with surprising candour:

> We literally played back to them: 'You have got to change your brand. What do you want to call yourselves besides the YPG?' With about a day's notice they declared that they [were] the Syrian Democratic Forces. I thought it was a stroke of brilliance to put democracy in there somewhere. But it gave them a little bit of credibility.[16]

The US–Kurdish partnership was an operational success. Largely Kurdish ground forces rooted ISIS out of its stronghold in the city of Raqqa with US air support and special forces' planning assistance. Only a relatively small number of American special-operations and advisory military personnel were required on the ground. Politically, the Syrian Kurds favour not the original PKK's Cold War-era Marxist–Leninist militancy but rather progressive democracy that is opposed to brutal jihadism.[17] Their actual conduct is more opaque, as substantiated reports of human-rights violations in Kurdish-controlled areas have emerged.[18] Nevertheless, they have effectively cast themselves as Western-leaning freedom fighters. Aiding minorities fleeing ISIS, such as the Yazidis, enabled the PYD/YPG to gain sympathy and respect in Western circles.[19]

The conversion of the YPG into the SDF also at least cosmetically shielded Washington from potential accusations that it collaborated with terrorists, given that the US recognises the PKK as a terrorist organisation, and demonstrable links between the YPG and the PKK would open the US to this charge. And the small American presence served as a tripwire deterrent against Turkiye, discouraging it from conducting cross-border military operations in Syria against YPG forces.[20] It is ironic and certainly unorthodox that in this case, the tripwire operated against a formal US state ally in favour of an informal, non-state one.[21]

Limits of pragmatism

Not all US officials agreed with the rebranding stratagem, insofar as it risked provoking a larger strategic crisis between Ankara and Washington. One key dissenter was James Jeffrey, who was appointed as the US Special Representative for Syria Engagement in 2018. Jeffrey was sympathetic to Turkiye's security concerns and critical of CENTCOM's posture against Turkiye. He observed that 'were the PYD to form a contiguous state along Turkey's southern border it would dramatically increase the PKK's reach, forcing Turkey to deal simultaneously with the PKK insurgency inside the country and a PKK-allied state to its south'.[22] He managed to dissuade CENTCOM from reinforcing military outposts along the Turkish–Syrian border and creating a border-defence force – measures designed to enhance the YPG's security by deterring Turkish forces from attacking it.

Turkiye's main concern is that the PYD/YPG accepts Abdullah Öcalan, the founder of the PKK, as its leader. The PYD's communal system of government in northern Syria is based on Öcalan's concept of democratic confederalism, which, in his words, 'aims at realizing the right of self-defense of the peoples by the advancement of democracy in all parts of Kurdistan without questioning the existing political borders'.[23] Taking aim at the concept of the nation-state due to its hierarchical nature, the PKK leader has called for the establishment of a horizontal system of governance in an area that includes parts of Iran, Iraq, Syria and Turkiye.

At the same time, Turkiye has prevailed on some PKK figures to ameliorate its worries. In the run-up to the Istanbul municipal election in June 2019, Osman Öcalan, a top PKK official, appeared in an interview on TRT Kurdish, a state-owned television channel, and delivered messages against the opposition. During the same period, a hand-picked government intermediary was dispatched to İmralı Island, where Abdullah Öcalan is serving a prison sentence, and elicited from him a letter, subsequently shared with the public, urging Turkish Kurds to stay neutral in the elections to enable the government to win.[24] In the event, however, Kurds, apparently in reaction to the government's arrest of a large number of Kurdish politicians, voted overwhelmingly for the opposition candidate, contributing to his victory.

Meanwhile, the SDF's close, effective and valiant cooperation with the United States in neutralising ISIS has created mutual bonds of loyalty extending up the respective chains of command. About 11,000 SDF fighters were killed in the US-led campaign against ISIS. The SDF has deterred ISIS's reconstitution, thus continuing to advance an important American interest. The nearby presence of US troops, in turn, protected the SDF. In October 2019, however, Donald Trump decreased the number of US military personnel in Syria from over 1,000 to 500, redeploying the remaining troops farther south and acquiescing to Turkiye's expulsion of the SDF from border areas. The US appeared to be abandoning a trusted and proven ally, and US military and diplomatic officials vigorously objected to the move.[25] To fend off Turkish attacks, the SDF had to establish a temporary tactical arrangement with the Assad regime itself.[26] Backlash from Congress, the Pentagon and US allies, as well as a resurgence of ISIS activity, compelled the Trump administration to return some of the withdrawn troops.[27]

Roughly 900 US troops remain in Syria, mainly to prevent ISIS's resurgence and, secondarily, to inhibit Iran's transfer of weapons to Hizbullah, check the activity of Iran-backed militias, enforce local ceasefires and facilitate humanitarian access.[28] A light US military presence in Syria also impedes Moscow from restoring the pre-crisis status quo in Syria, whereby Assad would regain control of all Syrian national territory.[29] As of summer 2024, in northern Syria, the US–PYD/YPG coalition controlled significant territory, including Kobani, Tell Rifaat, Manbij and Qamishli. Turkiye and the Turkish-aligned militias held a much smaller area, though it included the key border towns of Idlib and Afrin, both close to the Mediterranean. Turkiye had also seized the provinces of Tell Abyad and Ras al-Ayn in 2019, dividing PYD/YPG-controlled territory east of the Euphrates River. However, territory it has retained extends to the Iraqi border, which allows the US to use Iraq as a logistical base to maintain supply lines with the YPG, much to Turkiye's dismay.[30] Although large-scale conflict between opposing forces has been avoided recently, intermittent clashes and sporadic rocket attacks have occurred, highlighting persistent tensions.[31]

*   *   *   *

The Kurdish predicament may not be completely intractable. Relations between Turkiye and the Iraqi Kurdistan authorities following the US invasion of Iraq were extremely tense. Turkiye perceived that the Iraqi Kurds – and their US backers – had failed to take action against the PKK when it found refuge in northern Iraq. Over time, however, Turkiye and Iraqi Kurdish authorities developed closer ties based on pragmatic political considerations and especially on mutual economic advantage. People-to-people exchanges have markedly increased, Turkish direct investment has poured into northern Iraq and cross-border trade has reached unprecedented levels. A comparably manageable association could conceivably arise between Turkiye and the Syrian Kurds. Two major differences between the two contexts make this unlikely, however.

Firstly, given northern Iraq's rugged and mountainous terrain, it is doubtful that local Kurdish authorities or the US could have taken decisive action against the PKK even if they had wanted to. Turkiye itself, which recently established military outposts in northern Iraq, is struggling to eradicate the PKK from the region, suffering significant casualties.[32] This practical limitation has diminished Turkiye's leverage. The relatively flat topography of northern Syria makes it difficult for the United States to cite geography as an excuse for inaction.

Secondly, the link between the Iraqi Kurdish authorities and the PKK has never been as strong as that between the Syrian Kurdish movement and the PKK. There were even armed clashes between the Iraqi Peshmerga and the PKK. A number of interrelated factors account for this. Firstly, although the PKK and Iraqi Kurdish actors, such as the Barzani faction, developed close ties during the 1980s, Turkish pressure and concerns about Turkish military incursions into northern Iraq caused Iraqi Kurdish leaders to distance themselves from the PKK. Secondly, there was pronounced ideological incompatibility between the Marxist–Leninist PKK and Iraqi Kurds, with Öcalan expressing condescending views towards the Barzani faction due to its feudal orientation. Thirdly, the PKK was seen by Iraqi Kurdish leaders as a barrier to fostering positive relations with Turkiye, hindering mutually beneficial partnerships in areas such as trade, investment and development.[33] The Syria- and Turkiye-based Kurdish factions are more closely integrated.

Tensions remain between the United States and Turkiye in northern Syria. Having become frustrated with the US, Turkiye has begun to collaborate with Russia and Iran, the strongest supporters of the Syrian regime, to address the Syrian crisis. Furthermore, Turkish President Recep Tayyip Erdoğan has raised the possibility of meeting with Assad, a marked departure from his previous position.[34] This outreach on Turkiye's part is best understood as an attempt to rectify past mistakes, as diminishing the Assad regime's power by backing armed opposition allowed destabilising non-state actors to fill the resulting power vacuum.

The Turkish government would now prefer that the regime re-establish its authority in northern Syria and extinguish Kurdish aspirations for autonomy. The US military presence in Syria prevents such an eventuality.[35] The US and Turkiye have continued to cooperate within NATO as the Alliance seeks to address the challenges posed by the Russia–Ukraine war. But new developments in the Middle East could set the two allies starkly at odds there. Should the Gaza war morph into a full-blown regional conflict involving Israel, Iran, Syria and Hizbullah, the Kurds – spread across four countries in the region – could see an opportunity to advance their agenda and even push for independence. Turkiye is aghast at such a prospect. The United States and its allies should be concerned about it as well.

Notes

1   See 'US Continues Support for PKK/YPG Terror Group: Security Source', TRT World, 8 March 2024, https://www.trtworld.com/turkiye/us-continues-support-for-pkkypg-terror-group-security-source-17273383.

2   See C. Todd Lopez, 'After U.S. Downs Turkish Drone in Syria, Focus Remains on Defeat ISIS Mission', DOD News, US Department of Defense, 5 October 2023, https://www.defense.gov/News/News-Stories/Article/Article/3550462/after-us-downs-turkish-drone-in-syria-focus-remains-on-defeat-isis-mission/.

3   See Behlül Ozkan, 'Turkey, Davutoglu and the Idea of Pan-Islamism', Survival, vol. 56, no. 4, August–September 2014, pp. 119–40.

4   See Republic of Turkiye Ministry of Foreign Affairs, 'Foreign Minister Davutoglu and U.S. Secretary of State Clinton Agreed on the Further Strengthening of Coordination on Syria', 11 August 2012, https://www.mfa.gov.tr/foreign-minister-davutoglu-and-us-secretary-of-state-clinton-agreed-on-the-further-strengthening-of-coordination-on-syria.en.mfa.

5   See, for example, 'Turkey, US Agree to Train and Arm Syrian Opposition', *Defense News*, 24 November 2014, https://www.defensenews.com/global/mideast-africa/2014/11/24/turkey-us-agree-to-train-and-arm-syrian-opposition/.

6   See, for example, Jonathan Stevenson, 'The Syrian Tragedy and Precedent', *Survival*, vol. 56, no. 3, June–July 2014, pp. 121–40.

7   See Wladimir van Wilgenburg and Mario Fumerton, 'From the PYD–YPG to the SDF: The Consolidation of Power in Kurdish-controlled Northeast Syria', *Studies in Conflict and Terrorism*, January 2022, pp. 1–20.

8   See, for example, Sevil Erkuş, 'Ankara Urges PYD Leader to Join Ranks of Free Syrian Army Against al-Assad', *Hürriyet Daily News*, 6 October 2014, https://www.hurriyetdailynews.com/ankara-urges-pyd-leader-to-join-ranks-of-free-syrian-army-against-al-assad-72545.

9   See, for example, Robert M. Gates, *Duty: Memoirs of a Secretary at War* (New York: Alfred A. Knopf, 2014), pp. 302–4.

10 See, for instance, Michael R. Gordon and Eric Schmitt, 'Trump to Arm Syrian Kurds, Even as Turkey Strongly Objects', *New York Times*, 9 May 2017, https://www.nytimes.com/2017/05/09/us/politics/trump-kurds-syria-army.html.

11 Cengiz Çandar, *Turkey's Mission Impossible: War and Peace with the Kurds* (Lanham, MD: Lexington Books, 2021), p. 191. See also Burak Bilgehan Özpek, 'Paradigm Shift Between Turkey and the Kurds: From "Clash of the Titans" to "Game of Thrones"', *Middle East Critique*, vol. 27, no. 1, January 2018, pp. 43–60.

12 Quoted in 'Every Weapon Obtained by YPG Represents Threat to Turkey, Foreign Minister Says', Reuters, 10 May 2017, https://www.reuters.com/article/us-mideast-crisis-usa-turkey-minister-idUSKBN18616I.

13 See 'US Suggested YPG Change Its Name to Shift Optics on Terror Links', TRT World, 22 July 2017, https://www.trtworld.com/americas/us-suggested-ypg-change-its-name-to-shift-optics-on-terror-links-406197.

14 See van Wilgenburg and Fumerton, 'From the PYD–YPG to the SDF'.

15 See İlnur Çevik, 'ABD Kelime Oyunlari İle Türkiye'yi Oyaliyor' [USA is playing Turkey with word games], YeniBirlik, 1 September 2016, https://www.gazetebirlik.com/yazarlar/abd-kelime-oyunlari-ile-turkiyeyi-oyaliyor/.

16 Quoted in 'U.S. General Told Syria's YPG: "You Have Got to Change Your Brand"', Reuters, 21 July 2017, https://www.reuters.com/article/idUSKBN1A62SS/.

17 For a detailed history of the PKK, see Aliza Marcus, *Blood and Belief: The PKK and the Kurdish Fight for Independence* (New York: New York University Press, 2007).

18 See, for example, Human Rights Watch, 'Syria: Abuses in Kurdish-run Enclaves', 18 June 2014, https://www.hrw.org/news/2014/06/18/syria-abuses-kurdish-run-enclaves; Adam Baczko, Gilles Dorronsoro and Arthur Quesnay, *Civil War in Syria: Mobilization and Competing Social Orders* (Cambridge: Cambridge University Press, 2017); and Thomas Schmidinger, *Rojava: Revolution, War and the Future of Syria's Kurds* (London: Pluto Press, 2018).

19 See Ishaan Tharoor, 'A U.S.-designated Terrorist Group Is Saving Yazidis and Battling the Islamic State', *Washington Post*, 11 August 2014, https://www.washingtonpost.com/news/worldviews/wp/2014/08/11/a-u-s-designated-terrorist-group-is-saving-yazidis-and-battling-the-islamic-state/.

20 See Brian Blankenship and Erik Lin-Greenberg, 'Trivial Tripwires? Military Capabilities and Alliance Reassurance', *Security Studies*, vol. 31, no. 1, February 2022, pp. 92–117.

21 See Rod Nordland, 'On Northern Syria Front Line, U.S. and Turkey Head into Tense Face-off', *New York Times*, 7 February 2018, https://www.nytimes.com/2018/02/07/world/middleeast/us-turkey-manbij-kurds.html.

22 James Jeffrey, 'Trump's Plan to Arm Kurds Lays Bare the Strategic Vacuum in Syria', *Foreign Policy*, 9 May 2017, https://foreignpolicy.com/2017/05/09/trumps-plan-to-arm-kurds-lays-bare-the-strategic-vacuum-in-syria/.

23 Abdullah Öcalan, *Democratic Confederalism* (London: Transmedia Publishing, 2015), p. 34.

24 See 'Teröristbaşı Öcalan'dan HDP'ye İstanbul seçimlerinde tarafsızlık çağrısı' [Terrorist chief Öcalan calls for HDP neutrality in Istanbul elections], Anadolu Ajansı, 20 June 2019, https://www.aa.com.tr/tr/turkiye/teroristbasi-ocalandan-hdpye-istanbul-secimlerinde-tarafsizlik-cagrisi/1511453.

25 See Elias Groll and Robbie Gramer, 'An Angry Congress Prepares to Rebuke Trump over Kurds', *Foreign Policy*, 10 October 2019, https://foreignpolicy.com/2019/10/10/congress-prepares-sanctions-syria-trump-kurds-turkey-erdogan-lindsay-graham-normandy/; Eric Schmitt et al., 'Pullback Leaves Green Berets Feeling "Ashamed," and Kurdish Allies Describing "Betrayal"', *New York Times*, 13 October 2019, https://www.nytimes.com/2019/10/13/world/middleeast/kurds-syria-turkey-trump.html; and Eric Schmitt, Maggie Haberman and Edward Wong, 'President Endorses Turkish Military Operation in Syria, Shifting U.S. Policy', *New York Times*, 7 October 2019 (updated 15 October 2019), https://www.nytimes.com/2019/10/07/us/politics/trump-turkey-syria.html.

26 See Ben Hubbard et al., 'Abandoned by U.S. in Syria, Kurds Find New Ally in American Foe', *New York Times*, 13 October 2019 (updated 23 October 2019), https://www.nytimes.com/2019/10/13/world/middleeast/syria-turkey-invasion-isis.html.

27 See Eric Schmitt, 'U.S. Resumes Large-scale Operations Against ISIS in Northern Syria', *New York Times*, 25 November 2019, https://www.nytimes.com/2019/11/25/us/politics/us-syria-isis.html.

28 See, for example, Lolita C. Baldor, 'A Look at the US Military Mission in

Syria and Its Dangers', Associated Press, 24 March 2023, https://apnews.com/article/syria-us-troops-drone-attack-6194dca97f594e3609914637463c4ce3; and Christopher M. Blanchard, 'Syria and U.S. Policy', Congressional Research Service, updated 8 January 2024, https://crsreports.congress.gov/product/pdf/IF/IF11930.

29 On US–Russian engagements in Syria, see Andrew Weiss and Nicole Ng, 'Collision Avoidance: Lessons from U.S. and Russian Operations in Syria', Carnegie Endowment for International Peace, 20 March 2019, https://carnegieendowment.org/files/Weiss_Ng_U.S.-Russia_Syria-final1.pdf. In February 2018, US forces killed scores of Wagner Group mercenaries, deployed to support Russian interests, after they attempted to cross into US-controlled territory in Syria and threaten American troops. See Thomas Gibbons-Neff, 'How a 4-hour Battle Between Russian Mercenaries and U.S. Commandos Unfolded in Syria', *New York Times*, 24 May 2018, https://www.nytimes.com/2018/05/24/world/middleeast/american-commandos-russian-mercenaries-syria.html.

30 See Esref Musa, 'US Dispatches Military Reinforcements to Bases in Areas of Syria Under Terrorist YPG/PKK Occupation', Anadolu Ajansı, 26 April 2024, https://www.aa.com.tr/en/americas/us-dispatches-military-reinforcements-to-bases-in-areas-of-syria-under-terrorist-ypg-pkk-occupation/3202455.

31 See Ömer Koparan, 'Münbiç'te yuvalanan PKK/YPG'li teröristlerin Cerablus'a düzenlediği roket saldırısında 6 sivil öldü' [Six civilians died in a rocket attack on Jarablus by Manbij-based PKK/YPG terrorists], Anadolu Ajansı, 1 September 2023, https://www.aa.com.tr/tr/dunya/munbic-te-yuvalanan-pkk-ypgli-teroristlerin-cerablus-a-duzenledigi-roket-saldirisinda-6-sivil-oldu/2981139; and 'Tel Rıfat'ta PKK/YPG ile Suriye Milli Ordusu arasında çatışma: 5 ölü, 6 yaralı' [Armed clash between PKK/YPG and Syrian National Army in Tell Rifat: 5 dead, 6 injured], *Haberler*, 29 July 2023, https://www.haberler.com/dunya/tel-rifat-ta-pkk-ypg-ile-suriye-milli-ordusu-arasinda-catisma-5-olu-6-yarali-16170048-haberi/.

32 See 'Turkey to Reinforce Military Bases in N. Iraq After 12 Soldiers Killed', Reuters, 28 December 2023, https://www.reuters.com/world/middle-east/turkey-reinforce-military-bases-niraq-after-12-soldiers-killed-2023-12-28/.

33 For details, see Marcus, *Blood and Belief*.

34 See 'Turkey's Erdogan Says He Is Open to Meeting with Syria's Assad', Reuters, 17 July 2023, https://www.reuters.com/world/middle-east/turkeys-erdogan-says-he-is-open-meeting-with-syrias-assad-2023-07-17/.

35 If Trump is elected again, of course, he may follow through on his earlier promise to withdraw US troops from Syria, which would leave the PYD/YPG vulnerable and exposed.

Book Reviews

Russia and Eurasia
Angela Stent

Collisions: The Origins of the War in Ukraine and the New Global Instability
Michael Kimmage. Oxford and New York: Oxford University
Press, 2024. £22.99/$29.99. 296 pp.

In his wide-ranging and insightful account of the three decades that have
elapsed since the end of the Cold War, Michael Kimmage places the origins of
Russia's ongoing war against Ukraine in the context of three main 'collisions'
that have taken place between Moscow and Kyiv; the United States and Russia;
and Russia and Europe. These collisions, he argues, were not inevitable, but ultimately acquired a logic of their own, culminating in Russian President Vladimir
Putin's decision to go to war. In recounting these events, Kimmage provides a
compelling explanation for why Russia's – and the West's – hopes and expectations for the post-Cold War world were mismatched from the beginning.

Over time, Putin became increasingly suspicious of both the United States and
Europe, viewing them as a threat to Russian interests, just as he became ever more
convinced that Ukraine had no right to independent statehood. But the timing
of his decision to launch a full-scale invasion only months after what appeared
to be a successful summit with US President Joe Biden in June 2021 was, writes
Kimmage, the result of three factors: Putin's fear that Ukraine was steadily slip-
ping out of Russia's orbit; the perceived weakness and disarray in both Europe and
the United States; and Putin's 'faith in himself, in his military, and in the Russian
people' (p. 192). He was sure that his invasion would succeed in decapitating
Ukraine's government and possibly ending its statehood. A week after the invasion, however, Russia found itself in a war for which it was seriously unprepared.

Survival | vol. 66 no. 4 | August–September 2024 | pp. 161–167   https://doi.org/10.1080/00396338.2024.2380207

The Russia–Ukraine war has shattered three assumptions of the last three decades, says Kimmage. The first was that Europe would be peaceful as the Europeans had learned from their difficult past to eschew war and the United States was serving as the effective guarantor of peace on the continent. The second was that Russia would eventually be integrated into the West, however challenging that would be. The conviction – most prevalent in Germany – that closer economic and energy ties would ensure better political relations was a key element in the West's misplaced expectations about Russia's inevitable integration into Europe.

The third assumption was that Russia had to be a part of Europe if peace was to be maintained. As Kimmage shows, Russia has historically lived in peace with Europe only when it has dominated Eastern Europe – in the nineteenth century and between 1975 and 1991. As the 'treaties' that Russia presented to the US and Europe in December 2021 showed, Russia's precondition for improving ties with the West is the recognition of Russia's legitimate right to a sphere of influence in the post-Soviet states and Eastern Europe.

Russia's relations with the West, Kimmage concludes, will be conflictual for a long time. Post-Putin leaders will also seek to control Ukraine. Putin's rejection of the West will be difficult to reverse as Russia seeks to build a new world order with China and countries in the Global South.

Our Enemies Will Vanish: The Russian Invasion and Ukraine's War of Independence
Yaroslav Trofimov. New York: Penguin Press, 2024. $32.00. 400 pp.

Yaroslav Trofimov, the chief foreign-affairs correspondent of the *Wall Street Journal* and a Kyiv native, was in Kyiv when Russia invaded Ukraine, and spent the first year of the war reporting from the front lines. He has written a gripping and compelling account of those 12 months, offering granular and sometimes horrifying detail. He interviewed a wide range of Ukrainians, from President Volodymyr Zelenskyy to villagers fleeing Russia's assault on their homes and lives. He even spoke to Russian soldiers who did not understand why they had been sent to kill Ukrainians. His book raises key questions about the war and its possible outcome that remain relevant as the war enters its third year.

Trofimov reminds us that Russia recognised Ukraine's sovereignty in 1991 because it expected that the country's independence would be nominal at best. Most Russians never accepted that Ukraine was a fully sovereign country. Before the invasion, Putin reinforced these views through the propagation of elaborate historical myths purportedly demonstrating that Ukraine had never been a nation in its own right.

The author argues that Russia might have won the war had it been confined to the Donbas area, but Putin wanted more. After the full-scale invasion began, few people in the West believed that Ukraine would be able to stop Russia from taking Kyiv and ousting Zelenskyy. Yet, by March 2022, it was clear that Putin's initial plan had failed. Ukrainians rallied and fought back.

The reason for the failure of the March–April 2022 peace talks between Ukraine and Russia in Istanbul is a matter of some controversy, but Trofimov, who talked to many of the participants, is clear that the discovery of 450 corpses in Bucha and evidence of Russian atrocities – fiercely denied by Moscow – made it impossible for the Ukrainian side to continue negotiating. As British prime minister Boris Johnson told Trofimov: 'I thought that any deal with Putin was going to be pretty sordid' (p. 160).

US concerns about Russia's possible use of nuclear weapons in autumn 2022 led the White House to warn Moscow of 'catastrophic consequences' should it do so. Yet, as Trofimov shows, US fears of escalation have led the White House to slow-walk its supplies of lethal weaponry to Kyiv and insist until recently that Ukraine not use American weapons to strike targets inside Russia as Washington tries to discern Russia's red lines. These lines, according to Trofimov, are in reality 'very elastic' (p. 222).

When Trofimov interviewed Zelenskyy in July 2022, the president thanked the US and Europe for their support, but said that the weapons were too slow in coming and too limited, especially when it came to air defences. Two years on, these remain Zelenskyy's chief concerns. 'All they can do is kill all of us', he says, 'and I fear that may be their goal' (p. 240).

Trofimov does not believe that Ukraine will disappear from the map again. But the war is nowhere near over. A long, gruelling fight lies ahead.

The Showman: The Inside Story of the Invasion that Shook the World and Made a Leader of Volodymyr Zelensky
Simon Shuster. London: William Collins, 2024. £22.00. 384 pp.

Time correspondent Simon Shuster has written a compelling narrative of how Volodymyr Zelenskyy was transformed from a popular Ukrainian comedian into an effective wartime leader. The author's in-depth interviews with Zelenskyy and his family, colleagues and competitors reveal his unlikely journey from the gritty, decaying industrial town where he was born to the descendants of Holocaust victims to stardom on the stage and television, which he gave up for politics. This is a critical portrait of Zelenskyy's surprising rise to power, revealing his strengths and weaknesses.

Russia's 2014 annexation of Crimea and launch of a war in the Donbas galvanised Zelenskyy into reassessing his ties with Russia, where he had lived and often performed. He stopped working in Russia and his comedy troupe performed for Ukrainian soldiers at the front. According to Shuster, the idea for a presidential run first germinated during these trips to the Donbas. Zelenskyy started to work on the script for a new TV series called *Servant of the People*, a show about a high-school history teacher who, disgusted with the corruption of Ukraine's political leaders, runs for office on a dare, and accidentally becomes president.

In 2019, life imitated art. Zelenskyy, promising to end the war in the Donbas and to revive the struggling Ukrainian economy, was elected president by a wide margin. But Zelenskyy's one meeting with Vladimir Putin in December 2019 in Paris, alongside French President Emmanuel Macron and German chancellor Angela Merkel, produced no results. 'It was one of those rare moments in his life when he found the limits of his gifts as a communicator', writes Shuster (p. 173).

Despite repeated warnings from the United States and its allies, and detailed American intelligence briefings, Zelenskyy refused to accept that Russia was about to launch a full-scale invasion in February 2022. By then, his popularity had waned, and he feared the economic consequences of informing the Ukrainian people of an imminent invasion. He had prevented the military from preparing adequately for a war, and believed that Russia would launch only a minor incursion into Ukraine.

Nevertheless, as Shuster shows, once Russian troops had crossed the border and were threatening Kyiv, Zelenskyy refused to leave the country, becoming a decisive, popular wartime leader. He succeeded in rallying the country behind him. The Ukrainian military, after many setbacks at the beginning of the war, retook important territory from Russia by the end of the first year – the period covered in this book.

Nevertheless, the outlook remains uncertain. As General Valerii Zaluzhnyi, former commander-in-chief of the Armed Forces of Ukraine, said to Shuster: 'Knowing what I know firsthand about the Russians, our victory will not be final. Our victory will be an opportunity to take a breath and prepare for the next war' (p. 316).

The Russia that We Have Lost: Pre-Soviet Past as Anti-Soviet Discourse
Pavel Khazanov. Madison, WI: University of Wisconsin Press, 2023. $89.95. 208 pp.

Vladimir Putin's obsession with his version of Russian history has defined much of his 25 years in power. A former KGB officer and Communist Party member, he is critical of the Soviet state he once served, even as he laments its demise as the 'greatest geopolitical catastrophe of the twentieth century'. He eschewed a public commemoration of the centenary anniversary of the 1917 Bolshevik revolution and has criticised Vladimir Lenin for creating the Ukrainian Soviet Socialist Republic in 1922, which he argues gave Ukrainians the idea that they could be a separate nation-state. And while he counts Peter the Great as his true forebear, he has evaluated Josef Stalin ambivalently, recognising his crimes but praising him as an 'efficient manager'.

The search for a useable past has long preoccupied Russians, as Pavel Khazanov's engaging analysis shows. In his account of how Russian culture has dealt with Russia's pre-Soviet past since Stalin, Khazanov argues that both the conservative and liberal intelligentsia in the late Soviet period converged in idealising elements of Russia's imperial past, from which they created an 'anti-Soviet project for Russia that would eventually be realized in post-Soviet social life' (p. 7). This glorification of Russia's imperial past laid the ground for 'post-Soviet authoritarianism by consolidating even the liberal opposition around key elements of the power discourse' (p. 7). This interpretation of 'the Russia that we have lost' idealised both the authoritarian and the more liberal currents in late imperial Russia.

Nostalgia for the imperial past and rejection of the Soviet system infused much of late and post-Soviet discourse, with novels and films emphasising the message that the Russian people should welcome being ruled by their betters. Putin has favoured 'gold-plated Imperial retro' (p. 5) and emphasised the importance of 'eternal' Russia, praising the symbiotic relationship between the strong Russian state and the Orthodox Church, in contrast with the secular Soviet state. Many Russians have accepted the Kremlin's message that, under Putin, they are returning Russia to its rightful status as a great empire, even if this means they must fight a war to regain lost lands that rightly belong to them.

Despite Putin's invocation of Russia's glorious imperial past and his stated goal of 'decommunising' Ukraine, the rhetoric surrounding the war has sounded distinctively Soviet, and Soviet symbols have been used in the occupied Ukrainian territories, notes Khazanov. He questions how the post-Putin elite will deal with Russia's past, speculating that a 'cautious recovery of Yeltsinism' (p. 147) may emerge, which some Russian opposition figures support. Is it possible, he asks, to envisage a post-Putin government which rejects both Russia's imperial and its Soviet past?

Khazanov argues that, as long as Putin remains in power, the discourse about Russia's past will focus on its imperial glory. Perhaps, he concludes, it would be better for the West to focus on supporting Ukraine rather than trying to articulate a future for Russia based on its contested past.

How Finland Survived Stalin: From Winter War to Cold War, 1939–1950
Kimmo Rentola. New Haven, CT: Yale University Press, 2023.
£25.00/$35.00. 304 pp.

How did Finland – once a part of the Kingdom of Sweden and then the Russian Empire – remain independent and avoid becoming a 'people's democracy' in the twentieth century? What lessons can we learn from Finland's success in preventing the Soviet Union from conquering it? This enlightening and deeply researched history of Finnish–Soviet relations during Josef Stalin's rule highlights Finland's dogged determination to preserve its existence as a state – and Stalin's willingness to modify his policies when confronted with Finnish resistance.

Kimmo Rentola analyses three instances when Finnish sovereignty was threatened by Stalin: the Winter War in 1939–40; the road to a separate bilateral peace treaty between Moscow and Helsinki in 1944; and Moscow's attempts to coerce Finland into joining the Soviet bloc in 1948. 'Each of these three episodes', writes Rentola, 'ultimately concluded with Stalin settling for far less than he had originally intended to get' (p. 2).

In November 1939, Stalin believed that the USSR could successfully occupy Finland, just as it had done in eastern Poland two months prior. Apparently, his intelligence services mistakenly believed that Finnish workers and peasants would greet the Soviet troops with flowers. Moscow also failed to anticipate how steadfast the Finnish resistance would be. Instead of a quick victory, Stalin was 'forced to wage a vicious war in awful conditions as an international outcast' (p. 30). By March 1940, Stalin accepted that he could not conquer Finland, and settled for annexing its easternmost regions. This was a partial victory gained at a high human toll – 126,000 Soviet soldiers and 26,000 Finnish soldiers lost their lives. But Finland remained sovereign and free, and joined the German side a year later.

In 1944, Stalin tried to impose a harsh peace treaty on Finland, pressuring it to break with Germany, cede more territory, pay vast reparations and install a Moscow-friendly government. After tough negations, Stalin, now more preoccupied with Poland and getting to Berlin, settled for less. Finland survived the war without occupation, concludes the author, because of its geography – it was not on the road to Berlin – and because of timing, but above all because Finns felt their country was worth defending and fought hard for its continued existence.

By 1948, with a sizeable number of communists in the Finnish government, Stalin tried to coerce Finland into joining the USSR's expanding sphere of influence, hoping that it would follow Czechoslovakia's path. After months of negotiations, the two countries signed an Agreement of Friendship, Cooperation, and Mutual Assistance. But Finland remained outside the Soviet bloc as a neutral country that carefully calibrated its foreign policy not to provoke Moscow yet remained a democracy. This, as in the two previous cases, was largely the result of skilful Finnish diplomacy, but also of Stalin recalibrating his ambitions.

Juho Kusti Paasikivi, who served as president of Finland between 1946 and 1956 and spent many years negotiating with Stalin, concluded that 'the survival of a small state required much stronger political skill than leading a great power' (p. 221).

Asia-Pacific
Lanxin Xiang

Asia After Europe: Imagining a Continent in the Long Twentieth Century
Sugata Bose. Cambridge, MA: Harvard University Press, 2024.
£29.95/$39.95. 288 pp.

In *Asia After Europe*, historian Sugata Bose, who holds Harvard University's Gardiner Chair of Oceanic History and Affairs, reflects on the fate of the so-called 'Asian dream'. The idea of creating a common identity in post-colonial Asia was espoused by members of the continent's twentieth-century intellectual elite, such as Indian poet Rabindranath Tagore, an internationally respected figure who believed that China, India and Japan should work together in promoting Asian universalism. According to Bose, the dream has remained unfulfilled because of two events that unfolded in the last century. The first was Japan's invasion of China in 1937 – which 'undermined the idea of Asia as never before', says Bose (p. 12) – and the second the 1962 China–India border war.

Bose explores how Western colonialism and imperialism led to a unique phenomenon in Asian nationalism, whereby Hindu and Islamic universalisms and Bolshevik/communist internationalism developed in parallel but also interconnected ways. Things took a turn in the 1950s, however, when newly independent China and India broke with transnational thinking, choosing instead to follow the European colonial-imperialist paradigm of nation-states by defending hard borders and embracing nationalistic notions of sovereignty. In true colonialist fashion, this triggered conflicts and rivalries, thus destroying patterns of cultural dialogue and exchange that had raised the possibility in the first half of the twentieth century of a rising Asia built on shared values and solidarity.

Bose expresses sympathy with the notion of a unified Asia, but it should not be forgotten that an ideology of Asian universalism also produced the 'Greater East Asia Co-prosperity Sphere' that provided an excuse for Imperial Japan to invade China and other parts of Asia – the very event that Bose identifies as having damaged the dream of a unified Asia. He writes that the fate of Asian universalism in the twenty-first century 'will depend to a significant extent on the ability of China and India to peacefully manage their simultaneous "rise"' (p. 17), but he also seems sympathetic to the emerging geopolitical concept of the 'Indo-Pacific', describing a speech by the late Japanese prime minister Abe Shinzo before India's parliament in 2007 as 'eloquently' describing the '"confluence of the two seas" and the imperative to build a "broader Asia"' (p. 218). It seems unlikely that progress toward the Asian dream will be made any time soon, given that all three of Asia's major powers are beset with internal problems – such as socio-economic inequality and various obstacles to economic growth – that are undermining their ability to manage even bilateral ties, let alone collaborative efforts to further Asian universalism.

Cornerstone of the Nation: The Defense Industry and the Building of Modern Korea Under Park Chung Hee
Peter Banseok Kwon. Cambridge, MA: Harvard University Press, 2024. £54.95/$65.00. 448 pp.

Cornerstone of the Nation raises an important question: 'how did an impoverished country that was fully reliant on US military support until the early 1970s modernize its defense and commercial industries in less than a decade?' (p. 4). This study highlights the extraordinary wisdom and business acumen of General Park Chung-hee, who served as president of South Korea from 1961 until 1979, and who seized the opportunity afforded by the Cold War to launch a well-designed modernisation campaign. Kwon describes the 1970s as possibly 'the most revolutionary decade in Korean history, one whose influence continues to be felt in the Republic of Korea's domestic politics, society, economic policies, industrial technology, and international relations' (p. 4).

According to Peter Banseok Kwon, South Korea's development under Park can be seen as a 'story of symbiosis between capitalism and militarism', one that challenges the received wisdom dichotomising capitalism and militarism and pitting 'guns versus butter' (p. 18). Park initiated an industrial revolution that would simultaneously build the South Korean economy and promote its security independence. 'In accordance with Park's ideology of self-reliant national defense', writes the author, 'civilians were treated as the main drivers of the development of independent national security, and state strategies systematically merged national industries, the civilian workforce, and the body politic through the creation of the new indigenous defense industry' (p. 4). The high levels of industrial and export growth that resulted came to be known as the 'miracle on the Han River' (p. 5).

Interestingly, the pursuit of self-reliance during the Park regime mirrored similar developments in North Korea, despite the fact that the two countries had been bitter ideological rivals since the division of the Korean Peninsula in 1945. As Kwon puts it:

> The concept of self-reliance, which had its origins in anti-colonial and nationalistic responses to Korea's experiences under foreign imperialism

during the late nineteenth and early twentieth centuries, had by the end of
the 1970s crystallized into a sacred ideology for all Korean people. (p. 2)

Park's programme was spurred at least in part by doubts about US commitment
to South Korean security (pp. 46–7), while Kim Il-sung's policy prioritising the
simultaneous advancement of the national economy and the military in North
Korea came amid a falling-out with the Soviet Union and China (p. 2). Both
'systemically transformed themselves into heavily militarized garrison states
under totalitarian rule', says Kwon (p. 2). South Korea may have democratised
since then, but its commitment to self-reliance has endured, as have the effects
of its militarised development model (p. 6).

**North Korea's Mundane Revolution: Socialist Living and
the Rise of Kim Il Sung, 1953–1965**
Andre Schmid. Oakland, CA: University of California Press,
2024. £30.00/$34.95. 352 pp.

North Korea's Mundane Revolution challenges the cartoon version of North
Korea that tends to prevail in the Western media, whose coverage is dominated by depictions of a buffoonish dictatorship that might have been lifted
from a Charlie Chaplin film, complete with goose-stepping military parades,
mass public gatherings and leaders with curious coiffures. The book argues that
North Korea has developed in unique ways that set it apart from other communist dictatorships – ways that have enabled the country's socialist system to
outlast its Soviet counterpart. Rather than focusing on the Kim family and the
personality cult that surrounds it, Andre Schmid's study distinguishes itself by
exploring how the North Korean population took an active part in rebuilding
their country following the Korean War, with a view to ushering in what was
called 'New Living' in a socialist society. These efforts, he says, brought about a
'radical transformation in much of North Korea's economic and ideological life,
while at the same time serving to depoliticize the two main categories originally
used by the [Korean Workers' Party] to criticize contemporary society: gender
and class' (p. 4).

The invisibility of gender and class in the New Living project was a key
point of difference between North Korea and its larger communist neighbours,
China and the Soviet Union:

> Although all three emphasized individual ideological conformity,
> in neither of these neighbors did this emphasis translate into a similar
> depoliticization in their early post-revolutionary years. Class categories

remained a central part of Soviet and Chinese political culture, providing a central sociopolitical focus around which to define major campaigns. Not so in North Korea. (p. 10)

Instead, New Living glossed over the 'tensions and contradictions emerging out of a growing economy' (p. 4), displacing any class-based critique onto South Korea and the wider world, and reinforcing gender-based differences despite an official policy of gender equality (pp. 11–12). Schmid argues that these dynamics facilitated Kim Il-sung's rise to power but were not created by him, in contrast to studies that emphasise Kim's decisions and behaviour at the expense of wider societal trends (p. 4).

This is not to say that North Koreans themselves were unaware of the contradictions of New Living. On the contrary, Schmid explores the ways in which citizens interpreted New Living for themselves, sometimes offering 'flashes of criticism' of state policy or simply ignoring it (p. 230). This casts new light on the development of the personality cult in North Korea, which Schmid argues is difficult to understand without examining how New Living set the stage for it – for example, by presenting a particular ideal of family life that would later be expressed in the 'growing celebration of Kim's family' (p. 238).

Precarious Ties: Business and the State in Authoritarian Asia
Meg Rithmire. Oxford: Oxford University Press, 2023.
£64.00. 384 pp.

Since 2008, Chinese outward foreign direct investment has grown tenfold, and the overseas assets held by Chinese individuals, businesses and state institutions has quadrupled, making China a financier to the world. At the same time, however, large quantities of money have left China in ways that the state does not approve of – from 2012 through 2017, almost as much money left China in this way as through the country's formal outward foreign direct investment. If President Xi Jinping is as powerful as everyone thinks he is, why do we see behaviours like asset expatriation?

For most authoritarian regimes, a key factor in determining their success is whether political elites are able to control economic elites. The main argument of *Precarious Ties* is that the concept of cronyism is insufficient to account for the complexities of government–business relations in Asia's authoritarian regimes. Instead, the book outlines two major types of state–business relations that can be observed in authoritarian regimes such as those in Asia. The first is 'mutual alignment', which 'obtains when an authoritarian regime cooperates with business, formally or informally, to pursue regime goals and to facilitate profits and growth for cooperating businesses ... Economic and political elites both benefit, but society also benefits because resources are channeled into (at least mostly) productive uses' (p. 8). The system may not allocate capital perfectly, but most people will benefit in some way from the economic growth that it promotes.

The second type, called 'mutual endangerment', is not quite so beneficial. It describes a relationship in which 'economic and political elites are entwined in corrupt dealings and invested in perpetuating each other's dominance primarily because any loss of power on one side would bring about the demise of the other' (p. 8). In other words, the relationship is defined by fear. Meg Rithmire describes this phenomenon as 'cronyism without trust' (p. 87). Businesses cultivate ties with as many political elites as they can – not just with one faction, family or individual – to hedge their bets, but because both sides fear the downfall of the other, they each have incentives to try to outmanoeuvre each other. This happened in Suharto's Indonesia, and is happening in contemporary China – hence the asset expatriation. People seek to move wealth overseas and to obtain legal residency in other countries as a kind of plan B should things go badly domestically. Meanwhile, businesspeople are incentivised to collect incriminating information about political elites and business rivals alike, in case this can be used against them in anti-corruption campaigns. All in all, *Precarious Ties* offers an illuminating perspective on the economic and political dynamics in Asia's authoritarian states.

Cyber Security and Emerging Technologies
Melissa K. Griffith

Deter, Disrupt, or Deceive: Assessing Cyber Conflict as an Intelligence Contest
Robert Chesney and Max Smeets (eds). Washington DC:
Georgetown University Press, 2023. $36.95. 336 pp.

While there is now widespread consensus on what cyber conflict is *not* (namely, war), there is little agreement – in either the academy or the policy community – on what it *is*. In *Deter, Disrupt, or Deceive*, Robert Chesney and Max Smeets expertly weigh in on the question of how to conceive of the complex dynamics observable in cyberspace. 'Everyone knows that cyberspace has become a crucial battleground', Amy Zegart notes in the book's foreword, 'but understanding what exactly that means, how cyber conflict operates, and what to do about it has proven far more elusive' (p. ix).

The strength of Chesney and Smeets's book is that it does not land on a single answer to these questions. Instead, Chesney and Smeets offer a snapshot of current understanding, drawing together prominent experts to actively engage and debate with each other. Joshua Rovner kicks off Part I ('A Theoretical Debate'). Looking to historical examples of intelligence contests, he argues that cyber operations reflect the core conditions of spy-versus-spy battles – namely, competition to steal, protect and corrupt information and communications systems by rival intelligence agencies to gain and maintain an information advantage. In Chapter Five, Michael Fischerkeller and Richard Harknett stake out an opposing framework, strategic competition, arguing that cyber operations below the threshold of war can, in fact, have strategic effects. Those who subscribe to the intelligence-contest framework, they say, have correctly assessed that cyber operations are a poor tool for coercion, but are overlooking the fact that coercion is only one of the many ways states can pursue or achieve strategic advantages over other states. If these two chapters represent the poles of the debate, Michael Warner strikes a balance between them in Chapter Two, arguing that although a large subset of cyber operations may resemble intelligence contests, strategic cyber competition should not primarily be viewed as an intelligence contest due to its unparalleled scale and reach.

This theoretical debate is subsequently put to the test in Parts II (which offers country case studies) and III (on non-state actors). However, the first third of the book is largely US-centric, which tends to obscure the fact that while there are some core dynamics in cyberspace that are systemic – and thus faced by all states – many others are situational. Cyber conflict is shaped by geopolitical and domestic considerations as much as by the technical underpinnings of the domain itself. Does it make sense to frame the ongoing barrage of disruptive and destructive cyber activity between Iran and Israel as an intelligence contest? Moreover, does the term 'contest' – which may suggest a dynamic of clear victories in discrete windows of time rather than long-term, persistent and pervasive jostling – accurately convey the situation even for the United States?

While it can be all too tempting to see terminological debates of this kind as pedantic, they are fundamental to devising suitable policy. Depending on one's stance, different national-defence strategies may become more or less desirable, and different sets of cyber operations more or less worrisome. 'Countries that understand cyberspace faster and better will be able to bend the arc of history to their advantage', says Zegart (p. x). *Deter, Disrupt, or Deceive* offers one of the most comprehensive and theoretically grounded evaluations to date.

The Politics of Cybersecurity in the Middle East
James Shires. London: C. Hurst & Co., 2021. £35.00. 312 pp.

'Cyber security' is a term that appears in the names of institutions trying to understand it, private companies trying to sell it and defence strategies aiming to provide it. But what is it? In his recent book *The Politics of Cybersecurity in the Middle East*, James Shires suggests that cyber security is what states (and non-state actors) make of it.

Drawing on extensive fieldwork, Shires deftly examines the contours of cyber security – and who gets to define it. He discusses how actors have deployed the term in the service of their own domestic and international interests, a discussion that yields two key insights. Firstly, Shires offers readers a detailed glimpse into one of the most interesting, but also understudied, regions in the cyber-security literature: the Middle East. Secondly, he highlights when and how globally important concepts can be malleable, describing the 'reinterpretation of [their] meaning, scope, and content … for strategic gain' as a kind of moral manoeuvre (p. 310).

Such manoeuvres depend on high levels of symbolic capital (the pay-off must be worth it), as well as high levels of expertise, says Shires, because 'claims about what cybersecurity is, and should be, are nearly always couched in thickly technological language' (p. 311). Thus, in cases where moral manoeuvres are not performed by experts themselves, those doing so will usually rely on experts to gain legitimacy. As a result of these manoeuvres, different definitions and practices of cyber security have emerged, some mutually reinforcing and others antagonistic.

Understanding how moral manoeuvres contribute to defining cyber security helps to explain the full array of cyber-security practices that have emerged across the Middle East, according to Shires. For example, he notes that three separate incidents from 2012 – the Shamoon cyber attack on Saudi Aramco, the national oil company of Saudia Arabia; an update to the United Arab Emirates' Federal Law on Combating Cybercrimes targeting 'content crimes' in the wake of the Arab Spring; and the use of the FinFisher digital-surveillance tool against pro-democracy activists in Bahrain – were all defined by moral manoeuvres in that each represented 'distinct interpretations of the content and scope of the label cybersecurity', resulting in differing understandings of 'whom cybersecurity [should] protect and from what' (pp. 16–17).

Ambitious and deeply insightful, Shires masterfully weaves together politics, technology and the Middle East to explain cyber security in a way that is far broader and more subject to the interests of state and non-state actors than many might imagine.

Technology and the Rise of Great Powers: How Diffusion Shapes Economic Competition
Jeffrey Ding. Princeton, NJ: Princeton University Press, 2024.
£25.00/$29.95. 320 pp. Review is based on an advanced copy.

The rise of technologies such as artificial intelligence, semiconductors, biotech and quantum computing is fuelling scrutiny of their relationship to great-power competition. These technologies are seen as key components of economic innovation and growth on the one hand, and military and intelligence capabilities on the other. Capturing their benefits while simultaneously mitigating their risks continues to be a complex task, but one that states are keenly undertaking. Two countries, in particular, have found themselves at the centre of these geopolitical trends: the United States and China. Both countries view dominance in these technologies as essential to their geopolitical futures – a source of national power and a vital asset in the emerging competition between them.

In *Technology and the Rise of Great Powers*, Jeffrey Ding looks to the past to explore how technologies can influence great-power competitions like that playing out between the US and China today. Leveraging an impressive combination of qualitative and quantitative methods, he finds that technologies can and have contributed to historical power transitions, but not in the way many might expect. The steady diffusion of and adaptation to technologies across a country's economy is more important, he argues, than any given 'eureka moment' (p. 210) – instances of innovation or discovery that can be (wrongly) interpreted as setting the stage 'for a great power to leapfrog its rival' (p. 3). For example, the United States successfully exploited the technological opportunities afforded by British discoveries – particularly innovations in machine tools – to fuel interchangeable manufacturing techniques across American industries during the Second Industrial Revolution. Importantly, 'the United States did not lead the world in producing the most advanced machinery'. Rather, it led the world in adoption at scale. This was not a rapid process, requiring a 'long gestation period' (pp. 90–1).

Ding refers to this process as the 'GPT [general-purpose technology] diffusion theory', cautioning policymakers and academics alike not to learn the wrong lessons from previous industrial revolutions. Innovation in leading sectors is important, but has not led and likely will not lead to differential economic growth between great powers. Instead, the diffusion of general-purpose technologies is more likely to produce this outcome. Critically, some countries are better at diffusion than others.

To observe that *Technology and the Rise of Great Powers* has had a timely release would be an understatement. Anyone with an interest in the often misunderstood history of industrial revolutions, the evolution of disruptive technologies, the potential for artificial intelligence to reshape global economic power and the future of US–China relations should pick up a copy.

After *Stunde Null*: Reflections on Germany, Italy and Europe

Hanna Gesang

I

In northern Germany, some evenings have a special quality. Their soft warmth is nothing like the humid heat of Bologna, where I live now. These evenings are rare, so people treasure them, sitting outside until late – usually next to a barbecue. My mother, however, was relentless about bedtimes, especially on school nights. Maybe that is why a specific evening has stayed with me. A rather acquiescent child, I remember asking her if it was not time for bed by now – and her replying that tonight, I got to stay up longer. Across the table from us sat my grandfather, whom I called *nonno*. That evening, he was in an unusually talkative mood, speaking of the past. I no longer remember what he said, or how his voice sounded, but I remember listening with rapt attention.

Yet we never truly had a language in common. His German was broken, and my Italian was, at the time, non-existent. It was not something I questioned – this was just how things were in my family. My grandfather was one of the millions of *Gastarbeiter*, guest workers, who had come to West Germany starting in the 1950s. At that time, West Germany's economy was booming, lifting the country out of its post-war misery – and to keep wealth and welfare on an upward trajectory, labour was needed. Luckily,

Hanna Gesang is studying International Affairs at the Johns Hopkins School of Advanced International Affairs in Bologna, Italy. Her focus area is the rule of law in the European Union. An earlier version of this article appeared on the Eurac blog in June 2024 at https://www.eurac.edu/en/blogs/eureka/italo-tedeschi.

Survival | vol. 66 no. 4 | August–September 2024 | pp. 177–186   https://doi.org/10.1080/00396338.2024.2380210

there were plenty of places where people were looking for work. Bilateral agreements, the so-called *Anwerbeabkommen*, or recruitment agreements, facilitated this type of migration. The one with Italy was concluded in 1955, and at the time targeted mostly seasonal workers. As West Germany needed more and more labour, and as the freedom of movement increased thanks to the emergence of the European Economic Community (EEC), migration picked up through the 1960s. The German–Italian agreement would serve as a blueprint for similar treaties with other countries, including Spain, Portugal and Turkiye.

The term *Gastarbeiter* had been invented for people like my grandfather.[1] German has the wonderful quality of allowing for the creation of compound nouns whose meaning is more than just the sum of their parts. *Gast*, guest, *Arbeiter*, workers – through a kind of linguistical Lego, these nouns were combined in a term that came to mean much more than simply 'guest workers'. These were people who were not meant to stay. They were supposed to come, work, contribute to the post-war West German economic miracle and then go home. They were supposed to be young men strong enough for North Rhine-Westphalia's coal mines and Baden-Württemberg's factories. But the *Gastarbeiter* were no guests. Some left, but many did not. Instead, they had their families join them. By 1973, 620,000 Italian citizens lived in Germany.[2] Among them were my aunt and uncle, then nine and four years old, and my grandmother, soon to be pregnant with her third child – my mother.

II

German–Italian history obviously encompasses far more than my family history. Throughout the interwoven past of the European continent, an infinite number of ties can be identified. After Julius Caesar conquered Gaul, the tribes inhabiting modern-day Germany invaded Roman territory repeatedly, in a conflict that spanned decades. Later on, much of the current territories of both countries were part of the Holy Roman Empire. From the Renaissance onwards, scores of German artists, most famously Johann Wolfgang von Goethe, visited Italy and were inspired by its beauty. As per usual, the Germans even made up a word for this: *Italiensehnsucht*, or the longing for

Italy. The two countries have always been subject to different geographic, demographic, economic and political conditions. However, there are also notable parallels that have linked them for most of their existence.

The nation-states of 'Italy' and 'Germany' became political reality relatively late – in 1861 and 1871 respectively. As they sought to establish themselves on the crowded European political stage, ideas were traded between them. Benito Mussolini's fascism was an inspiration for the Nazi dictatorship, and by the early 1930s, both countries had descended into autocracy. Despite their initial alliance, relations were scarred by the last two years of the Second World War. After Mussolini's fall, Germany occupied large parts of Italy – deporting Italian Jews to concentration camps, and massacring partisans and civilians along the front lines.

After the Second World War came a *Stunde Null* – literally 'zero hour', referring to the German capitulation and its immediate aftermath. The liberation from the largely self-imposed plights of fascism and Nazism meant that Italy and Germany were both starting from scratch – or at least it felt like that at the time. With part of Germany increasingly closed off behind the Iron Curtain, relations between West Germany and Italy began anew after 1945. During their foundational years, both the Italian Republic and the Federal Republic of Germany were led by eminent Christian Democratic leaders – Alcide De Gasperi and Konrad Adenauer. The visions of the two men converged on many issues – most importantly, they both guided their countries towards Europe, which became central to their renewed national identities.[3]

The road began to fork in the 1970s. Both countries were haunted by 'red terror', in the form of the Brigate Rosse and the Rote Armee Fraktion. Yet economically, differences were emerging. Traumatised by past experience with hyperinflation, Germany's Bundesbank had adopted a stringent anti-inflationary course focused on stability, and became the EEC's economic poster child. Meanwhile, the Italian political system's design flaws had caught up with it, and an encrusted political class made questionable economic choices, leading to large debt increases. The changed hierarchy was visible at the 1976 G7 summit, where Germany pushed to make further aid to the Italian economy conditional on austerity measures.[4]

There was more bitterness when German reunification aroused anxiety and criticism from Italians, including then-prime minister Giulio Andreotti. Still, it is unlikely that he actually said he '[liked] Germany so much he wanted two of them'.[5] Overall, Italy was no more sceptical than most other European states about German reunification. It aligned with France on wanting a united Germany to be a deeply European one, and therefore pushed for greater integration into the EEC. Italian technocrats played notable roles in the conception of what was to become the euro.[6]

In the 1990s, as Germany was busy reunifying, the Italian political system collapsed onto itself. Widespread corruption and ties to the mafia were two of the many weaknesses that caused the political crisis, and the eventual destruction of practically all traditional parties. Whereas before, the most significant differences between Germany and Italy were economic in nature, there was now also a key political one. German political parties by now could look back on at least 45 years of history, whereas Italy became subjected to the whims of such political entrepreneurs as Silvio Berlusconi and Umberto Bossi, founder of the (then separatist) Lega Nord.

The decision to admit Italy to the eurozone, the conditions it was and should have been subjected to, and the impact of the euro more generally continue to be the subject of debate.[7] Whatever the euro's precise impact, when a financial crisis hit Europe in the early twenty-first century, Italy experienced a 'decline comparable with that of the Italian Great Depression of the early 1930s'.[8] The 2008 financial crisis and the 2009–10 eurozone crisis brought with them a 'new geography of power' in Europe.[9] Angela Merkel and her (literally and figuratively) austere finance minister, Wolfgang Schäuble, became the face of outright anti-German euroscepticism across the southern eurozone countries. In Germany, the Southern European economies were disparagingly lumped together as 'PIIGS' – Portugal, Italy, Ireland, Greece and Spain. Complicated economic dynamics were dumbed down to discriminatory stereotypes of lazy Southern Europeans who were wasting hard-earned German-taxpayer money to finance their corrupt politicians.[10] The countries' shared history of emerging from the ruins of the Second World War seemed forgotten.

III

Some of my earliest political memories are of this eurozone crisis. The negative depiction of Italy and Italians, especially in the popular press, angered me, even as I barely understood what was happening. Many Italians my age also remember that crisis – but as a period of genuine economic instability and fear, with unemployment looming over dinner-table conversations.

The economic difficulties soured German–Italian relations for years. Around ten years later, they would be put to the test once again. This time I was much more politically conscious. To be precise, I was in my second semester of an undergraduate degree in political science. In a spur-of-the-moment decision, no doubt fuelled by a constantly looming identity crisis, I had applied and been accepted to study in Milan. COVID-19 hit my new home early, and hard. An eerie silence hung over the usually dynamic city as I left it in February 2020, soon after my university had closed. In Germany, I was met with disbelief. My university had closed? That had to be due to the bad Italian healthcare system. For two weeks, I lived in a strange and scary limbo. My friends in Milan were confined to their apartments, my friends in Germany were out clubbing until the morning hours. In *La Repubblica*, I read about people dying in Bergamo.[11]

Germans who claimed that the Italian healthcare system was at fault for the COVID outbreak around Milan were clearly deluding themselves. Yet the reason that worked – at least for a week or two – was because of the lasting damage that recent history had done to the German–Italian relationship. In Italy, conversations about Germany are often laced with undue mistrust and unkind mockery. Media coverage of the Italian role in the 2008 financial crisis has left Germans with a bitter aftertaste and a lack of respect.

When I first moved to Milan at the age of 18, I was determined to resolve my identity crisis once and for all, but I confused quite a few of the Italians I met. At that time, I spoke practically no Italian, but I knew dishes, customs and even songs – especially the greatest Neapolitan hits from the 1970s. Like a 'proper' Italian, I would refuse cappuccino after midday – but I still have a cold dinner at 6pm. I soon grew tired of explaining my family's history at every encounter. Luckily, my native tongue

– an utterly pragmatic language after all – has a word for people like me: *Deutschitaliener*. It translates easily: *Italo-tedeschi*.

I have spent most of the past four years exploring a country I thought I already knew. This time has provided me with a deeper understanding of Italy's political struggles, and its complex history. It has both strengthened my connection with my family story and allowed me to build my own relations to the country. In many ways, living abroad has also made me understand how profoundly Germany has shaped me, and how I am very much not Italian in so many ways. Living in Italy has also changed my political views. The flaws of the European project are simply much more obvious in its southern member states. I still believe in the European Union, but not in the naive way that my 18-year-old self used to.

The EU's flaws will continue to be stress-tested by the ongoing rise of Europe's far-right parties. They have performed very well, much as polls have predicted, including in Germany and Italy. However, not all far-right parties are the same, and the differences between them will determine the extent to which they can leverage their newly gained political power within the European Parliament. Right-wing actors may share basic sentiments about immigration, euroscepticism and national sovereignty, but they are separated along a critical cleavage: their position towards Russia.

Russia is systematically seeking to gain influence in the EU. Recently, a fake media organisation calling itself the 'Voice of Europe' was uncovered as a Russian scheme that may have had the aim of bribing members of the European Parliament.[12] Less covertly, Russian President Vladimir Putin has invited members of some parties to visit Moscow, or even the occupied regions in Ukraine.[13] A key goal seems to be the bolstering of voices that disavow Ukraine and want to end European support for the war effort.[14] Parallel trends are also in evidence in the United States, where Donald Trump's ties to the Russian regime are a continuing source of worry.[15]

Geographic fate places Europe much closer to Russia. Russia matters on Europe's far right, and most of its parties can be neatly classified as either pro-Russian or broadly transatlanticist. For a long time, Hungary and Poland were lumped together as the 'sick men of Europe' when it came to democracy and the rule of law. They were largely isolated, facing criticism from EU institutions and other member states, and therefore natural allies. This changed with Russia's invasion of Ukraine. Poland, again by geographic destiny, has a long history of being 'anti-Russian'. Supporters of Poland's right-wing Law and Justice party (Prawo i Sprawiedliwość or PiS) are apparently just as negative towards Russia as their fellow citizens with much more pro-European views.[16] Hungary's Fidesz party, on the other hand, has invested enormous amounts of money and political capital in its relationship with Russia, which it has attempted to maintain even after the full-scale invasion of Ukraine.[17] Cooperation between Hungary and Poland, meanwhile, became 'limited'[18] – even before the election of Donald Tusk as Polish prime minister.

The divide also extends to the founding states of the European project. Members of Germany's Alternative für Deutschland (AfD) party have repeatedly been linked to neo-Nazi groups, despite the party's attempts to distance itself from them.[19] The party wants to end support for Ukraine and side with Putin, whom many AfD members seem to regard as a 'Eurasian' defender of 'Christian values'.[20] When Ukrainian President Volodymyr Zelenskyy spoke at the Bundestag on 11 June 2024, 73 of the AfD's 77 parliamentarians boycotted the session.[21] Meanwhile in Italy, Fratelli d'Italia, a successor organisation of the openly neo-fascist Movimento Sociale Italiano, has shown strong support for the West's embrace of Ukraine. Even before becoming prime minister, party leader Giorgia Meloni stated that 'Italy with us in government will never be the weak link in the West'.[22] Given that this is one of the first right-wing governments in Europe and has overall proven less extremist than previously feared, scholars are debating whether being in office has had a mitigating effect.[23] Undoubtedly, there are significant political pressures on European leaders of all political affiliations to side with NATO – even Hungary's Viktor Orbán has not been able to fully withstand this. However, attitudes towards NATO, Russia and the war in Ukraine remain a dividing factor among Europe's far right.

The departure of the United Kingdom from the EU left Italy as the EU's third-largest economy and population, yet the German–Italian relationship has tended to attract less attention than the Franco-German one, which has long been considered the motor of European integration. Bilateral relations between Italy and Germany, however, are also critically important. They stand for the successful emergence from the post-war *Stunde Null*, for the link between Northern and Southern Europe, and for welfare through trade.[24] Some of Europe's biggest challenges – such as migration and intra-EU economic disparities – will only be solved through German–Italian cooperation. This relationship has reached a delicate and somewhat surprising juncture. The German coalition government of centre-left and 'liberal' centre-right parties, challenged by Russia's aggression and the far right's strength, appears sometimes on the verge of paralysis. Italy's right-wing government, headed by a party that is descendant from Mussolini's fascists, appears unexpectedly restrained in its foreign relations and in any event is arguably the most stable of the leading European powers. Yet who knows what will become of Meloni's restraint if Europe's far right comes to power in Paris and elsewhere, and Trump returns to the White House? In that future, the EU's vital signs may well be measurable in the microcosm of German–Italian relations.

Notes

1 For a brief explanation of the term, see Bundeszentrale für politische Bildung, 'Gastarbeiter', https://www.bpb.de/kurz-knapp/lexika/glossar-migration-integration/270369/gastarbeiter/.

2 Grazia Prontera, 'Italienische Zuwanderung nach Deutschland', bpb.de, 7 November 2017, https://www.bpb.de/themen/deutschlandarchiv/259001/italienische-zuwanderung-nach-deutschland/.

3 See Tiziana Di Maio, 'Alcide De Gasperi and Konrad Adenauer: A New Approach', in Piotr H. Kosicki and Sławomir Łukasiewicz (eds), *Christian Democracy Across the Iron Curtain: Europe Redefined* (Cham: Springer International Publishing, 2018), pp. 57–89; and Gabriele D'Ottavio, 'Germany and Italy: The "Odd Couple" at the Heart of Europe', *Contemporary Italian Politics*, vol. 10, no. 1, 2 January 2018, pp. 14–35, https://doi.org/10.1080/23248823.2018.1436499.

4 *Ibid.*

5 Patricia Liberatore and Nino Galetti, 'Giulio Andreotti und Helmut Kohl. Die deutsche Wiedervereinigung, Lehren für heute', Konrad Adenauer Stiftung, 4 November 2021, https://www.kas.de/de/web/italien/veranstaltungsberichte/detail/-/content/giulio-andreotti-und-helmut-kohl-die-deutsche-wiedervereinigung-lehren-fuer-heute.

6   See D'Ottavio, 'Germany and Italy'.

7   See, for example, Gabriele Guzzi, 'L'euro è la moneta del nostro declino. Possiamo uscirne?', *Limes*, 11 March 2024, https://www.limesonline.com/rivista/l-euro-e-la-moneta-del-nostro-declino-possiamo-uscirne-15310398/.

8   Gianni Toniolo, 'An Overview of Italy's Economic Growth', in Gianni Toniolo (ed.), *The Oxford Handbook of the Italian Economy Since Unification* (Oxford: Oxford University Press, 2013), p. 24, https://doi.org/10.1093/oxfordhb/9780199936694.013.0001.

9   D'Ottavio, 'Germany and Italy'.

10   See Erik Jones, 'Merkel's Folly', *Survival*, vol. 52, no. 3, June–July 2010, pp. 21–38, https://doi.org/10.1080/00396338.2010.494873.

11   'Bergamo, non c'è più posto: 70 mezzi militari portano le salme fuori dalla regione', *La Repubblica*, 18 March 2020, https://www.repubblica.it/cronaca/2020/03/18/foto/bergamo_non_c_e_piu_posto_70_mezzi_militari_portano_le_salme_fuori_dalla_regione-251650969/1/. See also Jason Horowitz and Fabio Bucciarelli, 'The Lost Days That Made Bergamo a Coronavirus Tragedy', *New York Times*, 29 November 2020, https://www.nytimes.com/2020/11/29/world/europe/coronavirus-bergamo-italy.html.

12   See Nicholas Vincour, 'Russian Influence Scandal Rocks EU', *Politico*, 29 March 2024, https://www.politico.eu/article/voice-of-europe-russia-influence-scandal-election/.

13   See Kate Connolly, 'Far-right German Politicians Accused of Pro-Putin "Propaganda Trip"', *Guardian*, 20 September 2022, https://www.theguardian.com/world/2022/sep/20/far-right-german-politicians-accused-of-pro-putin-propaganda-trip.

14   See Vincour, 'Russian Influence Scandal Rocks EU'.

15   See Michael Crowley, 'All of Trump's Ties to Russia, in 7 Charts', *Politico Magazine*, 8 May 2020, https://www.politico.com/magazine/story/2017/03/connections-trump-putin-russia-ties-chart-flynn-page-manafort-sessions-214868.

16   Jacob Poushter, Clancy Christine Huang and Laura Clancy, 'Spotlight on Poland: Negative Views of Russia Surge, but Ratings for U.S., NATO, EU Improve', Pew Research Center, 22 June 2022, https://www.pewresearch.org/global/2022/06/22/spotlight-on-poland-negative-views-of-russia-surge-but-ratings-for-u-s-nato-eu-improve/.

17   See Péter Krekó, 'Viktor Orban Is the West's Pro-Putin Outlier', *Foreign Policy*, 11 April 2024, https://foreignpolicy.com/2022/03/20/viktor-orban-is-the-wests-pro-putin-outlier/.

18   Jennifer Rankin, 'How Soulmates Hungary and Poland Fell Out over Ukraine War', *Guardian*, 18 October 2022, https://www.theguardian.com/world/2022/oct/18/how-soulmates-hungary-and-poland-fell-out-over-ukraine-war.

19   See Maik Baumgärtner and Ann-Katrin Müller, 'Dangerous Liaisons: The True Proximity of Germany's AfD to Neo-Nazis', *Der Spiegel*, 27 July 2023, https://www.spiegel.de/international/germany/dangerous-liaisons-the-true-proximity-of-germany-s-afd-to-neo-nazis-a-e69c51d3-4b3c-49d2-8d54-d7b0a19c3f9a.

[20] Marcus Bensmann, 'Alternative for Russia: How the AfD Is Systematically Turning Towards Russia', Correctiv. org, 19 October 2023, https://correctiv. org/en/latest-stories/2023/10/19/ alternative-for-russia-how-the-afd-is-systematically-turning-towards-russia/.

[21] Nette Nöstlinger, 'Germany's Russia-friendly Parties Skip Zelenskyy Speech', *Politico*, 11 June 2024, https://www.politico.eu/article/ germany-russia-friendly-parties-afd-bsw-skip-zelenskyy-ukraine-speech/.

[22] Angelo Amante and Crispian Balmer, 'New Italy Government Will Be Pro-NATO, Pro-Europe, Says Meloni', Reuters, 19 October 2022, https:// www.reuters.com/world/europe/new-italy-government-wont-be-the-weak-link-west-says-meloni-2022-10-19/.

[23] See, for example, Gianfranco Baldini, 'From "Anomaly" to "Laboratory"? Fratelli d'Italia, Illiberalism and the Study of Right-wing Parties in Western Europe', *Political Studies Review*, 27 February 2024, https://doi. org/10.1177/14789299241231771.

[24] See Christian Wermke, 'Wirtschaftsbeziehungen: Außenhandel zwischen Italien und Deutschland auf neuem Rekordhoch', *Handelsblatt*, 23 March 2023, https:// www.handelsblatt.com/politik/ international/wirtschaftsbeziehungen-aussenhandel-zwischen-italien-und-deutschland-auf-neuem-rekordhoch/29056416.html.

Correction

Article title: Preventing Nuclear War
Author: Edward Ifft
Journal: Survival
Bibliometrics: Volume 66, Number 3, pages 129–144
DOI: https://doi.org/10.1080/00396338.2024.2357486

When this article was first published online, the sentence on pp. 136–137 read as follows:

If South Korean forces could stop such an assault with conventional means before South Korea, including Seoul, were devastated, the United States might decide to stop the offensive with a few tactical nukes.

This has now been corrected to read:

If South Korean forces could not stop such an assault with conventional means before South Korea, including Seoul, were devastated, the United States might decide to stop the offensive with a few tactical nukes.

This correction has been made to the online article.

Printed in the United States
by Baker & Taylor Publisher Services